I0103637

THE
SHADOW
STATE

Why Babita Deokaran had to die

JEFF WICKS

Tafelberg

Cover design: Nudge Studio
Cover photographs: Yeshiel Panchia/News24
Layout and page design: Marthie Steenkamp
Editing: Mike Nicol
Proofreading: Riaan Wolmarans
Index: Anna Tanneberger

Originally printed in South Africa
ISBN: 978-0-624-09494-4 (First edition, first impression 2025)

LSiPOD: 978-0-624-09614-6 (First edition, first impression 2025)

ISBN 978-0-624-09495-1 (epub)

To my wife, Bernadette, for her unwavering support in writing this book and telling Babita's story. Living under threat was never something she signed up for. I would not have been able to do this without her.

To the Deokaran family, for their time and patience during the innumerable visits, phone calls and interviews. I know Babita through you, even though I never had the privilege to meet her.

To the whistleblowers who risk their lives and livelihoods to do the right thing for the benefit of our country.

Contents

PART 3

List of abbreviations

ANC	African National Congress
CEO	Chief executive officer
CFO	Chief financial officer
CSD	Central supplier database
DA	Democratic Alliance
DPCI	Directorate for Priority Crime Investigation
DSO	Directorate of Special Investigations
HOD	Head of department
IPID	Independent Police Investigative Directorate
LCRC	Local criminal record centre
MEC	Member of the executive council
NHLS	National Health Laboratory Service
PPE	Personal protective equipment
RDP	Reconstruction and Development Programme
SAPS	South African Police Service
SIU	Special Investigating Unit

Foreword

Very little about proper investigative journalism is glamorous.

Often an investigative journalist, a unique breed within an unusual subset of the humanities, will tackle a story that no one else wants or, indeed, can even identify. And then the hard graft starts: tracking down documents and identifying patterns and anomalies.

Sometimes all of this leads to nothing, despite what your gut says or what your sources want you to believe. But every so often it guides you onto a singular trail. The longer you trudge down it – for investigative journalism is invariably a slow, arduous trek down a dark, winding road – the clearer it becomes that you've uncovered something remarkable, something that forces you to step back and inhale as you realise the true magnitude of what lies before you. And you know that, whatever lurks at the end of this obscure path, it will have a significant effect both on the body politic and on the lives of ordinary South Africans.

Long before Jeff Wicks, the author of this exceptional book, reached the point where he could declare with some measure of certainty that this was a 'big story', he had to put in the hard yards far away from his colleagues, who were publishing lead stories and collecting silverware at award ceremonies, and from his wife and family.

When Babita Deokaran was murdered in August 2021, her story was covered by the news desk at *News24*. But Wicks' interest was immediately piqued, and he notified his editor that he would keep an eye on the matter. Which was fine, because Wicks – a journalist-turned-medic-turned-journalist – is a keen observer of the human condition, and he can always spot a good news story among the everyday drama and tragedy of people's lives.

He started attending the court appearances of the hitmen accused of murdering Deokaran, and he asked the important questions. Why was she murdered? And who wanted her dead? Simply having the *izinkabi* in custody didn't mean Deokaran's case file could be closed. In fact, the arrest of the six signalled the start of an investigation that continues to astound Wicks' editors and the public.

Throughout 2021 and 2022, he followed the bail applications, regular postponements, applications and rebuttals in a rundown courtroom at the Johannesburg Magistrate's Court. At first, he just attended the proceedings to see whether something was afoot (there was), and then he started connecting with those who were directly involved.

And once Wicks started tugging at a very fine, nearly invisible thread he'd spotted in the courtroom, he couldn't stop. The work that he put in to answer the 'why' question took him off diary – not filing any other news reports for the foreseeable future – for large parts of 2022 and 2023. And while the rest of South Africa was carrying on with their own affairs, Wicks started building a network of connections, contacts and underworld figures in the Gauteng crime landscape.

What he found made even Paul Pretorius, senior counsel and evidence leader at the Zondo Commission of Inquiry into State Capture, sit up and take notice. In Gauteng, an insidious extraction network, rivalling the Zuma–Gupta network, had stolen billions of rand from the Health Department. 'This is part of State Capture 2.0,' Pretorius said after sharing notes with Wicks and his colleagues one day.

Wicks, following in Deokaran's footsteps, has uncovered a wide and sophisticated network of brazen corruption involving almost the whole value and supply chain at the department and its most senior

officials – officials who are supposed to look after the wellbeing of the most vulnerable in society. It was remarkable to see Wicks unpick this network of corruption and fraud thanks to Deokaran's forensic skills. She might have been killed in cold blood, but between them the investigative journalist and the deceased whistleblower traced the officials, the crooks and the liars who stole billions.

They were found in single-storey houses in townships, in shacks on the periphery of Gauteng's cities and in the boardrooms of Tembisa Hospital. There were fake companies, tender dons and crooked officials who had violated the public health system with false invoices and lies.

Wicks connected the dots, but Deokaran had laid out the bread-crumbs.

This is an upsetting account of Deokaran's death because of the threat she posed, but it also reveals the severity of the fractures in our criminal justice system. The police and the Hawks have failed to deliver justice to Deokaran, her daughter and her extended family because of a system that is unable to respond to crimes promptly and professionally. Wicks' account of how the crime scene was mismanaged is infuriating.

But even worse is the level of mismanagement by the Gauteng provincial government. Billions of rand meant to help the most vulnerable in our society have disappeared into the greedy pockets of the unscrupulous and shameless. These officials are shielded by the impunity handed to them by a misfiring criminal justice system and defended by the ineptitude of a government and bureaucracy that seek to serve themselves and their patronage networks first.

Deokaran is a South African hero. She worked within the system, and she refused to condone what many others not only facilitated but encouraged. And Wicks is an investigative journalist with exceptional courage and tenacity – a unique breed among an unusual species.

This book is a testament to their commitment to justice and truth.

Pieter du Toit
Johannesburg, 28 April 2025

Introduction

One August evening in 2021, as the Highveld winter loosened its grip on the city of Johannesburg, a group of men gathered at a house in Rosettenville.

The suburb south of the city has transformed over time, and the house at 32 Victoria Street harked back to the past. What had once been a small garden had become a cramped line of back rooms, each with a decaying corrugated-iron roof and ubiquitous satellite dish, a signal of a move into the present.

The men had been drawn to the house in search of wealth. Their secret rendezvous took place in a cramped courtyard behind high walls. The mood was buoyant. As they drank, they spilt beer onto the concrete floor.

Then, a bag was delivered. It contained R400 000 in crisp R100 notes. The drinking party was to celebrate a job well done, and the money was their payment. Their chilling task had been an assassination, carried out three days before. The target: Babita Deokaran, an unassuming accountant and single mother to a teenage daughter. The hitmen had lain in wait, and as she pulled her car into her driveway, they shot her. Twelve bullets ruptured her body.

I often linger on these moments, some of the last of her life. I imagine the searing pain from the hot lead passing through her. The sonic crack of bullets meeting metal. A mist of shattered glass. The tacky feel of blood on bare skin. Pain. Panic.

She survived just long enough to reach Netcare Union Hospital in Alberton, where she took her last breaths with her daughter and her siblings at her bedside. Her brother, Rakesh, told me about those final moments. Through a mess of cables, tubes and sensors, they embraced her. Each held her hand, spoke to her and said goodbye. The chorus of machines around her fell silent. The rhythmic whoosh and hiss of the ventilator stopped. She was dead at the age of fifty-three.

Babita was attacked in Winchester Hills, an enclave of multi-unit complexes that have become mainstay developments as Johannesburg pushes outward into every sliver of available land. It lies just seven kilometres from the Victoria Street safehouse where the gang of triggermen was drinking. They were awaiting the arrival of Phakamani Hadebe, a 33-year-old taxi owner hailing from KwaZulu-Natal. He was the gang's leader, and his life was a window to a murky underworld rarely seen – a realm where *izinkabi*, notorious hitmen schooled and hardened within the minibus taxi industry, operate as guns for hire. They are cold, callous assassins who kill for a fee.

Since the 1990s, internecine feuds between rival taxi owners and associations – either over access to specific routes or over positions of influence within association structures – have exacted a bloody toll, claiming the lives of drivers, proprietors and innocent commuters caught in the crossfire.[1] More recently, assassins who have proved themselves in the taxi wars have become free agents who outsource their deadly skills for the targeted killing of police officers, politicians, government officials, businesspeople and whistleblowers.[2] This is a dangerous shadow economy where supply and demand are always high. *Izinkabi* like Hadebe have shaped South Africa's democracy and undermined the rule of law with the barrel of a gun.

For the gang holed up in Rosettenville, the adrenaline rush from snuffing out a life and the high of a payday did not last long. A team of police officers soon traced Hadebe and others to the Victoria

Street house and two other homes in Rosettenville. Six men were arrested and charged.

Hadebe was the only one among them to offer a complete confession. Some made partial admissions, and others refused to cooperate with the police altogether. Each told his tale with varying degrees of completeness and detail. The statements, as much as they are elucidating, are also vexing. Finding the truth in it all is like putting together a puzzle: the picture is vaguely discernible but some pieces are missing, and the tabs and blanks of those you have don't align.

But Hadebe's confession, reduced to writing in the rough scrawl of a policeman, was a cold exposition of a hit-style killing from the moment he was recruited to the night he divided the pile of cash among his coterie of killers.[3] His recollection of what happened was recorded in an office in the bowels of Kagiso Police Station at precisely 00:52 on 27 August 2021, four days after the murder. Hadebe told the police he was paid R40 000.[4]

'I do not know the reason why the lady was shot and killed. Maybe the others might know,' he said in his confession.

If any of the men knew why Babita had to die, it was never recorded. She was always referred to only as a woman or a lady. The one who had to be killed. I doubt any of them even knew her name. To them, she was as good as inanimate. Killing Babita was a means to an end.

News reports filled in the details the six *izinkabi* apparently didn't know. Babita was the chief accountant at the Gauteng Department of Health, an arm of the state that has been mired in corruption and mismanagement for decades. Her death drew much unwanted attention.

When the six shuffled into the dock at the Johannesburg Magistrate's Court, they faced a veritable firing squad of TV cameras. Faces covered, they huddled together, hemmed in by the cramped wooden balustrade.

Had Babita been eliminated as an act of revenge? Had she been murdered to cover up the involvement of the political elite in graft?

Regardless of the motive, a key witness of the Special Investigating Unit had been murdered. It was national news.

When I watched the *izinkabi* in the dock for the first time, in the midst of the maelstrom of clicking cameras, I was fixated on the *why*. It was the inescapable question, and the answer would complete the impossible puzzle. What followed was a pursuit of that answer – a journey that set me on a track that would change my life and become the most challenging assignment of my career. For years, I feared that what I wrote would see me meet my end in a car pockmarked with bullet holes. I carry that fear with me even today, but Babita's assassination remains too important a story to be left untold. What she found in the weeks before she died was sinister. She had seen the first insidious shadows of a tender racket and money-laundering enterprise operating at an industrial scale. Her Tembisa Hospital investigation was buried and covered up before it could be seen through, and the price she paid was her life. I have tried to finish what she started.

PART 1

CHAPTER 1

Going home

It was 2am, and Rakesh Deokaran stood smoking outside his sister's Winchester Hills home. He couldn't sleep. A cold wind was blowing, but he did not feel the chill. With each pull at the cigarette, an orange glow pulsed like a beacon in the darkness. His eyes were fixed on Babita's car, pockmarked with bullet holes.[5] Minutes morphed into hours. He kept adding cigarette butts to the growing pile at his feet. Three days earlier, his sister had been brutally murdered just metres from where he now stood, her death so sudden and bloody that he had been rendered numb.[6]

Just before dawn, a sleek black hearse arrived. He took his seat beside the driver, and they headed for Durban. Rakesh was taking Babita home. Her funeral was to be held later that day in Phoenix, where he and his sister had spent their childhood. Her body was to lie in state in the same school hall where she once sat as a pupil.[7]

As they snaked southward along the N3 towards the Indian Ocean, Rakesh rested his hand on Babita's coffin. He had been unwavering in his determination that he would be the one making the journey with her. Even in death, she would not be alone.[8]

By 26 August 2021, South Africa had been in lockdown for 518 days because of the Covid-19 pandemic.[9] The status quo – 'adjusted alert level three'[10] – still enforced a daytime curfew, and all manner of public venues remained shut in an effort to curb the spread of the pathogen which had by then claimed the lives of more than 80 000 people.[11] That day alone, in the surge of the Delta variant, 357 people succumbed to the virus.[12] The restrictions meant that Babita's body could not be flown to Durban. Her final trip home was a seven-hour journey by road.[13]

Rakesh was in a haze during the trip. His pain and grief were interrupted only by the intermittent ping of messages in a family WhatsApp group. The Deokaran family is large. Babita and her seven siblings had sixteen children and five grandchildren between them, and most were on the group.[14] Those who were awake were checking in constantly, asking after Rakesh – how he was coping, what he was feeling. His staccato responses were focused on Babita.[15]

I'm bringing her.

She's safe.

I've got her with me.

The Deokaran family was right to be concerned about Rakesh. He was the one who had arrived at the scene of the shooting to find Babita in an ambulance outside her home. He had grasped her hand before the paramedics urged him aside as they rushed his sister to hospital. Later, when her life-support machines were turned off, he held her hand again, asking why she had to go. He broke down. 'Don't do this to me,' he begged.[16] He was a man overcome.

His sorrow had taken root two months earlier when he made the same, painful journey, in the same hearse, to bring home the body of his older brother, Sunil.[17] He had been in the ambulance with Sunil when he was taken to Netcare Union Hospital, his lungs unable to cope without a steady supply of medical oxygen. While Sunil was being admitted to a Covid investigation ward, Rakesh was at the reception desk, filling out admission forms.[18] A paramedic came to him while he was buried under the pile of paperwork, beckoning him to his brother who wanted to tell him something. But Sunil was wheeled off to the ward before Rakesh could get to him. He was off limits to all except the doctors and nurses who were straining beneath the onslaught of the pandemic.

It was the last time Rakesh saw his brother. Sunil's message was lost. He took his last breath in a Covid-19 ward in the same hospital where Babita later died.[19]

When Rakesh arrived in Durban with Babita, some of his nieces and nephews were waiting. As they hugged him, he wept.[20]

At the school hall, Babita's white coffin was draped in a fountain of pink, white and lilac: St Joseph's lilies, statice and chrysanthemums. Standing at the lectern, her niece Reola Haripersadh delivered an obituary.[21]

> Babita was a mother, daughter, sister, aunt, a cousin. Nothing will ever be able to fill the huge void left in our family. Our world has come crashing down. Her daughter, Thiara, was born in 2005. Thiara was and will forever be Babita's world. The bond they shared is second to none. She was her mum, best friend and confidante. Her entire world and routine revolved around the love for her daughter. She was an exemplary civil servant who diligently served the people of South Africa for more than 30 years. Her integrity and courage to stand up for what was right was second to none.
>
> Babita, you died a hero, not only to your family but for all peace-loving, honest citizens of South Africa. A strong and courageous woman who stood up for what was right and was not afraid to speak out against ruthless wrongdoing. Your legacy, Batha, lives on in each one of us, every day. You will never be forgotten. Watch over our precious Thiara.[22]

The epitaph summed up Babita neatly: a doting mother and a loving sibling in a tight-knit family. She was an everywoman, but at the same time, she was a civil servant quietly operating within a den of corruption. She could not stay silent when confronted with wrongdoing.[23] The prevailing narrative at the time was that she was murdered for this stance, a casualty that could be traced back to corruption at the Gauteng Department of Health. David

Makhura, the Gauteng premier, had said as much and acknowledged the connection between Babita's death and the multimillion-rand personal protective equipment (PPE) procurement scandal at her department three months before she was killed.[24]

How he could have known this within 24 hours of her death still eludes me. Perhaps it was an instance of Occam's razor – it was the simplest, most convenient explanation. There is no way Makhura could have been speaking from any position of authority, as the hitmen were still in the wind. No one could have cemented the links between her death and the PPE deal. They were just easy dots to connect.

Babita's murder was scandalous in many ways: a career public servant and known whistleblower had been the victim of an assassination; a high-ranking official had been eliminated by persons unknown. Her killing was a tragic example of how those in positions of authority, expected to act ethically and within the bounds of the law, were no longer protected by status.

Against the backdrop of the state-capture epoch, her murder was a brazen attack on the culture of ethical governance. In the three days after she was killed, her name appeared in bold headlines as journalists seized on the story. *Daily Maverick*'s Vincent Cruywagen reported that Babita had been a key witness in the Special Investigating Unit's probe into, among other matters, fraudulent Covid-19 PPE contracts. The police's cybercrime team was scanning her cellphone to see if she had been tracked by her murderers.[25]

In an editorial, *News24* questioned why Babita had to die: 'Here is a senior civil servant, the acting chief financial officer of the Gauteng Department of Health, being murdered before she could testify against corrupt businesspeople, politicians and civil servants who have looted millions from the department.'[26]

Millions of people watched a livestream on news channels *eNCA* and *Newzroom Afrika* of several hundred mourners in a twisting, social-distanced line that ended at her casket.

The funeral also drew the political class. Ravi Pillay, who was the KwaZulu-Natal MEC for Economic Development, Tourism and Environmental Affairs at the time, was among the guests. Pravin Gordhan, then Minister of Public Enterprises, sent an emotive message. It read:

> I join thousands of South Africans in applauding her efforts to expose and oppose corruption in the government health sector. Clearly, her assassination has revealed the underworld of criminal corruption which harms the poorest of South Africans, those in greatest need among our health workers, and patients, who need the best care.
>
> But the rogues inside the government and the business community get rich. She was a hero. She must be commended and celebrated. She must be the example of a dedicated public servant. Her life and work must inspire hundreds of thousands of politicians and officials to emulate her integrity, honesty and courage.
>
> To the Deokaran family: honest South Africans in government and among all our communities share your sorrow and loss. Babita sacrificed her future so the generation to come can live in a better, corruption-free and safer country. You can be proud of the work she did, the bravery and values she displayed in challenging corruption and the symbol she is and will become of a truly dedicated public servant. We stand in solidarity with you against corruption as we build a better SA.[27]

Gordhan's letter signalled that Babita's death had rippled upward to the highest spheres of the state.

Then there was Babita's own political principal, the Gauteng MEC for Health, Dr Nomathemba Mokgethi, an ANC appointee placed at the tiller of what is, by budget (R65 billion), the largest provincial department in the country. It is a department on which millions of South Africans – among them the most needy and vulnerable – depend. Mokgethi, who holds a doctorate in philosophy and literature, is in fact a nurse.[28] She did not deign to attend the memorial herself but sent a message.

Her emissary delivered a stilted, plodding tribute that sounded more like a workplace performance appraisal. With no particular flair, Mokgethi's words mapped Babita's climb through the ranks of the department. She was praised for being efficient and hard-working. Mokgethi couched the homage in soft terms such as 'maladministration and waste of public assets'.[29] This masked the reality of the realm in which Babita had worked: fraud, looting and corruption, with the connivance of the Gauteng Health Department's management suite, were rife.

Politically, a corruption scandal and the embarrassing backlash looked bad for Mokgethi only eight months after her appointment. Her dispassionate missive missed the mark and did nothing to shape the public's perception of her.

For Rakesh, the letters, homages and eulogies were a blur. He is a tall man, and his lanky frame can sometimes be spotted in the livestream video. To me, he looks restless, never seated for long and frequently heading towards the door. In earlier pictures taken at family gatherings and functions, he smiled broadly, looming upright over his sisters. But here his shoulders are slumped, as if weighed down by the yoke of mourning. By the time the attendees shuffle out of the hall, Rakesh again takes up his station with his sister as the hearse weaves through the narrow Phoenix roads to the crematorium. There, surrounded by her family, a Hindu priest performs Babita's funeral rites. Then her body is committed to the fire.

Rakesh's journey ended when Babita's ashes were cast into the sea, symbolising the start of her body and soul's new pilgrimage towards liberation and reincarnation.

CHAPTER 2

'My mom, my best friend'

Netcare Union Hospital. Monday, 23 August 2021.

A doctor standing at the doors of the trauma unit broke the news to Thiara Deokaran that there was nothing more they could do for her mother. The hail of bullets from the hitmen had done too much damage, and Babita had lost a lot of blood. In a steady, sombre tone, the doctor said they had tried their best, but they could not avert the inevitable. Her mom would die.[30] In those brief moments, Thiara's world was upended. She was sixteen years old.

Just hours before, Babita had dropped her at school as she had done many times before. It is a short drive from their home on Dungarvan Avenue to the gates of Abbotts College – less than three minutes. There was nothing to suggest that this Monday was different from any other. But on this fleeting journey, Thiara spoke to her mother for the last time.

Thiara's life was shattered when a lesson was interrupted by a crackle over the intercom, calling her to the principal's office. She hastily gathered her books and stuffed them into her bag. Her immediate thought was that she was in trouble, but waiting for her was Rakesh.[31] Her mother was undergoing emergency surgery and, seemingly knowing that their efforts would be in vain, medical staff had encouraged Rakesh to gather his relatives. There was not much time left for Babita.[32]

Thiara asked what was wrong, and Rakesh was at a loss. On the drive there, he had tried to marshal himself and rehearse what he would tell the teenager, but now he couldn't find the words. His mind was racing, trying to process what had happened that morning. He was grappling with the reality that he was to lose his sister. All he could muster was that Babita had been in an accident. He couldn't tell Thiara the blunt reality – that Babita was the victim of an assassination.[33]

The doctor told Thiara that Babita could hear her, even though the ventilator and breathing tube keeping her alive made it impossible for her to respond. Thiara sat with her motionless mother for a quarter of an hour. Rakesh thought if there was a twitch or a movement of her eyes, or if she squeezed his hand, things would be different. But all hope faded. There was no response.

He turned to Thiara and asked her what they should do. The family members who had rushed to the hospital decided to turn off the machines keeping Babita alive.

If by some miracle she survived, it was likely she would be in a vegetative state, the doctor had said. But that was never an option for Rakesh. His sister was a strong woman who refused to be dependent on anyone. It was not what she would have wanted.[34]

Shortly after 11am, Babita was declared dead.

In anticipation of taking Thiara home later, Rakesh had parked Babita's bullet-riddled car in her garage at her home, out of view. When the ambulance left the crime scene, so did the police, abandoning the car on the road – but Rakesh couldn't just leave it there. He did not want Thiara to see it.[35] It was enough that the duplex where she had lived with her mother was reduced to a cold shell. It was no longer a home.

Thiara was born on 1 February 2005 and became the centre of Babita's being. In all the time I spent with the Deokaran family, the consensus was always that Babita had lived for her daughter. She was a single parent, and the two of them were inseparable. Babita had never married, and Thiara's father has only featured sporadically in her life. I asked about him because I wanted to know what her future would look like. For the most part, Babita was all that Thiara had. Now her mother was gone.

During the research for this book, I asked to speak to Thiara, but she declined. I didn't feel snubbed because I understood why. My questions would again rip off the scab of pain and grief that was slowly healing. My very presence was a stark reminder of the darkest day of her life. Who was I to force her to relive that day and take stock of her loss, of her mother being taken from her, when she had already endured so much?

For Thiara, Babita's murder was a personal tragedy that played out vividly in the press because of who her mother was and how she was eliminated. As much as her relatives did everything possible to shield her from the journalists pursuing an interview, they always deferred to her. If a reporter requested an audience, they allowed her to decide whether to grant it.

Thiara has only spoken about her mother in a handful of interviews. On the first anniversary of Babita's murder, she spoke to eNCA's Heidi Giokos. Since the murder, Thiara had lived with her aunt Renu Williams, her husband, Dominic, and their two children. Now, for the eNCA interview, she was back in the home she had once shared with her mom – a place that seemed frozen in time. The apartment had been left as it was on the morning Babita died. Not a single piece of furniture had been moved. Pictures of Babita and Thiara's joyful moments were still fixed to the fridge. Religious icons and Hindu deities had pride of place. A cleaner visited dutifully, even though no one lived there. Nothing had changed.

Thiara told Giokos how, in the year since her mother's killing, she had struggled in the void she left behind.[36] 'Everyone's saying, oh, the time has gone so fast, but, like it's actually gone very slow, you know, a lot has changed for me and my family and, like, we all miss my mom. It's still not easy. I feel like, you know, if something interesting happens or if something fun happens, I don't have anyone to tell. Like, when I got my learner's licence or did well in school, I can't tell her about it.'[37]

On 22 September 2023, nearly a full year after Thiara spoke to Giokos, I was helping to produce a documentary about Babita, and Thiara agreed to meet us. I couldn't be there that day but had briefed the team on the line of questioning. I was mindful of not losing the essence of Babita's persona in our telling of her work as a civil servant and how she had blown the whistle on corruption. She had become a public figure only in death, but I felt we had a responsibility to tell the whole story. I wanted to show the person that she had been outside of office hours. I was trying to sketch Babita as a human being, with a family and friends and living a rich life, who had sacrificed herself in aid of honesty and integrity. Who better to speak for her than her daughter?

I had stressed the need to be circumspect and gentle. From the transcript of her interview it is clear that the pain Thiara felt had not dulled, and that her childhood died with her mother.

'I think I might have matured more in the last two years because I've had to. There have been a lot of changes. Like, I had to literally move house and stuff, and now I understand that I need to take my schoolwork more seriously.[38] She was my best friend, you know. She was very kind and everybody that knew her loved her.'[39]

While the cameras rolled, the reporter followed my brief and handled Thiara with care. The transcript sets out his lengthy preamble explaining that he would be asking her some difficult questions, some of which might be hard to deal with, but that her comfort was his primary concern. She was not obliged to answer, and if she felt overwhelmed and wanted to stop, she could – and should.[40]

The memories of the hours spent watching Bollywood movies with her mother, cuddling together under blankets, drew out Thiara's smile. Those were the easy questions to answer – the soft start. The reporter asked her about the day Babita was killed, and she recounted in detail her abrupt and jarring exit from school, how she had walked with a quick step to the principal's office and how Rakesh had ushered her to his car.[41]

Reporter: Can you tell me about what happened next? What happened when you got to the hospital?

Thiara: I don't want to. Can we skip that one?

That's where the questions about the hospital and the timeline of her worst memories ended.[42] She shouldn't have to think about that. I know we caused Thiara pain that day. I still feel guilty about it.

In the four years since Babita was murdered, as I have been trying to unpick the *why* behind her assassination, my encounters with Thiara have been brief. I can't say that we have ever had a real conversation. The only thing we have in common is her mother's death, and I evoke memories of a day she would rather forget. Every time I published a story that thrust 23 August 2021 into sharp focus, I worried that she would read it and that the pain would seep into her chest all over again.

From time to time, I get a brief glimpse of Thiara's life. She wore a floor-length, blindingly cerise dress to her matric dance; there are pictures of her getting ready for a night that is pencilled into every schoolgirl's calendar. She learnt to drive and got her licence on the first attempt. She matriculated with an 82 per cent average and five subject distinctions. Babita never got to see any of these milestones and achievements. Six hitmen, acting on orders, had seen to that.

At the time of writing, Thiara was in her second year at the University of the Witwatersrand, studying towards a Bachelor of Commerce degree. She still lived with Renu, Dominic and her two cousins.

New Cottage

In the days following Babita's murder, her relatives gathered to mourn in the home where she was raised. A diya – a small oil lamp made of clay – was burning.[43] In Hindu custom, death is not treated as the endpoint of life. Rather, it is held as a moment when the atman, or soul, begins a journey through the afterlife, either for reincarnation in some form or for moksha – a final release of the tether that held Babita's soul to this plane. The flame of the diya was lit when news of her death reached her family in Phoenix. Her siblings and their children took turns sitting vigil through the day and night for thirteen days, making sure the flickering light never burnt out.[44] Prayers were offered daily. Food was prepared and sacrificed in line with the *Garuda Purana*, a guiding scripture that details what happens to one's soul upon death.

After her body arrived in the hearse, Babita's sisters and nieces prepared her for the journey into the afterlife. She was bathed and dressed in one of her beaming yellow saris. She always loved wearing shawls, and her favourite was chosen, along with lotions and per-fume. All were gently placed in the coffin alongside her.[45]

In life, Babita had taken part in these same rituals when her parents, Mothilall and Sisilee Deokaran, made their journey into the after-life. She, too, took up her seat at their diyas and made offerings for each parent's odyssey towards emancipation. Now those left behind had converged in the same house on Ladygreen Place, Phoenix, for Babita. When her body was cremated and her ashes committed to the sea, the flame of her diya was snuffed out.

Babita's parents had settled on Ladygreen Place in 1977. Their home, number 7, was one of many built in a harsh blockhouse row, part of a low-cost housing expansion as Phoenix burgeoned as a settlement for the Indian community. In what is perhaps a testament to its resilient construction, it stands today almost exactly as it did when ground was broken nearly half a century ago. One of the only noticeable changes is the block's plastered walls, painted in beige, that abut the road. Stencilled black numbers – '1994' – mark the year this upgrade was completed.

Babita was nine years old when her family moved to Phoenix. Her parents and seven siblings shared three rooms. A life of poverty was a fait accompli for those who were not born white – a devastating design of apartheid. Their home was small, but it was considered a step up because it had electricity and running water. She had come from even humbler beginnings.

Babita, her parents' sixth child, was born on 30 November 1968. Like her siblings before her, she was born at home, in a two-bedroom red-brick house in a workers' compound on the Tongaat Hulett plantation.[46] The company was one of the most prolific benefactors of cheap labour.[47] Its main mill was established in 1903, built on the banks of the Amanzimnyama River.[48] The compound was called New Cottage and no longer exists. This land, along with the rich heritage of those who worked it, now houses the picturesque Mount Edgecombe, a luxury gated golf estate.

Babita's father worked as a clerk at the sugar plantation, tasked with overseeing the men who laboured in the cane fields, just as his father had done before him. Her paternal grandfather had grown up in the same compound house – one of ten siblings. Babita's mother was a housewife, and life for the family was often hard. Her father did not earn well, and when money was short, her mother would make samosas. Hour after hour, she folded yellow potato or mince into each tiny pastry sheet and fried them in oil on an open fire. She packed them into baskets and dispatched the haul with Babita and her siblings to be sold. The children would walk from house to house selling her mother's food before returning home with their meagre earnings.[49]

In a photograph that has long lost its colour and vibrancy, Sunil – one year Babita's senior – stands in a grey safari suit with his arm around her shoulders. She is sporting a bowl haircut and is barefoot in a white dress. In the background is the hedge line of their modest home at New Cottage. Exactly when the photograph was taken has been lost to time and faded memory.

Among the many keepsakes held by the Deokaran family are Babita's school reports. The dog-eared and yellowed pages are a window to the past and a schooling system designed entirely around segregation. In a Standard Three mid-year testimonial, carried home by Babita on 19 June 1979, her teacher, Ms Perumal, set out her remarks in cursive: 'Babita has produced very good results. A consistent worker who always gives of her best. She should keep up the good work.'

She had not missed a single day of school. She was first in her class. This snapshot was typical of Babita's academic life. She loved school and schoolwork, and she performed well.[50] But despite all her efforts, the colour of her skin and the circumstances into which she was born meant there were few opportunities. She wanted to be a lawyer, and her parents, struggling to provide for their children, simply had no money for university. Babita would need to work, not only to provide for herself but also to send money home.[51]

In 1987, she started her first job in Durban as a casual worker, without pay, for the House of Delegates, the parliamentary chamber established for Indian South Africans under apartheid. She received a living allowance of R8 a day to cover the costs of getting to and from the office, and for her meals.[52] This was Babita's entry into public service, and she was destined for greater prospects.

When opportunity beckoned, she left Phoenix and the house on Ladygreen Place. Within six months, she took up a post as the personal secretary to the then-executive director of education of the House of Delegates at Parliament in Cape Town. She was still working for free, and only a modest increase in her stipend kept her alive. Once the five-year term of that parliament ended, she returned to Durban to a permanent job as a finance clerk. Promotions followed as she climbed the ladder, something her siblings have ascribed to her work ethic.[53]

In the year 2000, she obtained a diploma in government finance from Technikon SA. She was hailed for her diligence in everything she did. She had come a long way from living in New Cottage, sharing a bed with her sisters and selling samosas in the neighbourhood. Her mother would have been proud.

Babita's story was a testament to success, rising from the depths of poverty and largely making her own way, yet her career was always secondary to her family. Calling them tight-knit is somewhat reductive: they maintained constant contact, whether through daily visits or frequent phone conversations.

Once Babita had broken free of the bonds keeping her in Phoenix and moved to Johannesburg for work, many of her siblings followed her lead. Among them was her youngest sister, Renu.

'She was my support system in Johannesburg, and we had a bond like no other,' Renu told me. 'We did everything together. We spent birthdays, Christmas, New Year's and Easter together. We didn't see each other every day, but not one day would pass by without us communicating in some way. Anything special that we cooked or baked would be dropped off or picked up. I relied on her for everything. Advice, assistance with my children, help with anything that I needed – I knew I could always count on my sister.'[54]

Babita's death hit Renu particularly hard, and she had a dream about her sister on the day of the killing: 'On the night of the twenty-third, after a day that cannot be described in words, I dozed off next to a sobbing Thiara. I know it was not a dream, but I believe it was a vision that Babita showed me. She was much younger, with long, straight hair and a flowing white dress with flowers in her hand in a beautiful garden. She looked like an angel, and I believe so strongly in my heart that that is what she is, and she wanted me to know that.'[55]

When Babita's body was washed and dressed in her favourite sari, Renu couldn't bear to see her sister like that. To her, Babita exists in memory as she was in life, in happier times. Because she didn't see her sister's body, she still clings to the hope that one day she will walk into her house to find Babita there. It's a comforting dream.[56]

Babita's career in the civil service ended cruelly because of her diligence and honesty. Her path to that point began on 7 March 2006, when she took up a post at the Gauteng Health Department. It ended fifteen years later.

Cold-blooded murder

On Monday, 23 August 2021, the last day of Babita's life, she followed an unseen ritual she had repeated many times before. Shortly before 7am, as she sat behind the wheel of her car, she clasped a small gold effigy of the Hindu god Ganesha in her hands and prayed.

Babita was never comfortable driving. When she first got her licence, she would avoid getting behind the wheel – and since then, every journey she took began this way. In Hindu custom, Ganesha is revered as a remover of obstacles. With the body of a man and the head of an elephant, he is the god of beginnings, wisdom and good fortune. She invoked the deity and asked for his intercession to keep her safe.[57]

It was to be a busy day for Babita. She and other officials were still working from home – part of her new normal in the age of the Covid-19 pandemic. She had spent most of the weekend on the frenzied preparation of the Gauteng Health Department's annual financial statements. The deadline was looming, and she had a string of meetings lined up to finalise the project, the first of which would start at 10am. But an exchange of messages between the Deokaran family that morning on their WhatsApp group showed that her mind was elsewhere.[58]

Babita's brother Sunil had contracted the coronavirus and died several weeks before. That Monday would have been Sunil and his wife Jenny's twenty-ninth wedding anniversary. It was a hard time for the family. Of the eight siblings, Sunil was the first to die, and they were still in mourning. They shared messages of support with Jenny, but the conversation then moved on to Babita's health with a message from her sister. Nothing in this exchange hinted at the tragedy that was rising over the horizon with the sun.[59]

> 06:40:47 | Shamilla – How is your troubling finger?
> 06:43:25 | Rakesh – It seems Fine. Cos when she came Yester-
> day no complaints. She was only in a meeting from 6am.
> 06:44:17 | Babita – Yes true not as painful now that it's get-
> ting warmer. Only finished at 7[pm]. Such a hectic day
> yesterday. Gonna be like that till month end.[60]

At precisely 06:56:32, Babita's iPhone registered that it had disconnected from her home Wi-Fi network, indicating that she had just driven her charcoal-grey Mercedes out of the garage and was moving along the cobbled driveway to her gate.[61] Her first obligation was getting Thiara to school. She could not have known that she was being watched. In fact, she had been under surveillance for days.

Babita drove away from her home along Dungarvan Avenue and turned right towards Columbine Avenue – an arterial road cleaving her suburb of Winchester Hills in half. After a short series of turns, she dropped Thiara at the gates of Abbotts College, a private school located beside the Columbine Square strip mall.

At 8.14am, CCTV cameras dotted around the Checkers supermarket at the mall captured Babita moving through the aisles. She queued and paid for her groceries before the short walk back to her car. She was heading home.

Less than two hundred metres from her gate, Babita spotted her helper, Elizabeth Khumalo (a pseudonym), standing by the roadside. She pulled over, and Elizabeth climbed into the car. At that moment, a white BMW that had followed Babita to Thiara's school, to Checkers and now to her home raced up alongside them. Shots were fired.

Elizabeth was frantic. In the haze of the attack, she had dipped her head down between her knees. Only after the BMW had sped away did she realise what was happening. Babita, bloodied and groaning, begged her to call an ambulance.[62]

At 8.26am, an ambulance was dispatched to Dungarvan Avenue. The only information given to paramedics was that they were responding to a shooting incident. They arrived to find Babita bleeding and barely conscious. In her final act in life, she had shielded Elizabeth from the salvo of pistol fire.

When news reached Rakesh, he rushed to his sister's home. He doesn't remember what he was told on the phone, only that his sister had been wounded. In his mind, he reckoned that Babita had been the victim of a hijacking.[63] 'I didn't even look at her car when I got there. It was still just standing in the driveway, and Batha was in the ambulance. I ran to the [ambulance] door, and I saw her lying there on the bed. I looked at her and she turned her head to acknowledge me.' It was important to Rakesh that Babita knew he was with her.[64]

After the ambulance left, Rakesh tried to process what had just happened. He walked over to Babita's bloodied car. He knew then, from the spray of bullet holes, that this had been no carjacking.[65] 'I just shook my head. I knew there was no chance she was going to survive,' he told me. 'You could see that all the bullet holes were strategically placed. The holes were all along the driver's side of the car. This was not random gunfire. They wanted to make sure she was dead.'

Inside the car he found Babita's handbag and cellphone on the passenger seat. In the boot were her groceries: bottled water, bread, milk.[66]

'I was thinking . . . these people didn't take a damn thing. If they didn't want the car or her money, then what was the purpose of all this?'

This is a question that would haunt him for years.

It was Dr Bozena Krysztofiak, a forensic pathologist at the Germiston Mortuary, who conducted a detailed examination of Babita's body. She noted small gold stud earrings and a gold dental inlay between her front teeth. The examination was clinical and impersonal. Babita was identified by a cardboard tag attached to one of her toes.[67]

Death Register No 1151/2021

> Chief postmortem findings in this case were: Multiple gunshot wounds to the neck, torso, right and left upper limbs, associated with injuries to the chest wall, right lung, diaphragm, liver, inferior vena cava and left kidney.

Krysztofiak had taken care to map each wound on Babita's body – and there were many. Her report is a chronicle of Babita's injuries. All in all, the pathologist noted 23 'defects' – a medical term denoting the gunshot injuries. Some of the projectiles had grazed her skin; others had coursed through her flesh and were lodged in muscle and bone. Some had tracked through her body entirely. Twelve bullets had pierced metal and glass before finding their target.[68]

During the autopsy, Krysztofiak took bullet fragments from Babita's neck, chest, armpit and right arm. These gnarled pieces of lead were cleaned and sealed in an evidence bag with the evidence number PW4000980047.[69]

A key observation in Krysztofiak's examination was the presence of stippling around many of the gunshot wounds. Stippling is a pattern of tiny marks on the skin caused by particles of unburned gunpowder that spew from the barrel of a gun when it is fired. Krysztofiak recorded it on Babita's cheeks, chin, neck and arms.

The findings told a chilling story. The men who shot Babita did so at point-blank range. At least one of the gunmen had been close enough to press the barrel of his weapon against her skin.[70] Her body was riddled with bullets; it was overkill. The hitmen paid to eliminate Babita had made sure that all their bullets found their mark. Rakesh was right to believe this was no random act of violence or a hijacking gone awry.

For a long time, I have picked apart every second of Babita's last day. On more occasions than I can count, I have asked her siblings to tell me the story of that morning. I know where each of them was when their world was upended. What time did you get the call? What time did you arrive at Babita's home? But their memories have been eroded by time and grief.

Then there was her cellphone, silently logging every keystroke, internet search and step. Overlaid on this, the dispatch logs from the ambulance that raced to Dungarvan Avenue provide a timeframe of her murder that played out in seconds.

It was 9.05am when the ambulance screeched into the emergency unit at Netcare Union Hospital. In the frantic rush, the paramedics had left Babita's phone in her car, obviously more concerned with stopping her bleeding. Two minutes later, at exactly 09:07:28, Babita's phone rang. It was the newly appointed acting chief financial officer at the Gauteng Department of Health, Lerato Madyo.

No one answered. Seconds later, a WhatsApp message from Madyo flashed across the screen: 'Are u ok?????!!!!'

Madyo was appointed in late 2020 as part of the department's revamped leadership. Her predecessor, Kabelo Lehloenya, had resigned amid a Special Investigating Unit probe into PPE procurement during the pandemic – a scandal that had enriched the politically connected elite. It also led to the axing of chief procurement boss Thandiwe Pino and the department's political head, MEC Bandile Masuku. Babita had acted as CFO, and Madyo was brought in to right the ship.

Madyo had been in constant contact with Babita and the rest of the management collective all weekend. In a department already so beset by furore and corruption claims, the deadline for its annual financial statements could not be missed. Babita had spent Saturday and Sunday glued to her laptop.[71] She and Madyo had scheduled a virtual meeting for 10am that Monday to iron out the remaining kinks in the reports.[72]

At 08:20:04, Madyo sent a message to the Gauteng Health management WhatsApp group: 'Morning colleagues, just check if there's still a need to meet this morning? We worked on the reports over the weekend mos neh. so I can cancel the meetings?'[73]

Another manager responded: 'Morning CFO, thank you. Few people attended so far and I told them that we met over the weekend. They must use this time to address specific outstanding issues/responses, if that is alright?'[74]

Madyo replied: 'Yes thnx. Let u and your team, Babita and myself meet at 10 as planned.'[75]

As this exchange played out, Babita was being rushed to hospital. By the time Madyo checked in with her, she was under the scalpel in a concerted attempt to save her life. Babita was not okay.

Later, Madyo surfaced again on WhatsApp, this time at 11.31am: 'Colleagues good morning pls let's pray for Babita. I've just heard some not so pleasant news. Pls don't share the news with anyone until HOD has made a formal announcement. I'm so emotional right now. I mean we just worked so well on the audits last night ... pls let's all pray for her recovery ...'[76]

At 1.24 pm, Madyo passed on the news of Babita's demise: 'Guys we have lost one of our own ... may her soul rest in peace.'[77]

It was already clear to Rakesh and others that Babita was not collateral damage in a botched hold-up or robbery. None of her possessions had been stolen, and her attackers had made no attempt to steal her car either. It was a hit – something that should have been clear to the police officers at the scene.

The Ganesha that had protected Babita on so many journeys was left in her car. All forms of protection had failed her that day.

PART 2

The hunt is on

The sun was setting when a group of police officers arrived at Babita's home. They had travelled in convoy in three unmarked cars, pulling up to the curb outside the Tampa Springs complex on Dungarvan Avenue just as the streetlights in Winchester Hills flickered to life.[78]

They parked on what had only hours before been a crime scene. It was there, in the driveway, that Babita's car had been peppered with bullets. Now, nearly ten hours later, there was no barrier tape or forensic technicians working under lights. All that greeted them was a closed gate and an empty street.[79]

Captain Freddie Hicks led the cohort of cops that night, a specialised unit attached to the police's provincial Serious and Violent Crimes Unit. This group was, in essence, a tactical detachment of the detective branch, tasked with pursuing dangerous criminals. These were not pot-bellied detectives in ill-fitting plaid suits but weathered cops who came from the trenches. When a police officer was murdered or an armoured cash van obliterated by explosives, this team was often the first to respond. A formidable group, they conducted surveillance, trailed their targets and then took them down. Gun battles were not foreign to them.[80]

Because Babita was a high-ranking official assassinated in an attack bearing all the hallmarks of a calculated hit, the shockwaves of her murder reverberated throughout the ranks of the Gauteng Health

Department. Hicks had been dispatched by the head of detectives in Gauteng, who, in turn, had been given his orders by the province's commissioner. This was a high-profile case, and the gravity of the situation was not lost on the police top brass. But by the time these orders trickled down, there was no crime scene left.[81]

Hicks is a gruff character. He's a stocky man with a barrel chest and thick, meat-cleaver forearms. He has a stern, abrupt demeanour, which I am sure is borne of a career in the police, where orders are given and followed. He struck me as a man who didn't suffer fools gladly, someone not to be trifled with.

Hicks retired from the police in 2023 and took his skills to the private security sector, so he was no longer bound by the constraints of official secrecy when we met late in 2024. He could tell me what really happened.

'There was no scene when we got there,' he said. 'It was over hours before, but her family was still at the house.'[82]

Police officers who had been called to the shooting that morning had, in effect, abandoned the crime scene and its evidence without processing it. The local criminal record centre, an oddly named forensic unit of the SAPS, had not been called out. No photographs were taken, and Babita's bullet-scarred car had been moved out of the roadway by her brother.[83]

Inexplicably, standard protocol had been abandoned. Babita's car should have been seized by police and towed away to an evidence store. The car should have been wheeled into a hermetic booth where its windows and door handles could be tested for touch DNA – the invisible genetic traces left behind with every contact. Analysts would have measured gunshot trajectories and looked for bullets lodged in the seat and dashboard.

Babita's handbag, cellphone and laptop were recovered by her brother. Everything should have been taken into police custody as evidence, yet none of this was done. The failure to process her car and the evidence it contained was a serious misstep. The chain of custody had been broken, and any good defence lawyer would seize upon this lapse. But these were problems for another day; Hicks didn't even have any suspects yet. He had to fix the mess of a crime scene and salvage what he could.[84]

The sixteen-year police veteran and his team were professionals. Operating in a high-stakes arena – surveilling and intercepting society's most dangerous elements – they were always the first to secure the scene. It was here where good police work could mean the difference between acquittal and conviction. Their methods were battle-tested: scenes were cordoned off, access closely guarded and evidence preserved. Everything was documented in a mountain of paperwork once the adrenaline had worn off, ensuring that when the detective compiled the docket, everything was in order and they could not be challenged on their procedures.[85]

'So, when there's an operation and we make an arrest, there is a crime scene. We follow the rules. We do things the right way. No shortcuts,' Hicks said.

But in Babita's case, the crime scene had been mishandled – badly. Hicks saw to it that Babita's car was locked away and arranged for a tow truck and a team to comb it for evidence. He sealed her laptop and cellphone in evidence bags. The murder docket registered at Mondeor Police Station was collected. The case would now be handled by a specialised unit. It would be several days before Hicks and his team would sleep again. The tables had turned for the men who hunted Babita.[86]

The blunt police commander sent his men, on foot, into the neighbourhood.[87] 'If you have a crime, people always look for footage of the actual incident. They become focused on that. I said to my guys, we do what we always do. Go down the road. Speak to people. Maybe someone saw a car speeding away.'

The old gumshoe strategy paid off. At a house less than fifty metres from the scene of the shooting, one of Babita's neighbours had snapped a picture of a white BMW speeding away on the morning of the attack. The single, grainy image of the car – with the number plate BV 56 FG GP – was their first lead. Police officers traced the vehicle to a man in Pretoria, but it was a dead end. Although he had a white BMW with the same registration, his licence plate had been cloned – a popular tactic among carjackers to hide stolen cars in plain sight.[88]

Hicks enlisted analysts from a private security company – trusted people who had previously worked with his team on high-profile and dangerous investigations. They had access to a resource beyond the police's reach: a blanket network of more than six thousand cameras dotted across Gauteng, operated by Vumacam. Nineteen individual camera masts stand at intersections and along main roads all around Winchester Hills. Each camera in this surveillance network reads and logs car number plates. Cars can be flagged as stolen on the system, with alerts sent to investigators. But they can also dial back the clock and examine footage from days past.

The analysts keyed in Babita's car registration and traced her movements. In the process, they saw two Volkswagen Polos tailing her. It was clear she was being followed, and now the cops had a new avenue to pursue.[89]

Having retraced Babita's movements, the analysts created a near week-long timeline of how she was tailed. They charted the routes of both the BMW and the two VWs and found that all three vehicles had been in the area on 18 and 20 August – days before Babita was killed. The cars followed patterns along her street and the nearby roads. Cameras captured footage of the cars stopping together, dropping off men and then fetching them hours later. The BMW had distinguishing features: a sunroof, a licence disk fixed to the bottom left corner of the windscreen, unique mag wheels and a missing tow hook on the front bumper.

For the hitmen, this activity served as a calculated reconnaissance of their target. Hicks saw to it that all the number plates were flagged in the system as 'vehicles of interest' in a murder investigation.[90]

Babita was killed on a Monday, and as the week stretched on, Hicks was informed that the Serious and Violent Crimes Unit – to which his crew was attached – would hand over the investigation to the Directorate for Priority Crime Investigation, better known as the Hawks. This didn't come as a surprise to him. Someone with a lot more brass on their shoulders had pulled rank.[91]

'So, then they said the docket was going to the DPCI, and that was fine,' he said.

Hicks was annoyed, as competent people were already following actionable leads and piecing together the botched crime scene. Now it would be signed off to another team, coming in cold, when time was of the essence.[92] But he was trenchant and stood his ground.

'I told my commander that we were following up on information. We were gonna work on it. It didn't matter who had the docket. A lot of people don't like me. They say I'm an arrogant cunt, but I am honest. I will never lie. If I say I am going to do something, I will do it.'

His commander begrudgingly gave him the go-ahead. Hicks didn't care about politics. He would follow the electronic bread-crumbs left by the cars that had shadowed Babita and see where the trail might lead.

On Friday, 26 August, he caught a break. As the day inched toward evening, the camera network captured one of the VW Polos in Rosettenville.[93]

Hicks and his team had to act, and fast. The alert was a single pulse of light in the darkness. All they knew was that the VW Polo was somewhere in the suburb. An invisible dragnet of unmarked police cars flooded the area, and cops rushed to choke points, fearing they would lose the car if it slipped past them. But the rush to Rosettenville paid off, and the car was spotted pulling up to a Spar. Cops gathered in the parking lot and waited.[94]

Hicks had a decision to make. He wanted to hit the car when it was in motion, to be sure that whoever was behind the wheel could be linked to the vehicle. But the roads were busy, and he knew that if the takedown played out there, it would draw a crowd. The entire road would be cordoned off, and evidence technicians would need hours to process the scene. It would be a spectacle, and Hicks worried that the rest of the *izinkabi* would scarper if they were tipped off. If the police let the car leave, they risked losing their only suspect.

Tense moments ticked by. Then a man approached the car and slid into the driver's seat. Hicks drew back the slide of his pistol and racked a bullet into the chamber.[95] The burly cop was out of his unmarked car and running. He wrenched open the door of the VW Polo, heaved the driver out of his seat and pushed him into a pile in the passenger floor well. Hicks was holding a bewildered Phakamani Hadebe at gunpoint.[96]

'It was quick . . . quick-quick,' Hicks recounted. 'He didn't know what was going on. Once I was in the car and we had him, I think he realised, "OK, now I know why these guys are here."'

With his team in tow, Hicks drove Hadebe to a deserted parking lot on the outskirts of the Turffontein Racecourse. It was quiet there, so his men could work. It gave them a brief respite after days of suspense. Of course, the Hawks had no knowledge of this operation, but Hicks didn't care. Solid policework had got them to this juncture. They had a suspect.

And then the suspect started talking.[97]

CHAPTER 6

'Wait there . . . don't move'

At the deserted parking lot, under the soft yellow glow of distant street-lights, Hicks considered Phakamani Hadebe.[98] He had surrendered without a fight. He had asked no questions. He had not protested. He appeared calm. The veteran policeman figured that these were signs of guilt, and he thought Hadebe had come to terms with his moment of reckoning.[99]

Hicks was joined by other cops. In the glare of their headlights, Hadebe was pulled from his seat, handcuffed and searched. He was not armed, but his cellphone was taken from his pocket and set aside.

Hicks told me that his team was like a brotherhood. The long hours and the shared threat of death while treading dangerous paths had forged an *esprit de corps*. Trust was high and the unit was close-knit. These were men who knew their job and followed protocol to the letter. Their work as lawmen was a calling. They were straight cops when many others betrayed the badge.[100]

Corruption is endemic in the police ranks, from the lowly station cop right through to the upper echelons. For bent detectives, every docket they carry is a veritable wad of cash. A statement or document strategically removed from a docket spells doom when the case arrives before a court and the matter is withdrawn by design. Then there are officers who are complicit in crimes, moonlighting as cash-in-transit highwaymen or drug runners. These cops pull the triggers, feed intelligence to their accomplices and quietly derail investigations from the inside. It is why Hicks kept his team small.

Now they had their first suspect who could be linked to Babita's assassination, and it was time for Hicks to inform his counterparts at the Hawks. The investigating officer, Captain Masenxani Percy Chauke, was leading a team of detectives assigned to the case.

When Hicks was told that the investigation would be taken away from his unit, he had defiantly assured his commander that he was following leads – and now one had panned out.[101] 'We informed the Hawks. We said we have a guy, and they said they were going to send someone to us. They were going to send a team,' Hicks told me.

I suspect that there was a level of animosity in this exchange, as Hicks took the case being shifted to the Hawks as a personal affront. After all, he had done the scutwork at the crime scene after the first-responder cops had neglected to process it. It was his unit that had turned to the traffic-camera network, which led them to this moment. Though he was used to the police's internal power dynamics, Hicks assumed that they were all working towards the same objective.

While they waited, Hicks spoke to Hadebe, who stood leaning against a car, eyes downcast and his hands cuffed behind his back.[102] 'So I told him, "Okay, this is the story. We know that you were there, so how are we gonna do this?"'

Hadebe remained calm and cooperative. Hicks was surprised. It was not the stolid silence he had come to expect when he handcuffed someone and started peppering them with questions.[103]

'He said to me, no, he will talk to us. He's not going to fucking jail alone, and not for just a cut of R400 000. That's what he said they were supposed to be paid.' Hicks wrote down everything Hadebe said.[104]

I asked about Hadebe's demeanour in these moments.

'He was expressionless. There was nothing. I think he knew what was happening to him. You know when you know you're really fucked . . . that's the sense I got from him.'

Hadebe then dropped a bombshell. He said that Babita's murder had been ordered by Health Minister Zweli Mkhize, who had just days before stepped down from his post amid a corruption and kickback scandal.

'The names that came out . . . fuck! This was a big thing now.'

Hadebe gave Hicks a detailed account of a planning meeting he had attended. The vividness of his description lent credibility to his story.[105]

'At first, I thought it was bullshit. But then he started. He described meeting Zweli Mkhize in a black van near Brits. He was even describing the shoes they were wearing,' Hicks said.

Hadebe was singing. He told the team of cops where the safehouse was, and that they used three houses in Rosettenville as fallback positions. At that very moment, members of the gang were at the Victoria Street hideout, celebrating a murder and dividing their spoils. He also told the cops where they had hidden the other VW Polo used to track Babita. It was an opportunity to take the entire cohort down.[106]

Hicks ordered his men to Victoria Street to keep the house and car under surveillance while he relayed the information to the Hawks.[107] 'They [the Hawks] told us to wait. They didn't want us to move until they got there. Yet they [the assassins] were all there together waiting for the money. What if the money comes and they just decide to leave, and then we have nothing. I said, fuck that. I told my guys, go there, secure the fucking house and make arrests.' He would take the lashes later.[108]

Soon, a team of heavily armed policemen huddled on a dark stretch along Victoria Street, several houses down from their target. It was a plan hatched on the fly, and they would take the safehouse by rushing the front entrance. After breaking down a heavy steel gate, a column of rifle-wielding officers breached the courtyard. Hicks told me that, aside from a brief scuffle, the men offered little resistance. In no time, five members of Hadebe's gang lay cuffed on the floor.[109]

Hadebe had also directed Hicks to a complex of flats in Kempton Park where the white BMW and the guns used in the attack had been stashed. Hicks wanted to send his men there to watch the car. The vehicles and the guns were crucial evidence. They would link the men to the crime, underpinning Hadebe's admissions. But Hicks was ordered by the Hawks to wait. Not to move until they arrived. He had already defied one order; outranked and overruled, he could only push the envelope so far. He told his men to wait. The Hawks were now running the show.

But something Hadebe had said under questioning made Hicks uneasy.[110] 'To have a suspect who says, "No, no, I don't want any nonsense." We were talking to him, and he said, "Oh, you guys are from province." He knew exactly who we were. This guy knew about our structures and what we were working on.' This alarmed Hicks.

Hadebe's knowledge can be explained in two ways. Either he was well-versed in the shady workings of the criminal underworld and had insight into the men pursuing the gang, or he had been tipped off that Hicks and his team were leading the hunt. It was disquieting.

When the Hawks and Captain Chauke arrived, there was trouble. They were irate that Hicks had moved on the safehouse without their say-so, and now they quibbled about process and protocol.

Hicks said they tried to find fault with the way his team had logged evidence, specifically the nineteen cellphones they confiscated when the gang was arrested.[111] 'We told them, we did everything right. If you look at our statements, everything is set out there. We had the LCRC [local criminal record centre] on standby, and they could start processing evidence immediately. It was a big fight over nothing,' he told me.

The delay stalled the move to seize the BMW and the murder weapons. By the time the cops arrived at the house where the car had been secreted away, it was gone – and the guns with it.[112]

Chauke shifted his attention to Hadebe and his gang. Hadebe was taken to Kagiso Police Station to make a full confession in front of an independent commissioned officer. The Hawks had lost crucial evidence, and now they had to shore up their case in other ways.

As for Hicks, his gut told him there was more evidence to be found at the complex of flats where the BMW had been hidden, so that was where he focused his efforts.[113]

'When we hit the Kempton Park flat, people told us that the men had just left. There was also a bakkie standing in one of their parking bays. I thought that someone could have come in the bakkie and left in the BMW. I put one of my guys on surveillance.'

Hicks was acting in the grey area outside his chain of command again, but his gut told him he was onto something. He questioned his hunch for five days while the bakkie didn't move from its parking bay.[114]

Then, on the evening of 1 September, a full week after Babita was murdered, the bakkie left the complex of flats and turned onto the N3, travelling in the direction of KwaZulu-Natal.

Hicks was resolute not to lose this lead. He strongly suspected that the bakkie could be linked to the gang, so he deployed his team. They caught up with the vehicle and moved in when it stopped at a petrol station. Their arrival interrupted a meeting. The bakkie driver had rendezvoused with another character, and both were arrested.[115]

The news reached then-Minister of Police Bheki Cele, who was on a press junket in Durban, and gave him an opportunity to crow about the breakthrough.[116] 'Interestingly, it looks like they have been arrested with a lot of cash in their cars. The story was that it was an expensive exercise, people were getting a lot of money each to pull the mission of killing Babita,' he told journalists.

Back in the real world, Hicks was certain that these two men were somehow linked to the killing. Their arrest led police to another flat, this time in Alberton. There they found bundles of money in envelopes. Some bore the names of police officers. The pair were arrested and detained in the cells of Johannesburg Central Police Station, while their cars and cash were seized as evidence.

'The guy in the bakkie from Kempton Park was involved, I know it. He was definitely part of that whole fucking shooting group. When we took him, he did not say one word. He kept trying to tell us that he is a Zulu and he comes from inner Zululand and doesn't speak English at all. But I could see he was listening to what we were saying. He understood us.'

The arrests were a promising development. The police investigation into Babita's murder had scored two early successes. But before the men could be charged and appear in court, Hicks received a phone call from Chauke. He was instructed to release them.

'He said I must go release the guys. I said I can't, I'm not a detective, and they were detained on his case. He was insistent. I told him straight I am not going to do that.'

Chauke then had the pair freed without charge. The cellphones they carried were never analysed or forensically examined. They walked away with all their money too, and investigations into who was renting the safehouses for them were never pursued further. 'The Hawks didn't follow up on anything. They just let them go.'

The crime scene at Babita's home was a mess, and the delays and bungles meant police lost pivotal evidence in the white BMW, including the guns it supposedly contained.

Hicks felt there was a dark force at work.[117] 'Those guys stashing the BMW. Somebody must have warned them, saying, "Hey, there's a fuck-up, you must get out." We never found that BMW, not even burned out somewhere. Nothing.'

The two men who were released disappeared into the ether.

Confession, torture

Phakamani Hadebe's candid admissions were somewhat out of step with the world of the *izinkabi*, especially his claim that former Health Minister Zweli Mkhize had contracted him and his gang to eliminate Babita.[118] His exact words to the police officer who took down his confession were that the clandestine meeting had taken place outside Brits Mall in the North West on 16 August, a week before Babita was killed.[119]

'We arrived at Brits Mall, and the people we were to meet were driving a black Mercedes-Benz Viano already parked along the road. We parked our car and got out and then got inside the Viano.'

Of the three men he found sitting inside the car, he said, one was among his accomplices who were arrested when police descended on the Rosettenville safehouse. Two others he didn't recognise.[120]

'We greeted them all, and the unknown men were introduced to me as Zweli Mkhize, and the man who was driving was his brother. I will be able to point out the Mkhize brothers if I see them again. They said there was a job they need us to do. We asked what it was, and they said there was a female who needed to be killed and that they would pay R400 000 for the job to be done. We agreed.'

In his version of events, Mkhize and his brother had shown the hitmen to Babita's residential complex and even guided them along the route she travelled. Referring to the day of the murder, Hadebe's statement wove in elaborate detail of the role each *izinkabi* played in executing the murder, as well as how they had conducted their surveillance in the preceding days.[121]

His statement concluded: 'I voluntarily elected to submit this statement. No one threatened me or promised me anything to write it.'

Hadebe had told both Hicks and the officer who recorded his confession that he was willing to cooperate. He had not been threatened or coerced, and there were no visible signs that he had been beaten. He had certainly not raised the spectre of torture then. But that all changed when he appeared in the Johannesburg Magistrate's Court. With a lawyer on the payroll, all six accused walked back on the confessions and admissions they had made. They were innocent, they said, and they wanted to be released on bail.[122]

This was Hadebe's new 'truth': 'I was taken to the Turffontein Racecourse and we parked at what appeared to be an entrance. I quickly realised why the police had chosen such a quiet, secluded place. I was first met with a barrage of threats and accusations such as "*jou moer*", "*jy gaan kak*" and the like. Though I understand very little English and even less Afrikaans, the impact and import of those threats were quite clear to me.

'The police proceeded to assault me: I was punched in the stomach many times. I was ordered to lie belly down on the ground. My interrogators were accusing me of killing someone in Mondeor on the Monday which had just passed. As I denied any knowledge or involvement in this crime, the blows continued. My hands had been handcuffed behind my back, and I was extremely afraid.

'The questioning took the form of "Where is the car? Where are the guns? Where are your friends?" Whilst torturing me, they said that their information was that we had received R400 000 for the hit. When I persisted with my denial of being involved, a black policeman sat on my back. What I believe to be a thick plastic bag was then used to suffocate me. The bag was pulled over my mouth and nose so that

I couldn't breathe. It was removed each time moments before I was about to pass out.'[123]

By Hadebe's reckoning, the relentless torture took place over more than an hour. He said it felt like an eternity. This new narrative starkly contrasted with his earlier confession, where he was described as calm, relaxed and at ease. In his recollection before court, he claimed that the cops had forced him to finger Mkhize as his paymaster.[124]

'A considerable part of the interrogation involved the accusation that they [the police] knew that our former health minister had hired myself and others to kill Ms Deokaran. To be clear, I have never met Zweli Mkhize. I rarely watch the news, even during the Covid-19 pandemic. I was asked by my legal representatives if I would recognise Mkhize if he was standing in front of me, and I answered candidly that I would not.'

He alleged that, between beatings, officers had shown him pictures of 'black men in expensive suits' on their cellphones. In essence, he said, the police had forced him to confess to an assassination in which he'd had no role. The officers themselves had provided him with the details of his so-called crime.[125]

'The suffocation and torture that I have described was intense and excruciatingly painful. At some point I urinated in my pants. At several instances during this, I thought I was going to die. Eventually, to stop the torture and the death I believed would ensue if it persisted, I admitted to the accusations that had been levelled against me, including that Mr Mkhize and his brother had hired myself and others to commit the murder.

'After the torture and my agreement to confess, I was taken to the Kagiso Police Station. I was warned that an officer would come to the station later and take my confession. My minders, who had interrogated and tortured me, forewarned that if I did not comply, I would again be tortured. I was warned that, if need be, they would kill me if I did not cooperate, reminding me that no one knew where I was. They asked me if I wanted to be "tubed" again.

'I then proceeded to narrate what I expected my torturers wanted of me. Some of the content I gleaned from the lengthy interrogation. Some of the content I simply made up. The disclosure in the confession that we had met Mkhize and his brother at the Brits Mall was a complete figment of my imagination.'

How does one reconcile two conflicting constructions by the same man? On the one hand, Hadebe was a cold contract killer – tied to the assassination of a senior government official – who was willing to reveal all to the policemen who had captured him.[126] On the other, he appeared as a family man, caught up in a crime he knew nothing about, a taxi owner with a modest lifestyle and providing for his children by sending money home to his rural KwaZulu-Natal village of Nhlawe. Hadebe's co-accused who had also confessed to the crime followed his lead. Everything had been contrived, or so they said.[127]

('Tubing' is a brutal interrogation method often associated with the apartheid regime's security police. A section of thick rubber tubing is stretched over the person's face, preventing them from breathing. It's a mode of inquisition that has survived long into South Africa's democratic era. Hundreds of claims of tubing have been investigated by the police watchdog body, the Independent Police Investigative Directorate. In 2014, Zinakile Fica died in police custody in Durban. A forensic pathologist concluded that it was likely that tubing was the cause of the heart attack he had suffered.[128])

Police had managed to keep a tight lid on the supposed role of Mkhize in the days after the killing – but not tight enough. Long before the six hitmen appeared in court, my sources in the Hawks had told me that Mkhize had been named as the mastermind. At the time, I found it astounding. It made no sense. Babita worked in the Gauteng Health Department, and I thought that even if Mkhize was crooked, he would wield his influence over much larger and more lucrative contracts at a national level. I reported that a senior ANC figure who occupied positions at the highest level of government and was influential within the ANC was a 'person of interest' in the case.[129]

Even in court, the police had tried to keep Mkhize's alleged involvement under wraps. When copies of Hadebe's confession were filed, Mkhize's name had been redacted.[130] But whoever had done so had no control over what was drafted by Hadebe's attorney, and with much flair, they let the cat out of the bag. When Mkhize's name emerged during proceedings, he released a statement.

'Zweli Mkhize would like to take this opportunity to assure the Deokaran family and all South Africans who are still reeling from the trauma of this callous crime that he has absolutely nothing to do with it, nor [with] the alleged procurement irregularities which are believed to have driven it. It should be remembered that these alleged procurement irregularities took place at a provincial level, far away from the national sphere of government where he was deployed as a national Minister of Health.'[131]

Having Mkhize's persona at the heart of this bail application painted the prosecution into a corner. State Advocate Steven Rubin was in an invidious position, forced to show his cards earlier than he would have liked. Mkhize was either a suspect or a witness, but the investigation into Babita's murder was still so nascent that he could not commit to framing him as either. He fell back on this: Mkhize was a person of interest.

The claim that Hadebe and the others were tortured by police officers was not entirely unbelievable. As I've mentioned, tubing is a common practice, albeit hidden. Equally common are unsubstantiated claims by criminals, when trying to explain away confessions, that they were beaten into submission. I believe it was a hackneyed legal strategy meant to chip away at the strength of the state's case. Hadebe's confession was a sturdy piece of evidence, and now doubt had been cast on it.

Hadebe held that without his confession, the case against him and his cohorts was on shaky ground. He averred that his first and forthright telling of his role as an *izinkabi* would be inadmissible. If

Hadebe could prove that he had been tortured and his confession was tossed out of court, it would be a severe blow for the police and prosecutors. Beyond this, there was no evidence to link him to the crime, he said. The case was barely circumstantial.[132]

Hadebe's lawyers homed in on the mention of Mkhize. This alone made the contents of the confession absurd. It was proof positive, they claimed, that words had been placed in Hadebe's mouth under the threat of violence. He had never met the ANC leader, let alone consorted with him.[133] Hawks Captain Masenxani Chauke, who had taken control of both the docket and the investigation, needed to counter this, and strongly, if he was to keep the six men behind bars while they awaited trial.

'I wish to state that the case against all the applicants is not, as some of them describe, barely circumstantial, but rather circumstantial and I believe it to be a strong case,' his affidavit opposing bail read.

Chauke leant heavily on the hours of video footage gathered by Hicks and his team. A detailed analysis of the footage was not yet complete, but he was confident that he could identify members of the gang by physique. One of Hadebe's accomplices had a picture of Babita's front gate on his cellphone, taken days before the murder. His explanation that he was looking for a flat to rent was hard to believe, Chauke suggested. An analysis of the men's movements, tracked by the cellphones they carried, would place them at the scene of the crime.[134]

He dismissed Hadebe's claims that he did not know Mkhize, holding that it was a story so wild that no policeman could have dreamt it up. Chauke said he had been at Turffontein on the night of the arrests and insisted that no one had been tortured in his presence.[135] But without the white BMW and the murder weapons, the case was by no means watertight.

The bail application of the Deokaran six played out over weeks. Ultimately, Magistrate Simon Sibanyoni consigned them to a remand section in prison where they would remain until the case went to trial. He ruled that a bail court was not the arena in which the admissibility of Hadebe's confession could be tested. That was for a trial court to decide.[136] Then Gauteng Premier David Makhura publicly advanced the theory that a provincial PPE corruption scandal had cost Babita her life. So, how was Zweli Mkhize in the mix?

I still found the notion that the former minister was the mastermind behind the murder fantastical. If it were true, Mkhize would never have been stupid enough to meet the triggermen in person, let alone drive them to Babita's home. In the shady underworld of targeted killings, layer upon layer of proxies and fixers separate the hitter and their assassins. Perhaps he was a convenient red herring, a lead meant to waylay and confuse?

Still, I couldn't simply dismiss his mention out of hand. I didn't know enough. I decided that I needed to look into the lives of the six *izinkabi*. My own pursuit of Hadebe, his cousin Zitha Radebe, Phinda Ndlovu, Sanele Mbhele, Siphiwe Mazibuko and Siphakanyiswa Dladla took me to the village of Nhlawe, in a sun-scorched valley in the KwaZulu-Natal hinterland.

Hitman's hollow

The R74 is a treacherous road. The single tar track snakes through the wide expanse of central KwaZulu-Natal. Wild veld and an endless stretch of acacia trees meld the hills and valleys together before giving way to citrus orchards on the outskirts of a small town called Weenen.

A wave of heat hit me as I got out of the car. It was October, a little more than two months after Babita was murdered, and the sun burned down. It had been a long six-hour drive from Johannesburg. I stood on the dusty shoulder, smoking and thinking. The mission to Weenen had been guided by a single word: 'Nhlawe'. It was the name of a village in the foothills that surrounded the town. I had found the name buried in a pile of court documents, an ever-growing collection of charge sheets, affidavits and other paper flotsam. On a perfunctory arrest form, filled out when one of the hitmen was detained and processed, the word 'Nhlawe' was scrawled in the space left for his residential address. My sources in the Hawks told me that the *izinkabi* had all come from KwaZulu-Natal and that they had visited a traditional healer two weeks before the killing, seeking muthi and rituals for protection. From what I understood, the police swoop on the gang had scuppered their plans to retreat to their home province.[137] Now this one word was a lead.

I had stopped the car to take stock and figure out what to do next. I was staring at the storefront of a panel beater and an adjoining petrol station. The colour had long been stripped from the once emerald-green walls by the unyielding sun. One lonely bowser was in the middle of the only patch of shade in sight. I lit another cigarette. The Weenen trip was a somewhat desperate bid to find another way into Babita's killing.

News24 had covered her assassination from day one and, by dint of her position in the Gauteng Health Department, it crossed my desk. By then I had been a member of the investigations team for a little more than a year, and I had fallen into the beat covering the criminal underworld. Prior to that, I had worked as a crime reporter for fourteen years, and experience had taught me of the vast intersection between crime lords and police, and how corruption hobbled crime fighting.

In my first months, I investigated the illicit cellphone surveillance and tracking of Anti-Gang Unit detective Charl Kinnear, with my colleague Kyle Cowan. We uncovered how gang bosses may have gained access to secret spyware and guided a hitman to Kinnear's doorstep. A criminal trial about these events is ongoing. I also unmasked a killing crew, operating in the illicit tobacco industry, who used stolen police rifles to kill eight people in a gang war. With Babita, we were looking at another targeted killing – this time of a whistleblower. It was an important story, and it fell to me to start digging. I started with the *izinkabi*.

I tore their lives apart. I went to the safehouses where they were arrested. All three houses had been rented just weeks before the murder. Some among the six had lived in Tembisa, and I drove through the maze that is the Winnie Mandela Section of the sprawling township, searching for four-digit house numbers that had no sequence. Over days and weeks, I visited companies that had previously employed them and spoke to their former coworkers. One hitman's address was Soweto's notorious Nancefield Hostel, a favoured retreat for criminals. No one would talk there, certainly not to me.

I was trying to piece together a puzzle. Why was former Health Minister Zweli Mkhize mentioned as the mastermind behind the murder? Had Babita been killed out of vengeance for exposing PPE corruption? I didn't know, and the only thread I had to tug on was the hitmen. I hadn't come up with much, at least nothing that could take the story forward. Was the planned escape to KwaZulu-Natal significant at all? Maybe I could track down the traditional healer? At least I would then know more about these men.

That's how I landed up in Weenen. I had company, then-*News24* reporter Lwandile Bhengu. She was a twenty-year-old journalism student at the Durban University of Technology when we first met in 2017 while I was working for the *Sunday Times* in Durban. In large parts of the province, being fluent in isiZulu is an essential tool of the trade; because I never mastered the language, I needed a translator. Bhengu was among a small group of eager students keen for time in the field. Together, we broke the news of an Islamic State terror cell operating in Zululand and its links to the murder of a British couple. Her career took her to Johannesburg, and now with me to Nhlawe.

The scalded petrol station along the R74 near Weenen was our starting point. All we had were the six names: Phakamani Hadebe, Zitha Radebe, Phinda Ndlovu, Sanele Mbhele, Siphiwe Mazibuko and Siphakanyiswa Dladla.

Bhengu crossed the road into the shade of the petrol station where a man lounged, propped up by a steel countertop. She asked for directions to Nhlawe. The petrol attendant was dubious. Why did we want to know? He stood up straight.

Bhengu explained that we were journalists following a story. We were looking for men who had been arrested for murder, and we thought they came from the area. She rattled off their names. When she got back to the car, she recounted his warning: be careful who you mention those names to – they are dangerous people.

We were directed to backtrack along the R74 and turn onto a gravel track that disappeared into the veld. We would be taking our chances in Nhlawe. We had to tread carefully.

Weenen is a violent place and a crucible for minibus taxi assassins. In 2019, thirty-nine people were killed in a bitter feud between rival villages, and much of the fighting played out in Nhlawe. The battle had been over land and how borderlines were demarcated. The death toll reflected only the region; others involved in the fight were assassinated in Johannesburg and Durban.[138]

The petrol-station portent made me uneasy. I didn't know what we would be walking into and exactly who we would encounter. One of the *izinkabi*, Dladla, when he was still talking to the police, said he had been promised R200 000 for his part in Babita's murder, but his fee was pared down to R25 000 because the group of triggermen had swelled. He revealed that there were twelve men in their gang, of which only six had been arrested before they could flee to KwaZulu-Natal. Had others made it back, and would we be knocking on their doors? I sat with that thought while we followed the dirt road into the valley.

In a place like Nhlawe, outsiders are viewed with suspicion. At first, I thought it was our Gauteng number plate that was drawing stares, but then I realised our dust-caked Toyota was the only car in the valley.

We stopped beside some women sitting at the roadside under trees and asked for directions. We repeated the men's names. Nothing. No one knew these men, their families or where they lived. We repeated this process for days. Each nightfall, we returned empty-handed to our dingy bed and breakfast in the town of Estcourt, forty kilometres away. I had a feeling that we were following the right path. We just had to keep going.

On the fourth day, we went back to Nhlawe and got the break we needed.

At a rondavel we had driven past too many times to count, an old man sat on a wooden bench. Scrape marks in the dust told me that his seat had been moved as the shade shifted. Bhengu asked the questions, repeating her script, and told him who we were looking for. He raised his arm and, with a weathered finger, pointed across a patch of bare soil at a house with a neat garden. 'One of them lives there,' he said.

Clearly the many who had shaken their heads at us, feigning ignorance, had been lying. The old man said others could be found near Nhlawe Primary School. 'Phakamani Hadebe lives there,' he told us.

We followed the road down into the valley. The house where Hadebe had grown up was on a small hill of arid soil, surrounded by gashes in the earth carved by flowing water. The cattle in the area had ripped the top cover of wild grass away, and all that was left was sand. It was there we found his brother, a schoolteacher.

When he emerged from a rondavel, Nokhi Hadebe flashed a look that said he was anything but surprised to see us. It was mid-afternoon. School had finished. The teacher had already stripped down to his shorts for some respite from the heat. I suspect he had heard of our presence, and our business in Nhlawe, long before we arrived at his kraal. When we asked about the arrest of his brother, he was indignant.

'All these things we are hearing about them are not like them at all. They are said to have gotten a lot of money, but where is that money? As you can see, there is no money here,' he said, pointing to his home. In his mind, the loot from the murder of Babita would have funded construction or cars, and look, there was nothing to show for it. The same was true for the others in the gang. Zitha Radebe, Phakamani Hadebe's cousin, had grown up in the same house where we found Nokhi. Standing in the dust, he pointed across the valley.

Phinda Ndlovu, Sanele Mbhele and Siphakanyiswa Dladla, too, came from this place, and all had left in search of a better life in Johannesburg. Each had a connection to the minibus taxi industry. Siphiwe Mazibuko was the only outsider, but Nokhi knew him. He was from Nquthu in northern KwaZulu-Natal, but he had come with the others to Nhlawe on 9 August, two weeks before Babita's murder. Nokhi said they had returned to the village for a traditional ceremony, although he was evasive when pressed for details. He did, however, ask whether Deokaran had children. Read into that what you will. Homestead by homestead, we tried to unpick the lives of these hitmen.

We found out that Phinda Ndlovu's mother was a traditional healer, which was, perhaps, grounds for the ceremony my Hawks sources had mentioned. Whether or not this rite was for protection from harm as they executed the brutal murder of a woman, I still don't know.

We established that Sanele Mbhele was employed as a general worker in the Inkosi Langalibalele Local Municipality in Estcourt and had been absent without leave for four months, yet he was still on the payroll. He was collecting his salary while he sat in a cell, and the town fathers were none the wiser.[139]

I felt like I had been on edge for days. I knew we were in an unwelcoming, often violent place, unsure if those we asked for directions were unknown figures who'd had a hand in Babita's murder. We left Weenen certain that the Deokaran six had ties that stretched back to childhood. Each featured somewhere in the minibus-taxi world, supporting the theory, circumstantially, that they could be *izinkabi* and not just a random collection of men rounded up because the police needed a success.

All in all, the assignment had been a failure. I was happy to leave Weenen, but why Babita had to die was a question I could not yet answer.

'I will fight for you'

Little more than a week before her death, Babita sent an abrupt WhatsApp message to her boss, acting Gauteng Health Department CFO Lerato Madyo: 'Morning CFO, I am just worried that the guys in Tembisa are going to realise we are not releasing their payments and know that we are onto something. Our lives could be in danger.'[140]

Several hours later, Madyo replied: 'Morning Babita I have requested [the] HOD grant approval for investigation.'

Babita responded: 'Thank you. I am praying that she grants approval soon so that we can start. Thank you for the support.'

It was laden with foreboding. Her words were chilling. Twelve days later, Babita was murdered.[141]

I wasn't the only one chasing this story. *Sunday World* first broke the story that Babita had feared for her safety in the days leading up to her murder, based on her brief exchange with Madyo.[142]

'Two weeks since her assassination, evidence has emerged showing that Deokaran had been concerned that her life was in danger because of the dodgy payments that she had stopped to some contractors at Tembisa Hospital,' the paper reported.

An atmosphere of fear had settled over the department after Babita was slain. Officials in the supply-chain management section – the gateway to the department's goods, services and infrastructure budget – were living in a perpetual state of unease.[143] If they flagged dubious payments and halted the flow of cash, would they meet the same end?

The brief interchange of messages between Babita and senior officials carried a lot of weight and was possibly the first tangible explanation for her assassination. My work began in earnest when politicians first speculated that Babita's murder was an act of vengeance. She had supposedly given evidence against officials who engineered a PPE procurement to go to a businessman who was a close friend of then-Gauteng Health MEC Bandile Masuku.[144] It was a neat explanation for her death, even if it seemed tenuous. Why would officials who had already been shown the door take on the risk of planning and executing a murder? Then there was the phantom figure of former Health Minister Zweli Mkhize, fingered by the gang of hitmen, which left more questions than answers.

My research into the assassins for any political links to either Masuku or Mkhize had turned up nothing. That the killing was a hit was clear, and the exchange with Madyo became critical. Babita obviously feared she had a target on her back. The timing of the messages, so close to her murder, was another aspect that could not be ignored. I thought then that her phone would hold the answers I sought, so I turned to her brother, Rakesh.

It took repeated phone calls over weeks to convince him to meet me. My first overture was swiftly deferred to Tony Haripersadh, Babita's brother-in-law, who the family had decided would deal with the journalists. I told Rakesh that I would call Tony and arrange to travel to Durban so we could talk. However, I was trying to make it clear to him that I was not simply looking for a quote. I wanted to tell the whole story.

On 22 September 2021, I sat in the Wimpy at Columbine Square Mall in the south of Johannesburg, waiting for Rakesh. He had already blown me off on more than one occasion. Now, a full month after Babita's killing, I had convinced him that all he had to do was sit with me. He didn't have to utter a word; he just had to hear me out. He reluctantly agreed.

When Rakesh's tall frame slid into the booth opposite me, I could see that he was a man in pain. His shirt hung loosely on his shoulders. He had lost weight. His countenance and the bags set deeply under his eyes told me that he had been struggling to sleep. Tears welled up when I said I was deeply sorry for his loss. Babita's death had broken him.

The coffees we ordered were cold by the time I finished talking. I told Rakesh that I had been a journalist for a long time, and I could see that there was more to his sister's murder than what was already in the public domain. I made him understand that I was serious about my work and would follow this story to the end. I was not in it to chase headlines. No, I cared about what had befallen his sister. The pain that gripped his family was something that no one should have to endure.

Hours passed, and he slowly opened up. I could see he, too, was looking for answers. He knew that the attack on Babita had been more than a hijacking, but what did she know that was so damaging that the only option was to eliminate her? I stressed that I had worked on complex investigations before, and that my role was to keep Babita's name in the headlines and maintain pressure on the authorities to act before the case slipped from memory and became just another killing in South Africa.

Rakesh didn't have much by way of answers. He knew that his sister was a high-ranking provincial government official, but the minutiae of her work were unknown to him. Babita had not mentioned her fear of 'the guys from Tembisa' to her siblings, and in the weeks before her death, she kept her work secret. But this was the start of a relationship with Rakesh, and I tried to see him once a week. Over cigarettes and black coffee, I would share what I had found with him, and together we tried to fit the pieces together.

I promised him that I would follow this story, no matter the danger, no matter how long it took, and he undertook to help me. I asked for any information that could be valuable. Mostly, I wanted Babita's phone, but that was not something Rakesh could give me.

It had been seized along with her laptop on the day of her murder, and the cops still had it.

By the time February 2022 rolled around, I was still no closer to understanding why Babita had to die. As far as the *izinkabi* were concerned, clearly, they were guilty. Safehouses had been rented strategically, long before Babita's murder. The men had returned to Nhlawe to seek the protection of a traditional healer. The video footage from the overhead cameras tapped by cops placed them at the scene of the crime and plotted their surveillance of Babita. It was all circumstantial, but it all added up. These were not innocent men.

Even so, I was nowhere in terms of trying to expose the motive behind the killing and the person who had ordered it. The police still held Babita's cellphone and her computer as evidence, but it was now nearly six months after her death. Surely the investigating team had finished their inquiry, at least as far as the digital evidence was concerned?

I knew the internal protocols for these situations. The devices are seized and transferred to a forensic analysis section. There, they are 'imaged'. Put simply, they are copied in their entirety, and this forensic 'image' is then examined and used as evidence in court if necessary. The process takes days, not months.

I had a plan, but I needed Rakesh onside. It would not work without him.

I asked Rakesh to call the investigating officer – Captain Masenxani Chauke – and request that the phone be returned. I suggested he spin a yarn: there were pictures and videos on Babita's phone that held sentimental value for her daughter.

On 28 February, Rakesh phoned me. 'I've got them,' he said. 'You need to come and see me.'

When I arrived at his home in Oakdene Park, southern Johannesburg, a stone's throw from where Babita had lived, he was waiting for me in the doorway, holding a tote bag. Inside were three laptops and Babita's cellphone, each in their own SAPS evidence bag. There was also a stack of random paperwork and diaries from years earlier.

This was all the evidence the cops had gathered from her home. Now I had everything. Our little scheme had worked.

I was elated on the drive back to the office. This story had been frustrating. Babita's colleagues in the Gauteng Health Department had closed ranks. One woman was convinced that if she spoke to me and the wrong people found out, she would be killed. I had been plugging away at the story for months without success, and now I held what I thought was game-changing evidence. If just one WhatsApp conversation published by *Sunday World* set out Babita's fear of the guys from Tembisa, I wagered there would be more in her discussions with her colleagues.

From her brief discussions with Madyo, it was clear that the latter understood what Babita was talking about. It told me there would be a trail. I was also buoyed by the fact that the police had handed over these devices to Rakesh. It was an indication that the investigation was on track and that the Hawks were following every lead. There was no scenario where the cellphone and primary laptop would be removed from police custody without first being imaged. It would be tantamount to throwing evidence away. But in my excitement I was getting ahead of myself. When I got back to our office in Randburg and pulled the devices from their evidence bags, I realised that they were all locked by passwords. The guys from Tembisa remained out of reach. I would need help to get into these devices.

The guys from Tembisa

I sat at my desk with Babita's laptop and cellphone in front of me. I was in the investigations team's office, a narrow strip tucked away in the corner of our effervescent newsroom. *News24* is a behemoth in terms of organisational size. Its success had allowed the establishment of a cloistered team of investigative journalists who could apply their effort, experience and skill to watchdog journalism. We often took the long road, and our projects spanned months and years. We worked with sensitive subject matter, and I held information that Babita had probably died for. Now, especially, I didn't want anyone to know what we had.

I had run out of space on my desk for files. Chasing down the *izinkabi* and gathering every piece of information I could find had created towers of paperwork on the desk and floor around me. But now, there was a new electronic trail to follow. Except the cellphone and laptop had lost their charge months ago, and I needed passwords to unlock them.

Neither Rakesh nor Babita's sisters or Thiara knew her passcodes. In one of Babita's diaries, I found a string of codes scribbled on the inside jacket. None worked. We work with a firm of digital forensic analysts when our team deals with large databases and troves of electronic information. They will remain anonymous because it would draw attention they don't want or need. Within days of Rakesh handing me the tote bag, I sat with it in the conference room of the firm's Pretoria office. I told my contact what was needed. He said they could do it, but at a cost – R32 000, to be exact.

I called my editor, Pieter du Toit, from the parking lot below the firm's offices. Pieter – who heads the investigations team – is a tall man with a firm handshake. When I think of him, I see him at his desk with a furrowed brow, hunched over his laptop, a patchwork of open books and stacks of documents teetering precariously around him. He's a dyed-in-the wool newsman, scathingly intelligent and a gifted writer.

He is also a man who calls a spade a spade, with a low tolerance for bullshit. He knew why paying for the devices to be unlocked was important. However, it was a lot of money to spend on a gamble. 'Give me two minutes,' he said. He needed to speak to Adriaan Basson, editor-in-chief of *News24*. Within two minutes, he rang back. 'We have the money. Do it.'

Midway through March 2022, I was still waiting on the tech experts. Our team's weekly planning meetings were uncomfortable. I had nothing to offer. The analysts said they would need time, but with each day that passed, I worried about blowing money on nothing. Adriaan had messaged me, gently prodding for an update. I reassured him, and myself, that we would find what we needed. When the call came from Pretoria, I hurriedly drove to the firm's offices. In the conference room, I was shown a database of sixty thousand emails they had managed to extract from Babita's laptop.

We keyed 'Tembisa' into the search bar and watched as hundreds of results came up. But the email at the top of this list was the most important. On 5 August 2021, at 8.02am, Babita had sent an email to Madyo with the subject line: 'Report on possibly fraudulent transactions'.

There it was. This single, ten-page document would become my unimpeachable lodestar.[145]

To provide a report to the Acting CFO as a follow up to my telephonic discussion on 3 August 2021.

On the 3rd of August 2021 during the analysis of the payment run it was identified that the greatest value of transactions that were on the payment run was for Tembisa Hospital (R104 million of the R166 million that was due for release). This immediately caused alarm, so an analysis was done of the transactions payable under Tembisa Hospital. On further analysis it was identified that most of the transactions was below the R500 000 value [quotation value]. A further search was conducted on the internet for some of the companies to whom payment was due for release and these companies could not be identified as legitimate. The payment run was immediately stopped at Provincial Treasury and all transactions relating to Tembisa Hospital was removed from the payment run. A further analysis was conducted on 4 August 2021 where a few more transactions were identified for other institutions. Since the payment run was already through, arrangements were made with the Provincial Treasury to have these funds recalled from the bank.[146]

Babita took time to lay out her concerns and how she had arrived at her conclusions. The spending by Tembisa Provincial Tertiary Hospital – commonly known as Tembisa Hospital – was anything but normal. A single facility was eating up the lion's share of the provincial budget, and purchases were at a high level. The accountant had examined payments processed in the four months between April and July 2021, when 2 453 individual transactions had been pushed through the facility's procurement office – worth R843 266 937. Tembisa was spending more than any hospital in the province's public health network. It was inexplicable. Another red flag she placed in the ledgers was the value of the contracts – all suspiciously just under R500 000.

It's an important figure within the context of the Gauteng Health Department. Buying below that threshold involves using a three-quote system. The supply-chain management section at the hospital would randomly approach three companies from the central supplier database and invite them to bid. The award would be signed off by the CEO of the facility. Spending above R500 000 would trigger a more rigorous public tender process. But Babita found that the hospital was gearing up, and it was all being done in-house.[147]

In the same four months, Tembisa Hospital approved 1 232 contracts, each valued at slightly less than half a million rand. These deals had a combined value of R603 394 651. It was massive. For context, the other nine largest facilities in Gauteng combined only processed 444 purchases for medical supplies and equipment during the same period. This disparity was glaring, and for Babita, it was impossible to ignore. If she overlooked these alarm bells, she too would be culpable. And she was a stickler for the rules.[148]

'Whilst this seems prevalent in Tembisa Hospital,' she noted, 'there is a high possibility that there are possible fraudulent transactions in other facilities as well. It is therefore recommended that the Acting CFO through the Acting Head of Department request an investigation into these companies as well as all Procurement transactions relating to these companies.'

In the interim, no payment transactions relating to Tembisa Hospital would be released pending the outcome of the investigations. Furthermore, any possibly fraudulent transactions linked to other institutions would also not be released on the payment runs.[149]

Babita had put the brakes on a flood of R104 million in cash that was about to leave the coffers of the provincial government. Once the money had been safeguarded, she asked Madyo for an urgent investigation into worrying transactions worth just shy of R1 billion. For the first time, I could understand the urgency in her terse WhatsApp message. I now knew exactly what money she had been talking about when she said she was worried that 'the guys from

Tembisa' would be on to her. This document was the reason she feared for her life. And, thanks to Babita, I knew who the Tembisa guys were. Annexed to her letter was a list of 217 companies she had identified as worthy of further scrutiny.[150]

Paydirt.

I also took delivery of an image of her iPhone, exported to a Microsoft Excel spreadsheet that contained thousands of lines of data. The phone had logged every keystroke, internet search, message and call Babita made. Now I could interrogate her entire dialogue with Madyo in the weeks leading up to her murder. It was clear that Madyo had known of Babita's fears just days before she was assassinated, and this report formed the foundation of Babita's concerns.

I was astonished when I read the document on her laptop – it was the result of a single search. Yet, there were still another 60 000 emails to pore over. The contents of her phone presented an equally daunting task, but I had gotten lucky. I now had a foundation to piece together a timeline of Babita's final months and to unravel her last internal investigation. At that moment, I thought the task would be Sisyphean, but it was doable. More information is always better than less.

As I was leaving, I asked the team of analysts in passing if they could identify the date and time when the police had imaged the devices. It would be an important milestone in the investigation, and knowing when it was done could indicate the Hawks' level of urgency. Did that process leave a digital imprint?

Indeed, it did. They found that no work had been done to process the phone or laptop as evidence. Within minutes, I had found the report and a list of suspicious companies numbering in the hundreds. Here was a viable motive for murder. There were 850 million reasons to ensure that Babita was silenced. Surely the elite investigators from the Hawks would pursue such leads? But they hadn't. Babita's possessions had sat untouched. The bags still bore the signature of Captain Hicks, the man who had seized them on the day of the murder. The cellphone and her primary laptop were never so much as turned on.

Hanlon's razor

*'Never ascribe to malice that which is adequately explained
by stupidity.'*

– Hanlon's razor

The Directorate for Priority Crime Investigation (DPCI) – the
Hawks – are meant to be the preserve of the South African law-
enforcement community. They are a team of police investigators
tasked with fighting organised, transnational and commercial crime
webs and dismantling networks of corruption.[151] Their mission is
both onerous and dangerous. The directorate was established in
2009 when then-President Jacob Zuma assented to the South African
Police Service Amendment Act of 2008. The very existence of the
Hawks was contentious, borne of the dissolution of the Directorate
for Special Operations (DSO), also known as the Scorpions.

The DSO was established in 1999 by Zuma's predecessor, Thabo
Mbeki, as an investigative force within the National Prosecuting
Authority that would take on organised crime networks, corruption
and complex commercial crime. The formula of the DSO was unique
in the South African sense, as police investigators would work
with prosecutors to guide difficult cases to court and, ultimately,
convictions.

The DSO – completely independent of the police – was an immediate success, boasting a conviction rate of between 82 per cent and 94 per cent. In 2002, a year after its establishment, the Scorpions arrested 66 people; by 2006, this number had climbed to 617. In 2002, the unit finalised 180 prosecutions, and in 2006, the figure stood at 214.[152] The DSO gained a reputation for taking on high-profile corruption cases involving powerful politicians or their acolytes, with lines of inquiry often tracing back to corrupt members of the ANC.

The DSO led the multi-year investigation into the arms deal, which resulted in the conviction of ANC politician Tony Yengeni and businessman Schabir Shaik, a close associate of Zuma, who was deputy president at the time. The same investigation drew in Zuma, and nearly two decades later, he is still trying to wriggle his way free of accountability. He faces two counts of corruption, one count each of racketeering and money laundering, and twelve counts of fraud in a criminal prosecution arising from a series of payments that the state alleges were bribes paid to Shaik, acting as a conduit for French arms company Thales.

Thales, or Thomson-CSF as it was formerly known, scored a R2.6 billion stake in the defence package for combat suites fitted in German-made warships. The payments to Zuma, via Shaik, were allegedly fees for Zuma's political cover and protection.

In another matter, the DSO investigated and prosecuted National Police Commissioner Jackie Selebi. Selebi was himself an ANC struggle stalwart with no law-enforcement experience who was appointed to lead the police in the democratic dispensation, serving from 2000 to 2008. He was convicted on corruption charges in 2010 for accepting bribes from drug trafficker Glenn Agliotti in exchange for favours and influence.

Zuma had fallen into the crosshairs of the DSO, as had other ANC politicians. When he deposed Mbeki and took control of the party at the 2007 Polokwane elective conference, he had a score to settle. His supporters cried foul, believing that the DSO was unaccountable and susceptible to political manipulation and meddling, and that unseen agendas were driving its pursuit of Zuma.

Zuma and those in his camp were the architects of a resolution to disband the Scorpions and incorporate its work into the South African Police Service. Many others countered that the Scorpions were an effective crime-fighting unit precisely because of their independence from the SAPS. The ANC had an outright majority in parliament, and the law was changed. The DSO was subsumed into the Hawks.

The Hawks, in their constitutional mandate, theoretically espoused the independence of the DSO: 'The Directorate should implement, where appropriate, a multidisciplinary approach and an integrated methodology involving the cooperation of all relevant government departments and institutions. It should have the necessary independence to perform its functions and be equipped with appropriate human and financial resources. The DPCI should be adequately staffed through transfers, appointments or secondment of personnel whose integrity is beyond reproach.'[153]

But for Zuma and the ANC, simply getting rid of the DSO would not be easy. Hugh Glenister, a businessman and lobbyist, challenged the legislation that had created the Hawks on a number of constitutional grounds, among them that the Hawks lacked independence and, as a body, was susceptible to government interference. The Constitutional Court found in Glenister's favour, specifically agreeing that the Hawks were not impervious to political influence.[154]

The apex court noted that the South African Police Service Act required the Hawks' activities to be coordinated by the cabinet. In addition, a ministerial committee comprising at least the ministers of police, finance, home affairs, state security, and justice and constitutional development, as well as any other minister designated from time to time by the president, would determine policy guidelines for the Hawks' functioning. As these ministerial positions were political appointments, the court held that the Hawks were vulnerable to political intrusion, which was inimical to its genuine independence. The judgment also found that the members of the Hawks lacked the security of tenure required for such independence.[155]

The genesis of the Hawks was fraught, and by the time Captain Masenxani Chauke took charge of Babita's murder investigation, the organisation was anything but stable. It did not enjoy the DSO's success in terms of convictions. Only 48 per cent of positions within the organisation were occupied, and the Hawks struggled to appoint skilled investigators in nearly 1 500 posts.[156] This dearth of human capital meant that investigations stumbled forward for years while the conviction rate slumped, Hawks boss Godfrey Lebeya admitted before a parliamentary committee.

That the Hawks would lead Babita's murder investigation was itself an oddity. According to its well-established mandate, the Hawks would take charge of murder cases only if the victim was a police officer.[157] One could argue that the presumption of serious corruption playing a role in Babita's murder would have been enough to see the docket fall within their ambit, but they didn't know it at the time. In fact, they didn't know much at all; in terms of their own guiding policies, the Hawks had no business leading this probe.

When Chauke was allocated the docket, I was watching him. As investigating officer, he bore the ultimate responsibility, even if he was supported by a team of officers. He would be the one driving the investigation. I was advised to be wary.

By the time I got access to Babita's cellphone and laptop, I had reason to be concerned about the veteran detective. Most significantly, the devices had not been 'imaged' and examined by police. As the man carrying the docket, this was a process Chauke should have led.

I asked some policemen I could trust to visit Mondeor Police Station and retrieve the evidence log. This would set out when the phone and laptop were logged in and when they were removed and transported for forensic analysis. The devices were booked into the store on the day of the murder, and removed by Chauke two weeks later. They only resurfaced when Rakesh demanded them back six months later. This begs the question: where were the devices kept all that time?

That Chauke and his team could have ignored the laptop and cellphone as items of evidentiary value was astounding and defied logic. I am no police officer, but it is an established principle that detectives, when seized with a murder probe, will try to understand the motive. Had Chauke and the Hawks examined this evidence, they would have found Babita's report filed with Madyo three weeks before the murder, when she placed a stop on R104 million in payments and called for a forensic investigation into expenditure from Tembisa Hospital worth R850 million. The Hawks appeared to be in a darkness of their own making.

It was clear to me that I would be investigating Tembisa Hospital's procurement processes on my own. Essentially, the Hawks and Chauke had thrown the cellphone and laptop away by giving them to Rakesh without first imaging them. The chain of custody had been broken. It was a significant misstep on the part of the Hawks, but now I was primed to expose what Babita had been looking into, which was likely to have resulted in her being killed. I had my work cut out for me. Trawling through 60 000 emails and thousands of lines of data logged by her cellphone was a big ask. There was no team of detectives and skilled forensic analysts working the leads. It was only me – a crime reporter.

When I confronted Chauke with these allegations, he shut down. He insisted that while he was not authorised to speak to me, he had 'done his part'.[158] The Hawks insisted that they had followed every avenue in the murder investigation and flatly denied that they had dropped the ball.

If the devices had been imaged by the police, there would have been a report from an analyst and an affidavit setting out the methodology of the examination in the docket. These documents would be needed if the *izinkabi* faced a murder trial. I asked the Hawks to produce the cover page of this report, with an undertaking that I would not publish it. I told them that if they didn't, it didn't exist – effective confirmation of my allegations that the evidence had been ignored. I was not asking them to reveal all; I merely wanted proof that they had done their job. The Hawks refused, claiming it was sensitive information that could jeopardise their prosecution of the hitmen.[159] It was a popular refrain that I had expected, and frankly, it could not have been further from the truth. That they refused to share this document was telling. It suggested, strongly, that the content on the devices had been ignored.

What confirmed my suspicions was that in November 2022, the Hawks' investigating team contacted Rakesh and asked for the phone and the laptop to be returned. If they had previously been imaged in line with police protocol, there would be absolutely no need to do it again. This did little to change the Hawks' official denials, and it came only after we started publishing. But now I knew for certain that an original examination of these devices did not exist.

The roles of Chauke and the Hawks in this saga are central. The Hawks took charge of Babita's murder investigation outside their mandate and frustrated a team of police officers who had managed to track and arrest the six hitmen. It was the Hawks and Chauke who instructed these cops to wait before surveilling the white BMW used in the killing – a vehicle that, along with murder weapons apparently hidden inside it, was ultimately lost. And what of Chauke's insistence that the men linked to the stash house and caught with a glut of money be released? They were set free and their cellphones, which were never examined, were handed back to them. This singular event would have dire ramifications years later.

From what I could see, the investigation championed by the Hawks had been mishandled at several junctures. The probe was entirely focused on linking the *izinkabi* to the crime and building what would become an entirely circumstantial case against them. It seemed that there was no desire on the part of Chauke to look beyond these men and try to reel in the mastermind and others who had helped to set the plot in motion.

Those who ascribe to Hanlon's razor would suggest the Hawks' missteps in the investigation stemmed from stupidity. For Chauke's handling of the matter and the success of arresting the hitmen – an accolade wrongly claimed by the Hawks after solid police work carried out by others – he was promoted to the rank of lieutenant-colonel.[160] While he basked in the afterglow of a pay rise and more authority and influence, I was doing the gumshoe work he had dodged. Babita's emails were a real treasure trove, and her cellphone provided other clues worth chasing down.

PART 3

'I don't like dealing with politicians'

For a good detective, a cellphone can be an invaluable cache of information. Every minuscule action is logged, timestamped and stored in the device's database. These data logs are populated in the background as the phone you carry in your pocket spies on you, silently and unseen. This is a worthwhile forensic tool. An investigator can stitch together a timeline of events using call logs, text messages, contacts, photos, videos, location data, browsing history, application data, calendar entries, social media activity and even deleted files, providing a detailed picture of the user's activity down to the millisecond. This invaluable chronicle on Babita's cellphone had been cast aside by the team of Hawks detectives investigating her killing, and now I had it all.

I set my sights on Babita's interactions with Madyo, her boss, who was acting CFO – a position of considerable power and influence within the Gauteng Department of Health – at the time of the assassination. Babita had compiled her report into thousands of 'possibly fraudulent' transactions out of Tembisa Hospital and sent it to Madyo just weeks before her murder.[161] She had also raised her concerns about her safety with Madyo days before she died.[162] Babita's pursuit of the guys from Tembisa – and establishing exactly where Madyo fit in – was my starting point. I could overlay the phone record with her emails and produce a pencil sketch of Babita's actions prior to her death. For days, I worked through 16 000 lines of data in the sprawling spreadsheet.

On 3 August 2021, the day before she formally escalated her report, Babita sent Madyo a WhatsApp message at 6.45pm that read: 'Hi please call me when you can. I need to discuss a matter with you urgently.' Within moments, Madyo placed a call to Deokaran, and the pair spoke for thirteen minutes.[163] Deokaran referenced the interaction in the opening line of her report sent two days later. As far as I was concerned, Babita's concern was patent, and she was dutifully creating a paper trail.

On 11 August, Babita pressed Madyo again.[164] The guys from Tembisa were a dangerous lot; why else would the accountant have feared the administrative exercise of investigating procurement deals and putting a halt on payments? It was a prescient exchange, and Babita now had the endorsement of her boss to keep probing. She herself lacked the authority to launch a forensic analysis at the hospital, as only the head of department had the clout to set something like that in motion.

For the record, Babita had raised her concerns with Madyo, and the latter had assured her that the happenings at Tembisa Hospital were a concern to management and the political leadership. Madyo had, according to the WhatsApp message to Babita, escalated the problem. Now they had to wait.

Babita was restless. I could see from the activity on her phone late at night that she was performing Google searches on companies trading with the hospital, all of which appeared on the list of entities she attached to her report. I believe that she was establishing if these companies had a track record supplying medical equipment and consumables. If they did, it was likely they would be well-established and have websites.[165] At the same time, she put her subordinates to work. She ordered them to generate reports on hospital procurement, and she singled out individual companies. One was a little-known shelf entity called Kaizen Projects.[166]

In an email to a colleague on the subject of this firm, Babita wrote that an 'events management company' was being paid millions as a Tembisa Hospital supplier. The woman responded, commiserating with Babita and saying that she, too, had queried payments emanating from the hospital but that the CEO, Dr Ashley Mthunzi, had berated her with accusations that nitpicking was somehow related to an anti-transformation agenda.[167] One would think that a hospital administrator would want to dot the i's and cross the t's when it came to the paperwork for which they would ultimately be held responsible.

On 17 August, Babita again looked to Madyo for guidance on the matter of Tembisa Hospital and its dubious suppliers. At 10.42am, she sent a screengrab of an Excel spreadsheet to Madyo. Highlighted were three payments to Kaizen, all processed on the same day, totalling just over R1 million.[168]

> 14:17 – Madyo: 'Yes babes.'
> 14:20 – Babita: 'Will ask for the documents. This supplier is delivering surgical items but when you google then its an events management company.'
> 14:25 – Madyo: 'Noted. Did u put them in the [payment] run?'
> 14:26 – Babita: 'We did. Will check the documents and if not in order will recall the money.'
> 14:54 – Madyo: 'Eish I just don't like dealing with politicians u know??Pls keep this private. Will speak to u soonest.'[169]

Two days after this interaction, Babita mentioned it to a colleague in an email. She set out how, despite her misgivings around Kaizen, Madyo had instructed her to pay them.[170]

'Almost a million rand to an events management company for medical related items. How does such a big company not have a company profile on the internet? How do they get business if they are not visible to the public?' she wrote. 'I highlighted this to the

CFO [Madyo], but she indicated that we must go ahead and pay them.'[171]

Madyo, in her own words, had no appetite to deal with politicians. Because of this, the company was paid on her instruction. Her response was informative. It suggested that Kaizen was not simply a letterbox entity controlled by an invisible hand but most likely headed by someone with political sway. Madyo must have known this.

What of the investigation that Babita had pleaded for? I had to establish what Madyo did when Babita warned her of possible procurement irregularities and a surge of payments that threatened to bankrupt the hospital and knock the entire Gauteng Health Department off balance. Madyo told Babita that she had asked the department head for authority to advance the probe and keep a freeze on payments. The acting head of the department was Dr Sibongile Zungu.

By the time I darkened Zungu's doorstep, she had moved on from the Gauteng Health Department. I wanted to know when Madyo had sent Babita's report, and what was done about it. What happened to the payment run, frozen in motion at the provincial treasury, that the guys from Tembisa were expecting? What happened with the investigation – when did it start and finish, and what did the findings set out? Was Babita right, or was there an innocent explanation for the mammoth expenditure?

Zungu was candid in her response and, in so doing, exposed Madyo as a fraud.[172] The CFO had never raised Babita's concern about Tembisa Hospital, either verbally or in writing, and Zungu had never seen Babita's report. The message Madyo had sent to Babita was a lie. Zungu told me she had heard of Babita's fears for the first time on the day of her murder.

Madyo had been an emotional mess, Zungu told me. 'She [Madyo] was responding to my question on how she was feeling. She indicated that she was still hurting and going through their [Babita and Madyo's] text conversations. Madyo did not communicate any request for an investigation. She did, however, share a screenshot of their WhatsApp conversation. [This was] not necessarily reporting or requesting an investigation but rather highlighting that it seemed like Babita had a premonition about the activities at Tembisa Hospital.'

It is also telling that Zungu seemingly just left the issue there. Why did she overlook it?

Madyo's deception was plain as day, and Babita's report had been buried. The red flags Babita raised regarding Tembisa Hospital disappeared when she died, and the implications were damning. And what of Kaizen and the politician Madyo had no desire to deal with? A simple search of the Companies and Intellectual Property Commission database set out that the firm Babita had homed in on was controlled by Sello Philly Sekhokho, an influential figure in the ANC in Ekurhuleni. This was the man Madyo didn't want to deal with – the man she wanted paid. And Babita was ordered to keep it secret.

When I started looking into Sekhokho, I found that he made a living off plush contracts and tenders, coincidentally while he was a figure of influence in a political party that controlled the awarding. The payments to Kaizen came ahead of the ANC's Gauteng elective conference, and Sekhokho was in the running for treasurer-general. But that was not all. Sekhokho was the director of three companies, and Babita had flagged them all for further investigation.[173]

Babita's phone and its silent logging of her actions made clear that Madyo was a point of focus. There was no investigation and no intervention. She released the payments, and the cash flowed freely to those who Babita feared.

CHAPTER 13

Covid corruption frenzy

History will remember Monday, 23 March 2020, as a day that changed the course of South Africa forever. These were uncertain times. The coronavirus, originating from the Chinese province of Wuhan, had already begun its rout of the world. Three weeks earlier, the first case of Covid-19 had been recorded within our borders. The virus was imported by a KwaZulu-Natal man returning with his family from a skiing trip in Italy, and now it was spreading.[174]

President Cyril Ramaphosa stood at a lectern, and in a 23-minute address beamed to the nation, he delivered the news that would affect the lives of millions of South Africans. In a black suit and a burnt-orange tie, his fatigue was visible and his message devastating. 'My fellow South Africans . . .' he began.[175]

The country was placed in a state of lockdown for 21 days, a drastic measure imposed to save lives. Companies not essential to the pandemic response would close. People were to shelter in their homes, leaving only to buy food or seek medical care. The economy was about to grind to a halt, and the army and police were deployed to maintain the rule of law.[176]

'Our analysis of the progress of the epidemic informs us that we need to urgently and dramatically escalate our response,' Ramaphosa said. 'The next few days are crucial. Without decisive action, the number of people infected will rapidly increase from a few hundred to tens of thousands, and within a few weeks, to hundreds of thousands. This is extremely dangerous for a population like ours, which has a large number of people with suppressed immunity because of HIV and TB, and high levels of poverty and malnutrition. [...] While this measure will have a considerable impact on people's livelihoods, on the life of our society and on our economy, the human cost of delaying this action would be far, far greater.'[177]

Leading up to this point, Ramaphosa and his advisors had tracked the spread of Covid-19 across Asia and Europe. The inundation of hospitals and dire global shortage of PPE and medicines foreshadowed what would soon arrive at the southern tip of Africa. The full heft of the state had already been mobilised to prepare for what was coming, and the gears of the government procurement machine were turning.

Ramaphosa was alive to the spectre of corruption in this realm. The mismanagement of public funds and the networks of patronage linking civil servants – often abetted or coerced by their political principals drawn from the rank and file of the ANC – and the private sector had become a hallmark of South African society. Tenderpreneurs were enriched by the public purse, and the dubious spending channelled their way had gravely impeded service delivery. The poorest and most vulnerable in our society were badly affected.[178]

'I want to make it clear,' Ramaphosa continued, 'that we expect all South Africans to act in the interests of the South African nation and not in their own selfish interest. We will therefore act very strongly against any attempts at corruption and at profiteering from this crisis. I've directed that special units [of the National Prosecuting Authority] be put together to act immediately and arrest those against whom we find evidence of corruption. We will work with the judiciary to expedite cases against implicated persons and make sure that the guilty do go to jail.'[179]

At the time of Ramaphosa's address, the Commission of Inquiry into State Capture, chaired by Chief Justice Raymond Zondo, had already sat for two years, and evidence before it laid bare how his predecessor, Jacob Zuma, had enabled the rise of the Gupta brothers – Indian businessmen who became billionaires from the cream of state contracts. Zuma had, with Machiavellian precision, denuded the capacity of the police, the State Security Agency, the National Prosecuting Authority and the South African Revenue Service by installing those loyal to his agenda to protect himself, his cronies and his benefactors. The quid pro quo had been bribes and crooked largesse dished out in spades. Evidence before the inquiry showed how some within the ANC had sold out South Africans to serve their own greed.

When Ramaphosa wrested back control of the party from Zuma at the ANC's 2017 elective conference, he campaigned on a clean-up ticket. Rogues had infiltrated the ranks and leadership of a lauded liberation movement, and support was waning after Zuma's 'nine wasted years'.[180]

He promised that in this time of calamity and global pandemic, the looting would come to an end. It was not so. One after the other, the coronavirus corruption scandals battered his reputation, and that of the ANC. Just days before Ramaphosa made his address to the nation, the Department of Public Works embarked on a spending spree for a 40-kilometre fence meant to secure South Africa's border with Zimbabwe.[181] Border posts had been closed to prevent the spread of the virus, but the demarcation between the two countries was notoriously porous. Navigating paths etched into the veld by tobacco and cigarette smugglers, illegal immigrants had easily crossed into South Africa on foot for years. Now this new fence, procured under emergency regulations with a price tag of R37 million, would stop that. Within two days of the purchase directive being issued, two contractors were appointed. Work was expected to be concluded within a month.

But this fence, intended to be an impervious barrier near the Beitbridge border crossing, was a joke. Spools of razor wire that had been stretched between hastily rooted fence poles did little, if anything, to prevent illegal crossings. It took less than five minutes for human traffickers to cut new holes in the 1.8-metre-high fence, and rivers of people flooded onto South Africa soil in broad daylight. A one-kilometre stretch of the fence was stolen and hauled back to Zimbabwe.[182] An investigation by the Special Investigating Unit found fraud, irregularities, deceit and misrepresentation at the core of the border-fence splurge. It was not a good start for Ramaphosa.[183]

The police, considered an essential service crucial to the pandemic response, had to equip their 180 000-strong force with PPE as they hit the frontlines and risked exposure. Top brass tapped their mammoth budget. All in all, the SAPS spent R1.56 billion on PPE, sanitiser and disinfectant. Sleuthing by social justice activist Mark Heywood revealed how a little-known company, Red Roses Africa, based in the slowly dying mining town of Barberton in Mpumalanga, received a most significant boon. It had no traceable history of supplying PPE products and was not registered to do so. Nor was it certified to produce sanitiser and disinfectant.[184]

But this didn't stop the police. The SAPS sourced 90 000 25-litre containers of hand sanitiser and disinfectant from the company, paying R5 405 per 25-litre unit. Each unit should have been priced at little more than R900. The result was an undue R486 million windfall.

Of all the profiteers in the Covid-19 pandemic, 32-year-old Hamilton Ndlovu had to be the dumbest. In May 2020, his braggadocio got the better of him when he took to social media to share a video montage of a fleet of luxury cars. He had just taken delivery of three Porsches, a Jeep Grand Cherokee and a Lamborghini Urus SUV worth R11 million.[185] I bet he was on top of the world. His video went viral, immediately raising questions about the source of his riches. As it turned out, his automotive shopping spree had been funded by the National Health Laboratory Service – an entity within the Department of Health – through a raft of PPE tenders worth R170 million.[186] His garish display drew the attention of the authorities, and a probe was launched.

Ndlovu had used a series of companies, controlled by close proxies, to bid for work. He scored nineteen different awards. R42 million had been channelled into his personal bank accounts but only R15 million had been spent on providing the National Health Laboratory Service with PPE.[187] His cars, houses and collection of Rolex watches were seized by the state, and his flamboyant image was in tatters. In South Africa, getting rich through corrupt means is so simple, you can be a dullard and still get paid.

The Gauteng provincial government awarded a R6 million tender – to retrofit taxis to allow for better ventilation – to a company controlled by Ramaphosa's son, Andile, amid claims of preferential treatment because of his political connections. The president, who had taken such a strong position on graft and put measures in place to staunch it during the pandemic, now wore a stain. Allegations of undue benefit were landing very close to home.[188]

The Gauteng Health Department, led by then-MEC Bandile Masuku, was also spending. It was understandable: the Covid-19 wave would soon break over their 80 000-strong complement of doctors, nurses, clinicians and support staff.

Among those to benefit was another ANC figure, former cabinet minister Nomvula Mokonyane, whose daughter's company secured a contract to supply soap for frontline workers. Mokonyane herself paid R1.6 million to the shelf company – formed just three months earlier – to buy the bars of soap.[189]

But it was yet another PPE procurement scandal that roiled the leadership of the Gauteng Health Department and Ramaphosa's presidency. Masuku's department had awarded a R125 million PPE tender to a company called Royal Bhaca Projects, whose only director was Chief Madzikane II Thandisizwe Diko. He was married to Ramaphosa's spokesperson, Khusela Diko.[190] This payment formed part of R2.2 billion worth of PPE acquisitions by the department, all within five days of Ramaphosa's announcement of the lockdown. Other companies, with deeper political ties, remained in the shadows.

The Masukus and the Dikos were close. The MEC and the presidential mouthpiece had risen through the ranks of the ANC together, from student formations into youth structures, before their ascension to the big league. They were family friends and part of the bridal parties at their respective weddings.[191] Money meant for the vital preparation of Gauteng was being diverted to those within the ANC's orbit. Moreover, the stink of corruption, which had been so widespread, had now oozed into Ramaphosa's own office. It was scandalous. Diko took a leave of absence from her presidency duties, and Gauteng Premier David Makhura replaced Masuku, who also took leave.

The SIU began an investigation into the tainted procurement, and its findings led to the ouster of Masuku and his management. In the end, the axe fell on the head of the department, Professor Mkhululi Lukhele, chief financial officer Kabelo Lehloenya and chief director of supply-chain management Thandiwe Pino. They either resigned or were dismissed.

At a press conference to announce Masuku's suspension, Makhura said that it had pained him to act: 'I must say that I am disappointed at this point. I am really, really disappointed to have an MEC, who has been leading from the front very well, facing allegations that I can't ignore.'[192]

What he told journalists was probative evidence that Makhura had anticipated abuse of the procurement system. It was a shocking indictment of the people he himself had appointed to lead. He described the financial scandal as the most significant of his tenure.[193]

For several months at the height of the pandemic, the department that oversees one of the largest, most complex and highly challenged healthcare systems on the continent was in a leadership vacuum. Critical positions were vacant. Politics, patronage and procurement had become intertwined. Officials installed for their party allegiances had let hospitals in the province fall to ruin.

The Gauteng Health Department has a legacy of political leaders embroiled in scandal. In October 2015, then-MEC Qedani

Mahlangu announced the end of a contract between her department and long-term psychiatric-care hospital Life Esidimeni. This facility had provided highly specialised chronic care to about 2 000 mental healthcare patients for years. What should have been a state service had been outsourced. Mahlangu moved these patients to NGOs and other psychiatric hospitals in an attempt to 'deinstitutionalise' mental healthcare and cut costs.[194]

Civil society reacted in shock and horror, concerned about the safety, health and dignity of these vulnerable patients – all of whom were indigent. The South African Society of Psychiatrists implored the MEC to halt her plans, detailing serious risks. This warning was ignored, and patients were discharged – some loaded onto the back of trucks – and dispersed to NGOs across the province. Their families were never informed. A total of 141 patients with mental health problems died in undignified conditions. Over 1 400 surviving patients were exposed to torture, trauma and severe violations of their human rights. The whereabouts of 44 people transferred from Life Esidimeni remain uncertain to this day.[195] It was a tragedy.

But the departmental mismanagement stretched back even further. Between 2006 and 2010, ANC strongman Brian Hlongwa was MEC of the department. He allegedly received massive kickbacks in the form of luxury spa treatments, trips for him and his wife, and a R2.6-million deposit on a plush Bryanston mansion from company 3P Consulting, which was blessed with contracts worth R1.2 billion.[196] The Hawks and the SIU were asked to investigate.

The corruption allegations lingered long after he was shuffled out of his post, but the pall they cast didn't matter to his party. He was an ANC member of the Gauteng legislature and had acted as chief whip. He resigned in 2018 when the SIU released a report detailing his culpability.

Babita had joined the Gauteng Health Department as a clerk around the same time Hlongwa was parachuted in.

Sometime early in 2019, she was suspended on allegations of misconduct – something she kept hidden from her family. She was one of only two senior managers in the finance section. Simultaneously, two senior officials in the supply-chain management unit were pushed out too, also on the strength of departmental charges.[197]

Exactly what Babita was charged with and what had occasioned the alleged misconduct remain unclear because she suffered alone and in silence. She did not say a word to anyone, and even her niece, who was living with her in Johannesburg, was kept in the dark. Babita would get dressed as if for work every day and drop her niece at university. Yet, for six months, her salary was stopped and she was barred from the office.[198]

What I know of this time in her life has been pieced together from WhatsApp messages she sent her family a year before she was killed. Her sisters shared the messages with me, and I was the first person outside the family to see them. They were sent in August 2020, around the time that Masuku and the other senior managers were being axed. Babita was of the firm belief that her removal was a stitch-up to allow funds meant for medical care to be stolen.[199]

'So this Women's month, let me tell you a story about the power of women,' she wrote in a WhatsApp message. 'I have been going through this for 18 months but I have not said a word to you guys. At work, since last year, they suspended a few of us for refusing to be part of their corruption. I was one of them and last year I sat at home for six months without working. Our approach was you can fire us but we will not be part of this genocide and theft of patients' money . . . Now if you look at what is happening, where would we be if we allowed them to use us? Our entire family would be brought into disrepute and our names would be all over the media. I didn't want to tell you guys anything because I know everyone will be stressed, and these are problems we didn't create ourselves.'[200]

Babita told them she returned to work, but she had ostensibly been demoted. Instead of taking up her post at head office, she was relegated to a district outpost in Hillbrow.

Among a pile of documents, I found a handwritten workplace grievance Babita had filled out, seeking to be returned to her post as chief director of financial accounting. 'I am aggrieved that my employer [Gauteng Department of Health] has unilaterally changed my terms and conditions of employment by removing me from my position and placing me at the Johannesburg Health District. This move has diminished my status.'

I can't be sure if it was sent, let alone received. I doubt her relatives have ever seen it. It was seized by police on the day of Babita's murder. Her WhatsApp messages provided the next step in her timeline.

'We received a letter to say all the charges were withdrawn. So after their corruption became public knowledge they quickly withdrew charges. We knew that one day they will be exposed, we just didn't realise it will be so soon. The PPE came as a bonus. They were stealing in other ways as well.'[201]

'And if you look at it, all the politicians say they don't sign anything. It's the officials who will take the fall. I always tell the other managers, you want to be able to sleep at night and not worry about the police knocking on your door. Not even the doctors who should have patients' interests at heart had the guts to say no. If we four were there this PPE fraud would never have happened.'[202]

She told her relatives that when she was pushed out, the department brought in a consultancy to do her work. She claimed that this unnamed company was paid R140 million for its services. Babita's account of what happened to her is drawn from the state-capture playbook, perfected during Zuma's nine wasted years. Any official unwilling to kowtow to political pressure was smeared, charged and removed. Zuma did it to some of his ministers, but it was a one-size-fits-all stratagem that was replicated and wielded against Babita at a provincial level. The charges were never meant to stick, and the disciplinary action was initiated only so that someone more pliable could be placed in her office.

At about the same time, she also shared her frustrations with Ahmed Kathrada Foundation chair and anti-apartheid activist Neeshan Balton. As for the department, she painted a fraught picture of a place where corruption reigned.

'I want to tell you how I see the modus operandi of the department and I have been there for over 14 years now.[203] They suspended us and they made the life of the payments director a living hell and she resigned. Once all the PPE orders were done and some payments made, they dropped all charges against the two supply chain management directors and called them back to work. They offered the payments director to come back on a contract and moved me to JHB Health District.[204]

'My biggest issue though is the Provincial Treasury. How do all these things happen under their watch and this is not the first instance. It's as if they are a silent partner and will start acting when the damage is done. With all that has happened at Gauteng Health it is no wonder we are forever struggling to pay our suppliers.[205]

'My assessment of the situation is that they wanted us out of the way because if these were real charges, why are they not pursuing them? I also see they do not want me back at the Province as they see me as an obstacle in payments they want to make to certain companies. I just want to tell you that not all of us are corrupt. Some of us are trying but you see how they are dealing with us.'[206]

Clearly, Babita's indictment is of the officials who, at the behest of other role players, corrupted the procurement system. What mattered to them appeared to be not the sick and dying or the medical staff who cared for them, but rather self-enrichment. Despite this, she had withstood the pressure and held on to her job. And now the department was under new management.

A message she sent to Balton was prescient: 'Every few years we have a different team of people who come in and loot and the funds seem to be a bottomless pit.'[207]

CHAPTER 14

Tembisa Hospital: a place to die

Tembisa Hospital was pushed to the point of collapse by the Covid-19 virus. Doctors and nurses in powder-blue smocks, their faces hidden behind layers of masks, vacillated between beds in the Covid section, trying to save those they could. For many, it was a losing battle. The mortuary, too, was overwhelmed. Bodies were piled up in storerooms. Others were left in their beds for hours.[208]

Three months after the pathogen arrived on South African soil, biting strictures and regulations imposed by the state – movement curfews, bans on public gatherings and interprovincial travel, and the use of masks and social distancing – had curbed its spread to a degree.

But now the pandemic was rampant: the number of infections had climbed to well over 100 000 during the first wave, the most virulent and deadly iteration of what was a modern-day plague.[209] Of this number, more than 40 000 infections were recorded in Gauteng alone.[210]

It was not surprising that the province emerged as the new national epicentre. Epidemiologists and infectious-disease experts had predicted it weeks before. While Gauteng is the smallest of the country's nine provinces by area, it is the most densely populated. More than

16 million people reside in its three metropolitan municipalities in cities, suburbs and sprawling townships.[211] Covid-19 struck hard, leading to a surge in caseloads that quickly reached a tipping point. In total, 8 301 hospital beds between private facilities and the public health network were full.[212]

Tembisa Hospital was established in 1972 to serve Tembisa township. It is a patchwork of distinct buildings on the eastern fringes of the settlement, flanked by the rapidly developing expanses of Midrand. Its 840 beds and 23 separate wards serve a population of nearly 2.5 million. It was upgraded from a regional hospital to a tertiary facility in 2012.[213] Put simply, after this transition, the hospital should have offered the full array of specialist medical care and an intensive-care unit under the supervision of an experienced intensivist. At the same time, it should have become a training institution, taking in referrals from the 26 clinics and community healthcare centres in its catchment area.[214] However, it is a perpetually overcrowded facility. Its structure was never ideal for the mammoth population it served. The supposed upgrade was a change only in name.[215]

Because of its status and location, Tembisa Hospital was chosen to deal with the local fallout of the global health crisis.

When the Gauteng provincial government announced its plans to prepare for the inescapable surge that was forecast by virus modelling teams, the focus was on increasing capacity in the public health sphere by adding hospital beds, augmenting the number of nurses and doctors, and equipping facilities to deal with the influx of the infected. Tembisa was one of three hospitals in the province that would act as a designated centre of care.

Dr Bandile Masuku, the Gauteng Health MEC, was at the vanguard of managing the health response in the province. He moved to allay fears, insisting the system over which he presided would not fail.[216] For Tembisa Hospital to be part of this response – a political decision with devastating implications – it needed to be well-resourced in terms of budget and decked out with the best equipment, operated by medical professionals well-versed in the ways of the virus and its effect on its hosts. It also needed dedicated high-care facilities and an ICU purposely fitted for Covid-19 patients. In essence, any person admitted to such a centre should have expected the highest quality of care. But Tembisa Hospital was by no means ready. It fell short in nearly every respect. The result of this ill-fated decision was that the hospital was reduced to a warzone.[217]

The dissonant public messaging from Masuku was heartening to those fearful of falling ill, but roundly misleading. Weeks had supposedly been spent preparing health facilities, both public and private. A massive procurement drive for PPE and ventilators was in high gear. Donations from abroad poured in. They were ready, they claimed. Surrounded by the Gauteng Provincial Coronavirus Command Council – a platoon of advisors and experts – Masuku was resolute that his team had taken every measure to prevent loss of life and the total implosion of the healthcare system – or so he said. At Tembisa Hospital, at least, this could not have been further from the truth.

In reality, there were no dedicated and staffed ICU and high-care wards. The hospital hastily established a temporary Covid-19 investigation ward in a tent adjacent to the accident and emergency unit. Two existing wards were ringfenced for those who tested positive – one for men and another for women. The recognised standard is such that an ICU has one nurse dedicated to each patient, with constant monitoring and every change in a constellation of vital signs noted. On Tembisa Hospital's Covid wards, two doctors, aided by a small clutch of nurses, were charged with more than 40 gravely ill patients at a time. Many nurses flatly refused to work on these wards because they had not been supplied with PPE and feared contracting the virus themselves.

The underqualified and inexperienced doctors and nurses deployed to these wards were immediately overwhelmed – little wonder when the hospital's response was managed by a paediatrician.[218] This patent lack of preparedness was the first link in the chain of disaster for one patient.

Shonisani Junior Lethole had taken ill several days before he was admitted to Tembisa Hospital. He had first sought care at Edenvale Hospital, also a public health facility. When he woke his father, Albert, in the dead of night, complaining of pain gripping his back and chest and that he was struggling to breathe, the elder Lethole drove his son to the hospital. They were turned away by a security guard who insisted that there were no doctors on duty and told to return in the morning.[219]

On 23 June, Albert woke Shonisani at 4am for what would be his last meal, a bowl of soft porridge. By 5am, they were back at Edenvale, where a queue of patients already lined the block. The pair eventually found a place in the queue at Kempton Park Clinic, where Shonisani was seen by a nurse. Armed with a referral letter, their journey took them to Gate 3 of Tembisa Hospital.[220]

By this point, Shonisani's father could see that his son was flagging, and he was getting desperate. On the Covid-19 casualty ward, he was first attended by an intern doctor who tried to turn him away. 'Go back and quarantine at home. You are a Covid-19 suspect,' Shonisani's father was told, despite his son's illness worsening. Albert stood his ground, and the encounter descended into an argument, ended only by the intervention of a senior doctor. This cold admonition hardly augured well for what was to come. But Shonisani was admitted and would get the care his family could not find anywhere else. Hospitals were straining, but Shonisani was lucky, Albert thought. He had a bed.[221]

The following day, Shonisani sent a WhatsApp message to his father: 'I am very hungry, please could you get me some food, I haven't eaten since arriving here.'[222]

At the time, Shonisani was still on the reception ward where Albert had left him. He had been tested for the virus, but medical staff were waiting for the results before he was transferred to the male Covid-19 ward. Albert went out and bought a packet of bread rolls and some KFC to feed his son, but when he got to the hospital, he was barred from entering. A group of cleaners promised they would see that the food reached Shonisani, and Albert returned home, deeply concerned. Close to midnight, Shonisani was moved to the ward. The food never reached him.[223]

On Thursday, 25 June, Shonisani was placed on oxygen. He was deteriorating, but he still had his faculties and took to Twitter. To Health Minister Zweli Mkhize, he posted: '@DrZweliMkhize – can I respond to your tweets if the problems I have at one of your facilities continues [sic]? It is becoming unbearable, and they don't seem to care. Didn't eat for 48 hours.'[224]

I don't see a scenario in which Shonisani would have taken such a step as his first port of call. He could talk, and he surely must have told the nurses and doctors that he was missing meals and that breakfast, lunch and supper had not been delivered to his bed. I can only assume that his pleas were in vain. Even his overture to the health minister was ignored.[225]

A day later, Shonisani was weak but still in contact with his parents. He recounted how he had seen a ghost – the man lying in the adjacent bed had died, and his body lay covered in a sheet for five hours. He told them the nursing staff were callous and uncaring. He was unable to walk and needed a wheelchair to get to the bathroom. Instead, he was ignored and left to soil himself and lay in his own filth. It was the last his family heard from him. Unbeknownst to them, Shonisani's lungs were failing. He was sedated, intubated and placed on a ventilator. He died on Monday, 29 June 2021.[226]

In the wake of his death, his entreaty to Mkhize went viral. Some 25 000 people signed a petition under the hashtag #JusticeForShoni, which prompted a probe by the health ombudsman, Professor Malegapuru Makgoba. His investigation – based on a forensic analysis of Shonisani's hospital records, cellphone data and 113 separate interviews – laid out a timeline of torture, in some instances detailed down to the minute.[227]

After Shonisani was intubated, his doctors failed to insert a feeding tube, a standard procedure that had been completely cast aside. When he was conscious and able to feed himself, he begged for food and went hungry. When he was placed in a sedative coma and could no longer protest, his starvation continued until he eventually died.[228]

Makgoba's final report was a tale of woe. In 203 pages, he exposed the failures of hospital management and Shonisani's medical team in graphic detail. Regarding his starvation, Makgoba found that an established system for ordering meals for each patient – a boilerplate form of detailed dietary requirements completed every morning – had been inexplicably dropped. Instead, wards relied on scraps of paper, with a scribbled headcount, being delivered to the kitchen.[229]

When Makgoba called for CCTV footage, which would show meals being moved from the kitchen to Shonisani's ward, he was told by hospital management that the cameras were inoperable. Other, more candid staff told him that the cameras had been intentionally broken. The kitchen is next to the medical-supply storeroom, and the cameras had been disabled so that staff could steal supplies from the store.

Every clinician who saw Shonisani failed in their duty of care, Makgoba found. His Covid-19 test results – as well as those from a battery of diagnostic tests conducted on his arrival – were never examined by his doctors. His treatment was unguided and haphazard, and often delayed by hours, if not days. Nurses struggled to reach his doctors for instructions. They abandoned accepted medical practice at every turn. Worst of all, they didn't seem to care that a man had died through their negligence. They had ushered in the tragic conclusion of Shonisani's life. But Shonisani should never have been there in the first place.[230]

Makgoba cut to the quick: 'Tembisa Hospital should not have been designated a Covid-19 hospital – yes, there were systemic faults; yes, the management of the establishment had not done their job, but the individual healthcare professionals involved in providing care also failed to discharge their responsibilities and their conduct could not be fully explained by the broader systemic issues. The hospital and its medical team of health providers must take accountability and responsibility for this substandard and negligent care provided to Shonisani Lethole.'[231]

Makgoba knew what he was talking about. He is a medical doctor by training and the former vice-chancellor and principal of the University of KwaZulu-Natal. He is an internationally recognised molecular immunologist and celebrated academic. He acted as deputy vice-chancellor of the University of the Witwatersrand, and he has been both president of the Medical Research Council and chair of its board.[232] Given his gravitas, his scathing rebuke of all who had contributed to Shonisani's death was damning. It poured scorn over the lack of preparation for the Covid-19 onslaught as a result of misguided and misinformed decisions by politicians.

He recommended that each medical professional who mistreated Shonisani face disciplinary action on a raft of charges, each for a varying degree of negligence. But, ultimately, the buck had to stop with Tembisa Hospital CEO and administrator Dr Lekopane Mogaladi. If systems failed under his watch, he had to shoulder the ultimate responsibility. He was appointed in 2016 and was, at the time of Shonisani's demise, at the helm of a hospital in crisis. He had failed, abjectly so.[233]

Makgoba described the Tembisa Hospital boss as a smooth operator. In fact, when I asked for his impressions of the man tasked with leading a major hospital through a pandemic, those were his exact words.[234] 'I didn't think he was competent, and I don't think he understood medical practice. He's a dentist, I think,' Makgoba said. 'I don't know how good he is as a dentist, but as a medical practitioner he was beyond his depth, he was not there. I think he's a good PR person . . . maybe he should have been employed in that position.'[235]

Makgoba told me that in the early stages of his investigation, Mogaladi had fallen over himself to accommodate them. PPE was in short supply, and Makgoba needed to visit the hospital. Mogaladi offered to bus his team in and equip them. Makgoba said that he saw this as a charm offensive.

'The man would call and email me constantly. I believe he was fishing about [for] what we had found. When he was given our preliminary findings, and they were so damning, all of the charm stopped.'

Makgoba was astounded that Mogaladi had landed the job in the first place and said he regarded him as a politically connected figure. If true, the wrong man – appointed for political allegiances – was making decisions that would affect the most vulnerable, with lives at stake.[236]

'I couldn't believe it,' Makgoba said of the Tembisa Hospital leader. He sighed and then continued, 'But that's how things are in Gauteng.'

The academic said that during his time as health ombudsman, he had noticed a disturbing trend. Grossly underqualified hospital CEOs were parachuted in at the whim of the health MEC, the political head. 'The criteria they are using when hiring these people are really below standard. Anybody can become the CEO of a state hospital in Gauteng. If you have weak leaders in these positions, or worse, crooked ones, the services in the health sector suffer. You can see it happening in Gauteng. They are perpetually plagued by problems with health service delivery and the quality of healthcare. It doesn't matter where you go – it's every hospital.[237]

'The top people are poorly qualified with no experience, and all they can do is become treacherous because that's the simplest behaviour to default to, and they then recruit similar people [to key management positions] who are going to assist them. Their agenda is not to look after patients; it's to steal. That's the agenda.'[238]

In plain terms, hospital staff may have had a hand in Shonisani's death, and their conduct cannot be excused, but they were led by an underqualified 'crony', placed there for political means. It's the vulnerable who suffer most in this broken system.

In Shonisani's boyhood home, I sat in the dining room across the table from his elderly mother, Vhahangwele Lethole. A tall woman with a big laugh, she did not look 64 years old. She sat with her arms folded across her chest as she told me about her son. He was precocious as a boy, she said, and had grown into a man intent on forging his own path. Conventional academia was not something he enjoyed, but he had an entrepreneurial spirit that his mother didn't understand but accepted as part of who he was.[239] Pictures of Shonisani – either professionally commissioned paintings of him or rough sketches made by his younger schoolboy cousin – were fixed to the walls. I could feel a burning resentment, understandably so, when she recounted how she couldn't sleep not knowing what had happened to her son.[240]

After Shonisani was sedated, she and her husband had been called to the hospital to fetch his clothes and phone, lest they be stolen. They asked the nurses if they could take a picture or a video of Shonisani just to see how he was doing. They were refused permission and dismissed out of hand. They strongly believe that Shonisani was already dead by then, although Makgoba's findings differ.[241]

'I do have a lot to say, and it's also my culture to have something to say,' Vhahangwele told me. She had been restrained during most of the hour-long interview, letting Albert field the bulk of my questions. But this was near the end, and I felt that she wanted to be frank. She was also poignant.

'To be responsible for somebody's life is not child's play. Those people, all of them, were in positions of power. When you are there, as a servant, in every sphere of life, you have to look after the powerless. They failed my son. I feel very much beleaguered or looked down upon by those doctors.'[242]

Both she and Albert told me that they would never set foot in Tembisa Hospital again, and that they remain haunted by everything Shonisani went through in his final days.[243]

The principle of 'Batho Pele' is a well-worn government slogan that means 'people first'.

'There at that place . . . at Tembisa [Hospital], Batho Pele stops at the gate,' Vhahangwele said.

Mogaladi, the dentist-cum-hospital-administrator who had run the show for five years before Shonisani died, was suspended in January 2021, several days after the report was released.[244] He tried to gainsay Makgoba's findings and even went to court to review aspects of the report.[245]

Ultimately, a tribunal consisting of retired Constitutional Court Judge Bess Nkabinde and two doctors – professors Rudo Mathivha and Ebrahim Variava – considered Mogaladi's appeal. One of the grounds was that there was no valid complaint. Albert and Vhahangwele Lethole would disagree. But the evidence against Mogaladi was overwhelming. The panel ordered that he face disciplinary action for presiding over a hospital 'that on two separate occasions could not provide Lethole food for prolonged periods', and a 'health establishment that showed poor record-keeping'. He should also face charges relating to substandard care.[246]

But there would be no disciplinary process, and the hospital boss was never held to account. His contract had come to an end, and he walked away from the provincial health department. Now he is a businessman.[247]

In his final days, Shonisani was dehumanised and abandoned by doctors, nurses and hospital staff in a horrific series of missteps allowed to take place in a dysfunctional system. His death was a blight on Bandile Masuku's tenure and a case study of his failings in managing the pandemic. Politics had interfered in patient care, and lives were lost as a result. Already, another hidden virus was taking hold of Tembisa Hospital's procurement office.

Balancing the personal ledger

As an investigative journalist, at times, you must balance a personal ledger. In one column, the critical importance of a story, the public interest and the value of the truth. Offset against these is the threat of death and the risk to your own life. It's a disconcerting, existential accounting process that only someone who has been faced with the choice can understand. But a good journalist will move towards the danger – even when confronted by powerful enemies, some who may have killed before – because the truth must always out. I balanced my ledger when it became apparent what Babita had discovered. The cost of her report into Tembisa Hospital's spending had likely been her life, but the report had been suppressed and buried. I would try to finish what she started.

Using her access to the backend of the Gauteng Health Department's accounting system, Babita followed the money. Tembisa Hospital was steaming through its goods and services budget, and the demand for hospital beds, gloves, surgical drapes, ventilators and myriad other specialist surgical devices was high. Babita traced the endpoint of this procurement boom to 217 companies. She then generated a list of beneficiaries that she appended to her report.[248]

If there was to be the forensic investigation she called for, this list would be important.

In the space of little more than three weeks, the entire tenor of my project had changed. It started with my beleaguered profiling of the *izinkabi* arrested after the murder, characterised by an endless train wreck of dead ends and folly. I was tailing a police investigation that had all but stalled. Now, armed with the contents of Babita's phone and email server, I could follow leads the police had abandoned. I had to peel back the layers of ownership of the companies Babita had flagged and pin down exactly who was banking the missing millions. I asked to be taken 'off diary', meaning I was removed from our news publishing cycle so I could seal myself away in our office and just read, research and map Tembisa Hospital's network of suppliers.

I went to my editor, Pieter, again with the begging bowl. This network was massive, and I needed a whiteboard so I could expand the web and actually develop a picture of it. We ended up with a whiteboard cut to custom length – so large that, when it arrived, it took hours to negotiate it into the building and up four flights of stairs. There was a five-metre-long bank of windows separating our team from the rest of the newsroom. The whiteboard went up there, blocking us off entirely. I ordered extra computer monitors because of the extensive spreadsheets and expenditure ledgers Babita had been working with. My desk resembled that of an air-traffic controller. But I was left alone, and email by email, company by company, I sifted the wheat from the chaff.

Babita, in the simplest of terms, had raised three issues in her report.[249] What she found were indications that certain companies were illegitimate, and the evidence – specifically those thousands of transactions just below the R500 000 internal procurement threshold – suggested the practice of rigging. One such illicit ploy was split invoicing. This occurs when one large purchase is spliced into many to keep the buying process hidden at a hospital level. What Babita found also suggested that suppliers had been handpicked to bid against one another. The system was designed to allow an official to enter the type of goods or services required. Three companies from a list of registered suppliers were then selected at random to bid. How was Kaizen Projects, supposedly an events company, picked to deliver surgical goods to a hospital? This mismatch suggested that the central supplier database was not used and pointed to collusive procurement – or, at least, the warning signs of it.[250] Going beyond Babita's endpoint meant company director searches – hundreds of them. When I had an idea of who controlled these companies, I could map their reach.

The patterns in company ownership leapt off the page, so obvious that even the Keystone Kops leading the investigation into Babita's murder would have noticed them, had they only looked. I found an odd, repetitive trend in which one person would hold directorships in five separate entities, all of which had been formed on the same day and appeared on Babita's list. One of these directors worked in a bank as a teller and another in a cellphone shop; one woman was a packer in a warehouse. I found it curious that hyper-successful businesspeople whose companies invoiced a hospital for tens of millions of rand would still keep their day jobs.

The names of these companies added an additional layer of absurdity. It appeared that no attempt had been made to mask the fact that these were simple shell entities. Arantxa Chichi, Fenella Frooti, Mafaldaramp, Roguepalm and Stotleari were entities controlled by one man who worked as a sound engineer for a Johannesburg-based recording label. Another director, a 27-year-old who sold cellphones for a living, had five companies: Cielchauncey, Fleurnavy, Liralotte, Terrastarla and Umathora.

I managed to connect a man, his wife, his son and his brother to a medical-supply dynasty of seventeen companies in simultaneous trade with Tembisa Hospital. Another individual had nine companies under his control, and all had been flagged as dubious by Babita. While her list of suppliers stretched into the hundreds, the list of who controlled them was far, far shorter. This alone made it clear that syndicates were preying on Tembisa Hospital. My spiderweb on the whiteboard expanded all the way to the margins, and I now had a sense of the scale of these networks. I also mapped out a publishing plan and suggested that we publish a series of eight stories detailing Babita's last investigation. But there were other important considerations to iron out before we put words on paper and kicked the hornet's nest.

Informed by what I had found, I was more certain than ever that Babita was killed for this knowledge. What she had unearthed were the first signs of contract syndicates possibly inflating their prices, bidding collusively and splitting invoices, and she had advocated for further investigation to prove it. The probe would have brought the entire house of cards tumbling down, as the auditors would have found what I did. Both the suppliers and the Health Department officials who had engineered these transactions had a lot to lose. Babita had compromised their revenue stream, but any freeze on payments and calls for further inquiry died with her.

I knew that, by dredging up her report from its resting place and pursuing those who had made millions in the scheme, I would face similar danger. If my suspicions about Tembisa Hospital and its suppliers proved true, I was about to disturb some chancy people. I had to ask: was this a story worth dying for?

I had made a promise to Rakesh that I would follow the story, no matter the threat or danger, and see it through to the end. In hindsight, it was an easy promise to make until there was something on the line. A sacrifice is only valiant because of the prospect of losing something. I thought that if I pushed this mess into public view, Babita's enemies would become mine. What steps would these people take to ensure that what was secret stayed that way?

With Pieter and Adriaan, we resolved not to position me as the person leading the project. When we published stories, they would be under the collective 'News24 Investigations' byline. When we spoke publicly of the work, we hid that I was the only journalist working on it. We wanted it known that if a decision was made to eliminate me, a team of others would pick up the baton and continue. But these necessities for my safety and benefit would not last long.

I still had to track down these 'businesspeople' and interrogate them. My name might have been redacted from our reports, but it would have been glaringly clear to those running this extraction network that I was behind their looming exposure.

I also know how easy it is to dive into someone's life. Unscrupulous police officers, private detectives and lawyers could easily, and illegally, access my consumer profile without me knowing. All they needed was my cellphone number, which was easy to find. The profile would give my enemies my home address, my work address and details of cars registered in my name. They would be able to see if I kept up with my debt obligations and paid my accounts. In the same way, my cellphone movement data could be purchased. The *News24* byline would do little to protect me. If they wanted to profile me, this information was readily accessible if you knew the right people. I would be exposed.

If those who profited from these schemes were willing to go as far as murdering a high-ranking civil servant, they would have little compunction about silencing a journalist. This realisation kept me up at night. Hours in the dark were spent playing out scenarios. The worst permutation would have been an attack while my wife was in the car. How would I live with the guilt if she was killed and I survived? I was balancing my ledger.

It is not uncommon for journalists to be on the receiving end of threats and online abuse. Legal journalist Karyn Maughan knows this better than most. She has intrepidly covered attempts to prosecute former President Jacob Zuma and his arms-deal corruption case, which has spanned two decades. For her efforts, Zuma abused court process and tried to privately prosecute her and Billy Downer, the lead state advocate in the arms-deal case. The central issue was the supposed leaking of Zuma's 'confidential medical records', an aspect multiple courts have ruled as benign. But the assault on Maughan was amplified by faceless people on social media who threatened her with death and gang rape. Just to do her work, she has had to travel to court with bodyguards.[251]

Daily Maverick investigative journalist Pauli van Wyk revealed how the Economic Freedom Fighters and their leaders, Julius Malema and, at the time, Floyd Shivambu, had been the beneficiaries of shady loans and credit from the now collapsed VBS Mutual Bank. For her efforts, she was threatened. She was told her throat would be slit, and that she would be raped, necklaced and 'shot in the pussy'. Malema called her 'Satan' on X in 2018, and torrents of abuse from EFF supporters followed.[252]

When I first joined the investigations team, I was working on a project focused on the misspending of a slush fund controlled by the police's Crime Intelligence Division, something that was at the heart of a war for control of the SAPS. I was followed from my home and told my phone calls were being listened to – acts I saw as intimidation tactics.[253] I know that there was a file on me somewhere in the bowels of the police crime intelligence headquarters. My own sources in crime intelligence have told me so. In the file is my consumer information and bank records, as well as movement and call data from my cellphone. To obtain these lawfully, a warrant is required, but I am well aware that there are ways around it. My view remains that I operate in the open, and my life is an open book. The intrusion was illegal, but go ahead, have at it. I have nothing to hide.

My investigation into Babita's murder brought with it different risks. I can stomach online abuse. Really, I couldn't give a fuck what people behind faceless accounts think of me or what they say. I have received death threats before, but I am a firm believer that if someone really wants you dead, giving you – the target – a heads-up before the fact is asinine. In the Tembisa Hospital matter, I had started developing my own list of persons of interest, and when I shared these names with trusted sources, both in law enforcement and the underworld, I was given a warning: watch your back – there is a lot of money involved, and anything can happen. It would be stunningly stupid to eliminate a journalist, mostly because of the attention it would draw, but I was told that these were not rational people. They were desperate to keep the truth hidden.

I was scared – for what might happen to me, and for the people that I love – and conflicted. I could have walked away from this project because of the danger, and I think that few would have judged me harshly or thought less of me. But what would be the cost of abandoning the pursuit?

Babita could not keep quiet, even when she knew the guys from Tembisa were dangerous. If I did nothing and stayed silent, the pernicious networks of extraction would endure, and insidious actors in a shadow state would continue diverting money from a hospital and the millions of poor, desperate people who relied on it. Babita sacrificed her life in aid of doing the right thing, and those who killed her banked on the notion that others would be cowed into silence. What kind of man would I be if I stood by and let the status quo persist? This was bigger than me. There was too much at stake to walk away and break my promise to the Deokaran family. I had a duty: publish and be damned.

'My brother, please'

Sello Sekhokho is a brash, self-important character who had squeezed himself into a dark suit and tie for our meeting at his office in Edenvale, east of Johannesburg. He planted himself behind a polished oak desk, probably the only piece of furniture in his office worth anything, and interlaced his fingers as if girding himself. A Chinese guardian lion with red faux-jewel eyes was on display, and I felt as if it was watching me. It was early in July 2022. In the preceding weeks, I had pushed myself into seclusion while combing through Babita's email server before building out a vast network map of companies trading with Tembisa Hospital. Now, armed with Babita's report and a selection of her emails, I had questions.

The 40-year-old had been on Babita's radar in the weeks before her death. When she collated a list of entities driving a procurement boom at the hospital, one of his companies, Kaizen Projects, was tied to a single transaction of R534 750.[254] The company was to amass another R1 million – via three separate payments – in an ensuing payment run. Babita had been concerned, and when she raised her doubts about the legitimacy of Sekhokho's company, her boss, acting CFO Lerato Madyo, instructed her to pay the company and keep it secret.[255] 'Eish I just don't like dealing with politicians u know??Pls keep this private. Will speak to u soonest,' Madyo had written to Babita on WhatsApp.[256]

By Babita's reckoning, Kaizen was an events company, so the accountant found it strange that it was selling surgical equipment to a hospital. Kaizen is, to all intents and purposes, a shelf company. It has no website, and its official business address is a two-room Reconstruction and Development Programme house – #285 Isikelo Section – hidden away in the dusty alleys and lanes of Tembisa. I suspect that when Babita was searching the internet to verify if Kaizen was legitimate, she misunderstood what she found. A 'Kaizen event' is a business concept, and I think Babita wrongly connected the dots from a Google search. But she was not entirely off the mark.

She had also flagged two other entities, Nokhokho and Bollanoto Security. In the payment run she tried to freeze, they were due to be paid R423 200 and R411 700, respectively. She didn't know that all three formed part of Sekhokho's business empire. They operate from the house in Edenvale where the politician-cum-businessman asked me to meet him.

Sekhokho was a political player of some prominence in Ekurhuleni, where Tembisa Hospital is situated. He once ran for the position of ANC Youth League Gauteng chair, and his social media accounts are littered with servile posts fawning over the ANC and regional leaders, including former Ekurhuleni Mayor Mzwandile Masina, whom Sekhokho described as a personal friend.[257] His Facebook page is stocked with pictures of him in his party colours of green, black and gold. There are also trappings of wealth on display. Tailored suits, gleaming watches and nice cars contrast with portraits of Mandela, Oliver Tambo, Chris Hani and an AK-47-toting Fidel Castro.

When Masina was elected and installed as mayor in 2016, following local government elections, he announced that the city would increase disbursements of grants-in-aid. These charitable contributions would fund startups and NGOs in a push for the party's pro-poor policies. The princely sum of R100 million was ringfenced to this end.[258] But this ultimately noble project courted controversy in 2019 when Masina's friend Sekhokho became a beneficiary of this state-sponsored largesse. His company, Nokhokho, was paid

R1.2 million to build a science laboratory at Emmangweni Primary School in Tembisa. Sekhokho, speaking to the AmaBhungane Centre for Investigative Journalism, denied there was any conflict of interest and said his company scoring the grant had nothing to do with his ANC connections.[259] Now the smooth-talking politician was in the spotlight once more.

I had sent my questions to Sekhokho days in advance, but when it was time to answer them, he was evasive. I had found records of seven payments to his three companies, with a combined value of R2.3 million, but was aware that there could be more. I asked him exactly how much money he had made from Tembisa Hospital. He couldn't be certain, he said. He would have to check, but the figure I arrived at sounded right.[260]

'Honestly speaking, I had no idea any of this was happening, and I don't know why I am on this list,' he said. Sekhokho added that at the peak of the Covid-19 pandemic, his companies flogged soap to the Gauteng Health Department, and this deal was investigated by the SIU.[261]

'The SIU investigated me, and I was cleared. They could see that from my side I had done nothing wrong. I supplied soap to the department, and I gave the SIU my receipts and it was all sorted,' he added.[262]

When Babita queried the payments to Kaizen, Madyo said she didn't like dealing with politicians – a strong indication that she knew exactly who Sekhokho was. When I asked what relationship he had with the CFO, he claimed he had never heard of her and they had never met.[263]

That Sekhokho was using three companies to trade with the hospital was suspicious. It raised the possibility that orders had been spread between them, keeping figures low to avoid revealing that a single man was the ultimate beneficiary. He told me I was way off the mark. His companies would be invited to bid for contracts, and his staff would choose which would respond.[264] This, again, is curious.

Requests for quotations are typically issued to a specific entity and cannot just be passed around as Sekhokho described.

From Babita's email server I found purchase orders linked to both Kaizen and Bollanoto Security issued by Tembisa Hospital for the supply of headblocks and cervical collars, respectively.[265] Headblocks are used in an emergency medical setting and prevent the unconstrained movement of a patient who may have a spinal injury. Cervical collars serve the same purpose.

Kaizen sold headblocks to Tembisa at a hefty price tag of R4 485 each, and Bollanoto's cervical collars cost R2 106 per unit.[266] I approached a medical supply company and requested quotes for the same products in the same quantity. Sekhokho had gouged his pricing of the headblocks by 533 per cent. I could source them for little more than R700 each. The collars I could get for R120 each. If Sekhokho had sold collars at a fair price, his R423 000 contract fee would have shrunk to R25 000. This was money for jam.

When I confronted Sekhokho about this, he was caught off-balance. He spun me a long, incoherent explanation of how he had sourced the medical supplies, often from abroad, and tacked on his markup. He was not a producer of medical equipment; he was merely a middleman. He would buy goods, jack up the price and sell them to the hospital.[267]

'We look into the products, put our own markup and we will bid. We get our products from local and international suppliers. Usually, our markup is 30 per cent. I would love for you to be a buyer for me. I can't find products at the prices that you have,' he said. I doubted that was true. It had taken me less than fifteen minutes and one phone call to beat his rates.[268]

I asked him for invoices that would disprove predatory pricing practice. After all, he was an ANC man with leadership ambitions, and he would have to espouse the party's values, which focused on the upliftment of the poor and downtrodden. Knowingly bleeding funds from a hospital would be incongruent with these values. Sekhokho refused to divulge the documents, citing 'client confidentiality'.

'I think it is unfair and unjust that I am expected to provide my trade secrets and strategies. It should be noted that I cannot expose my methods of calculating my markup to [. . .] my competitors. I am sure you will understand this.'[269]

More evasion. I think it then dawned on him that I had done my homework and wanted answers. I wasn't going to let him get away with bluffing.

'I am trying to build a name for myself politically and business-wise, but of course when stories like this come . . . eish! No one wants to be in the newspaper,' he told me. He then asked me to stop recording our discussion.[270]

'My brother, please . . .' he began. He was an honest businessman who had done nothing wrong. He could not understand how his companies came to be identified by Babita as 'possibly fraudulent', and if I was to link him to the saga, it would be damaging. He knew of high-level corruption involving big-name politicians, and he would be willing to give me this information. He was a small player, he insisted, but he knew of other rogues more deserving of my attention.[271]

I turned the recorder back on, and I was forthright. There would be no deal and no negotiation. I don't operate like that. He could choose whether or not he wanted to answer my questions, and that was the only choice I was willing to entertain. Nothing he could offer me would change the fact that his shell company was among the first to pique Babita's interest – and, moreover, he had two other irons in the fire at the same time.[272]

Sekhokho had much to lose if he was exposed. Two months before our tête-à-tête, he had been elected as the ANC's treasurer-general in a fraught leadership contest. Masina – his close friend and cadre – was re-elected in the same process. I asked Sekhokho if the money he made through his network of companies had funded his campaign for this office. Another bald denial: those who had nominated him, he claimed, funded the contest.

I saw through Sekhokho's chicanery. There was a reason why he had latched on to my figure of R2.3 million when I first queried how much he had been paid by Tembisa Hospital. The real figure was much, much higher. Sekhokho's business relationship with the facility stretched back to 2019. Nokhokho scored 36 of the 55 total contracts awarded to his companies, supplying cleaning material, medical and office supplies, protective clothing and groceries. From boerewors to bandages, Sekhokho was the go-to guy. Bollanoto Security alone was paid R2.4 million for 'medical consumable supplies' and protective clothing worth more than R200 000. The cumulative value of his hospital trade is R14.5 million.[273]

When I looked wider, to other hospitals Sekhokho had boasted about, his total haul was more than R100 million via 225 contracts. He had hit the tender jackpot, and his proclivity for price inflation was ever present.[274]

A total of 108 'rain suits' of various sizes for men and women were supplied at a total cost of R1.88 million – equating to R17 000 each. He charged R196 000 for seventeen V-neck jerseys – R11 500 each.

In the space of a week, the company sold almost two tons of boerewors for nearly R1 million. This is equal to R490 per kilogram, far above fair market rates.

Also: R280 000 for 27 pairs of men's Parabellum brown leather shoes – R10 370 a pair.[275]

In essence, Sekhokho had become a business maverick, enriching himself through bloated contracts from hospitals in Gauteng's public health network. Orders were juggled between three obscure companies, the spread masking the true heft of his benefit. Because the value of a single contract was insignificant, the deals had avoided attention. But cumulatively, Sekhokho's heyday was blatant – and Babita had moved to put a stop to it.

Tender family affair

The Vaal River reaches out from the jagged crags of the Drakensberg range in central South Africa and flows southwest more than 1 200 kilometres to converge with the Orange River in the Northern Cape. The watercourse forms the border between the Free State and North West provinces, and on the western bank – 400 kilometres from Johannesburg – lies the town of Christiana.

The town is surrounded by farmland, and its 3 700 residents support an agrarian industry producing maize, potatoes, onions, sorghum, groundnuts and beef. Many of those who work the fields and feedlots live in a dusty settlement on the town's limits called Geluksoord, an arrangement of low-cost houses in the sparse veld. A company called Minzorex was based in this dour township.

This was the address used to register it: 2236 Extension 3, Geluksoord, Christiana, North West, 2680.[276]

Even though it was set in the middle of nowhere, Minzorex was a favoured supplier of Tembisa Hospital. From a single monthly payment run to suppliers in August 2021, this obscure entity was due just under R3 million.[277] But there were things about this company that set alarm bells ringing. There was, of course, the fact that it was so far away from the hospital it supplied – basically, Geluksoord is closer to Kimberley than to Johannesburg. As far as businesses go, it was young, less than two years old, and it had no public presence through a website or social media pages. Most conspicuous was that its sole director, 28-year-old Bhekumuzi Ntshangase, worked in a lucerne factory. The proprietor of a wildly successful business that was banking millions lived in an RDP house and loaded bags of animal feed onto trucks for a wage. It was within the realm of possibility that Ntshangase was a proxy.[278]

When I was picking apart Babita's list of 'possibly fraudulent' suppliers, I had focused primarily on those that were due the largest haul of cash, and Minzorex was among them.[279]

Ntshangase was something of an oddity. If the factory worker were indeed a businessman, Minzorex was his only going concern. But that was just at first blush. Among the tens of thousands of documents, images and emails saved on Babita's laptop, there was a spreadsheet saved under the heading 'Payment commitment GPDOH 2017 – 2021'. This was a ledger containing records of 57 819 payments stretching back five years. The detail it contained was a real coup for my investigation: purchase-order numbers, the dates they were created and processed, and the names of the hospitals doing the buying. There were product descriptions, prices and quantities, as well as the suppliers' contact numbers and email addresses. This was as complete a repository of the Gauteng Health Department's buying patterns as I could hope for.[280]

I knew Minzorex was due to be paid by the department, and when I found this spreadsheet, I could see exactly what it was selling. There were four purchase orders issued in favour of the company, all of which were processed within two days.[281] Spending on 'brush cleaning nylon bristles 1 x 5' for R234 500 and 'brush cleaning nylon bristles twisted 2.5mm' for R242 500 was combined into one purchase.[282] 'Crafts pipe cleaner 100 pcs assorted' for R242 500 and 'brush scrubbing 8cm diameter 20cm long' for R242 500 were amalgamated in another.[283]

Minzorex also supplied a consignment of 1 500 'pen electro-surgical w/blade and 3.1m' and was paid R488 250; later on the same day, another order was moved, this time for 500 'suction tube Luer

Left: A radiant Babita takes the podium at her niece Reola Haripersadh's wedding in Durban in 2015. When it fell to Reola to deliver the obituary after Babita's shocking death in 2022, she said: 'Nothing will ever be able to fill the huge void left in our family. Our world has come crashing down.'

Above: Babita's only child, Thiara, on the left at the wedding of Babita's niece Prativa to Nikesh Prithipal in Durban in 2019. Babita is on the right.

Above: The Deokaran family was very close and spoke to each other daily, even after Babita left Durban to work in Johannesburg. Here they are gathered at a school hall in Phoenix to celebrate Soorash Deokaran's birthday in 2019. Shamilla Haripersadh, Sunil Deokaran, Shaleen Ramgulam and Rakesh Deokaran are at the back, with Meera Mangali, Soorash Deokaran and Renu Williams, who gave Thiara a home after her mother's death, in the middle. Babita is in front.

Right: Babita and her brother Sunil at the family's home in New Cottage, the workers' compound on the Tongaat Hulett plantation, in the early 1970s. From this house, the Deokaran siblings sold samosas their mother made to supplement the family income. It is also where Babita, her father and her grandfather were born. New Cottage no longer exists. The land now houses Mount Edgecombe, a luxury gated golf estate.

Left: After Babita's death, her family found this photo of her reading among her belongings. They could not place the setting or the time, but it attests to her studious nature as a young woman. Even though she did well at school, there was no money for further education and her first job was as an unpaid casual worker. Babita eventually studied finance and worked diligently to rise through the ranks of the civil service.

Above: Babita's eldest brother, Soorash, walks toward the family's home on Ladygreen Place in Phoenix. The family moved here when Babita was nine. It is also where they gathered to mourn and keep vigil by her lit diya after her death.

Above: The entrance to Tembisa Provincial Tertiary Hospital. Established in 1972 in the rapidly expanding Midrand, its 840 beds serve a population of nearly 2.5 million (often poor and vulnerable) Tembisa residents. Babita wondered why Tembisa Hospital was inexplicably spending more than any other public hospital in Gauteng.

Right: Captain Freddie Hicks, now retired, whose old-school methods gave the police their first lead despite the mishandling of the crime scene. When Hicks was taken off the case, to be replaced by Masenxani Chauke of the Hawks, the investigation ground to a halt.

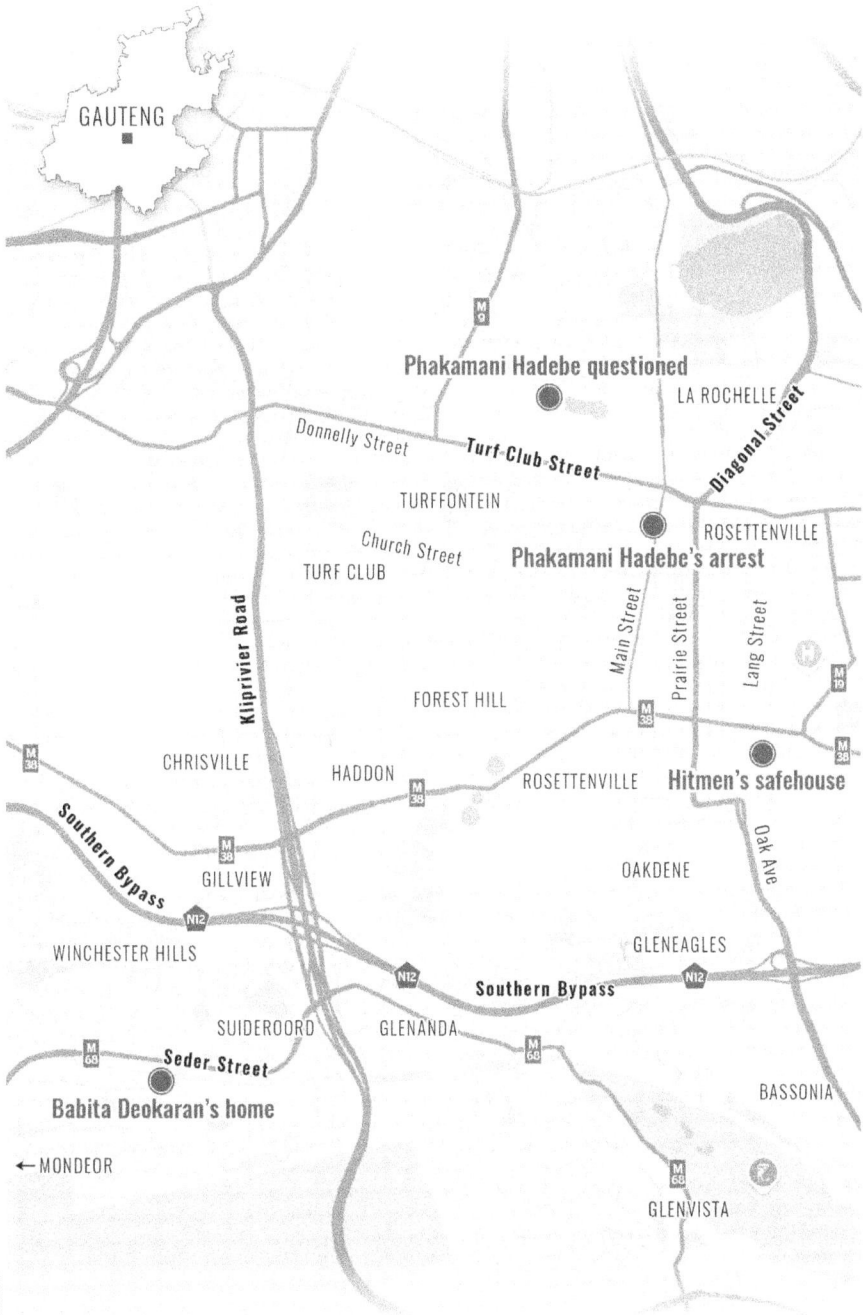

GAUTENG

Phakamani Hadebe questioned

LA ROCHELLE

Donnelly Street

Turf Club Street

Diagonal Street

TURFFONTEIN

ROSETTENVILLE

Church Street

TURF CLUB

Phakamani Hadebe's arrest

Main Street

Prairie Street

Lang Street

Kliprivier Road

FOREST HILL

CHRISVILLE

HADDON

ROSETTENVILLE

Hitmen's safehouse

Southern Bypass

GILLVIEW

OAKDENE

Oak Ave

WINCHESTER HILLS

GLENEAGLES

Southern Bypass

SUIDEROORD

GLENANDA

Seder Street

Babita Deokaran's home

BASSONIA

← MONDEOR

GLENVISTA

Rudi Louw

Above: A map showing Babita's home where she was gunned down, the safehouse where the *izinkabi* gathered afterwards, and the locations where Phakamani Hadebe was arrested and thereafter questioned by Hicks and his team.

Jeff Wicks

Above: Two months after Babita's murder, the author visited Nhlawe in rural KwaZulu-Natal, in search of the *izinkabi* cousins. When he asked about their whereabouts, he was told to be careful: 'They are dangerous people.' Persistent queries led him to this homestead.

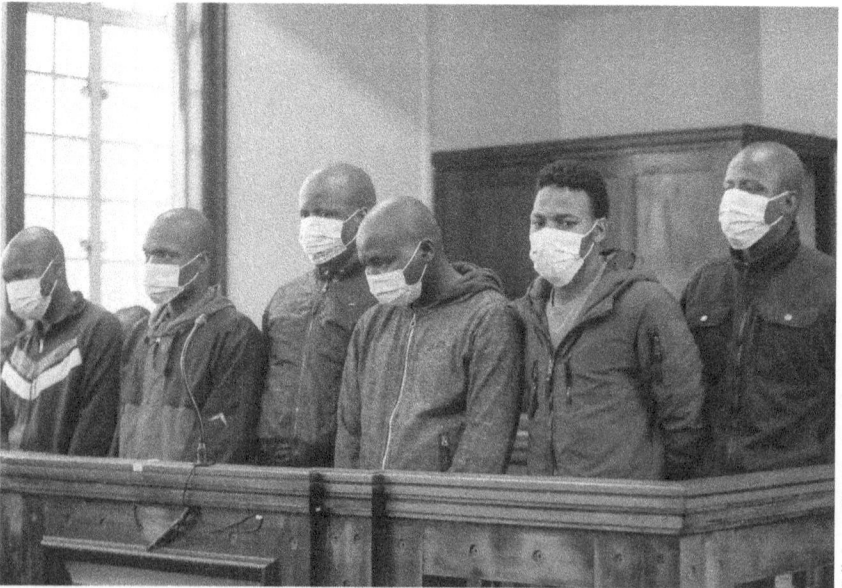

Gallo Images/Papi Morake

Above: Six of the triggermen in the Johannesburg Magistrate's Court just days after their arrest in August 2021.

Above: Gauteng Health Department chief financial officer Lerato Madyo. She resigned while she was suspended and facing 13 charges of misconduct. She now goes by Daniella Molapo. Madyo ignored Babita's WhatsApp message that said 'our lives could be in danger'.

Above: Tembisa Hospital chief Dr Ashley Mthunzi with his unionist wife, Lerato. He was at the tiller of the hospital and signed off on the dubious deals Babita later flagged. Mthunzi died in 2024 while on suspension and facing misconduct charges.

Above: Dr Nomonde Nolutshungu, who took over as head of the Gauteng Health Department shortly after Babita was murdered. When she suspended Lerato Madyo and Ashley Mthunzi, she received death threats but persevered.

Above: Dr Nomathemba Mokgethi, a nurse by training who became the ANC-appointed MEC at the Gauteng Health Department. In contrast to Nolutshungu, Mokgethi tried to shield both Madyo and Mthunzi from accountability.

Left: Shonisani Lethole contracted Covid-19 midway through 2020. After being admitted to Tembisa Hospital, he was ignored by medical staff and starved for days before his body gave out. Lethole was just one casualty of a dysfunctional public healthcare system.

Above: Professor Malegapuru Makgoba, who led the investigation into Lethole's death at Tembisa Hospital. Makgoba, an internationally lauded expert in immunology, found that 'the hospital and its medical team of health providers' were responsible for the 'negligent care' provided.

Above and left: For days, the author travelled the length and breadth of Gauteng in search of the registered addresses of companies flagged by Babita. Some addresses did not exist. Others were for churches, guesthouses or vacant veld. These are just two of the dilapidated buildings listed as company addresses.

Opposite: A whiteboard in situ at the *News24* investigations team's office in Randburg, Johannesburg. It was used to trace connections between the hundreds of shell companies invoicing Tembisa Hospital and the few masterminds who controlled these companies while raking in the stolen money.

Right and below:
While Khusela Diko was spokesperson for Cyril Ramaphosa, it came to light that her husband's company was awarded a R125 million PPE tender by Bandile Masuku's department. The Masukus and the Dikos were close friends. **Right:** Diko at Bandile's wife Loyiso Masuku's baby shower; **below:** the two couples together.

Facebook

Facebook

Left: Sello Sekhokho, tender don and ANC strongman in Ekurhuleni. His company received suspicious payments ahead of the ANC's 2021 Gauteng elective conference, where he was in the running for treasurer-general. Sekhokho was the director of three companies, all flagged by Babita.

Above: One of the three alleged main Tembisa Hospital syndicate leaders, Stefan Joel Govindraju, with his wife, Dhereshni, and their family. Govindraju became the sole director of 54 different companies that supplied Tembisa Hospital.

Right: Tenderpreneur Vusimusi 'Cat' Matlala with Cordelia Kabeng, his customary wife. The Matlala clan lived the high life with private helicopter charters, designer clothes and overseas trips, and they showed off their wealth on social media.

Below: Cordelia Kabeng shared this photograph online. She also bragged of using a blue light on her car to get the 'cubs' – her and Cat's children – to school on time.

Supplied

Instagram

Above: Cat appears in court on charges of attempted murder (unrelated to Babita's death).

Above: Advocate Andy Mothibi, head of the Special Investigating Unit, at a memorial service for Babita. The SIU, tasked with tracing and reclaiming stolen public money, can act only once it has been authorised by the president. Only in 2022, after a public outcry, did President Cyril Ramaphosa ask the unit to investigate procurement at Tembisa Hospital.

Gallo Images/Fani Mahuntsi

Above: A candlelight vigil for Babita, held in 2021 at the office of the premier in Johannesburg. The SIU and Hawks investigations are ongoing: justice demands more than vigils. Will the Deokaran family – and the South African public – have to go without answers?

s/steel 150x0.7mm' for R488 200.[284] I couldn't really make sense of the product codes, but the money the company was banking couldn't be disregarded as insignificant. When I looked at its email address in the ledger, there was an odd entry: 'elrosparkmed@gmail.com'.[285]

I knew I had seen the name before. Elrospark was another entity that had previously cropped up on Babita's list. In the payment run, this company was due to be paid R3 896 900, and it was controlled by a woman, Linhle Mazibuko. She used nine companies, including Elrospark, to do business with the hospital. Her husband, Rudolf, directed six others. Their son, Thadolwethu, steered another. And then there was Ntshangase, exiled in Geluksoord, who had a tangential link to what was a medical supply dynasty.

It's a long road to Christiana. The city skyline of Johannesburg disappeared as I took the R59 through the Vaal and its industrial heartland, with vistas of belching factory smokestacks. After five hours on the road, with blurred farmlands on either side, I finally arrived in Geluksoord. The township sprang up from veld flatlands. Everything was brown, save for the ubiquitous burnt maroon or grey terracotta roof tiles on the small, cramped RDP houses. If I was going to unmask syndicate activity at Tembisa Hospital, I was certain I was on the money with the Mazibuko clan. But I had to test my thesis that Ntshangase was connected to the cabal. It's easy to put the phone down on someone, but it's a lot harder to ignore them when they show up at your doorstep and won't leave. That was my plan, and I had to find one house, #2236, in a township of identical houses.

I drove around Geluksoord for hours, but for the life of me I could not find this house. I figured the home of a successful business owner would be conspicuous with upgrades, but I was wrong. Stop. Ask for directions. Follow them. Find nothing. I repeated this over and over until I was beaten. I couldn't find the house. Maybe it didn't exist, or perhaps my township navigation skills were wanting. But I knew of the factory where Ntshangase worked. When I arrived there, I told the receptionist who I was after. She confirmed that Ntshangase worked there, but said he was off duty and I should try his cellphone. Exactly what I didn't want to do.

I was parked on the shoulder, nearly defeated. I keyed in the number and hit dial. It rang. Ntshangase answered. I told him I was a journalist, and I had questions about his company, Minzorex. Stilted silence. 'You are the director of this company, are you not, sir?'

Almost stuttering, Ntshangase conceded. Yes, it was his company, but he 'had nothing to do with it'. His brother, Mduduzi, handled everything – bidding for work and delivering the goods. Ntshangase himself was merely a front, he admitted.[286] Mduduzi is Rudolf Mazibuko's middle name. Ntshangase may have been outside the Mazibuko nucleus, but he was in the family business. Now it made sense.

'He does the orders and delivers things. I don't know anything. I am just a shareholder,' he said. 'You should speak to Mduduzi.'

I had every intention of confronting Rudolf Mazibuko with this new information, specifically that his own brother had admitted to acting as a proxy for him to obscure his interest in the business. But it was an interview that would require preparation and forethought – not something I wanted to do from a car.

I was barely back on the road when my phone rang. On the other end was the Mazibuko family patriarch. Ntshangase had raised the alarm, and Mazibuko wanted to head me off at the pass. What did I want to know about Minzorex? I told him that Minzorex was just the start. I also had questions about the sixteen other companies controlled by the family.

Then came the swerve. He said his late wife had handled most of their interests, and that he would have trouble responding to questions in writing. This was accompanied by a sob story about how she died during surgery at a private hospital, and how he was suing them. I asked if he would be willing to meet me. I could be back in Johannesburg by the evening. He agreed to see me at my office. But when 9pm rolled around, Mazibuko was a no-show, and my calls and messages went unanswered.

The payment commitment ledger was incontestable, and from this document, I could see that the Mazibuko family's foray at Tembisa Hospital started in November 2019. In a matter of days, six companies controlled by the family saw a flurry of seventeen payments from the facility.[287] The lion's share of the deals went to Apollo Clothing, owned by the late Linhle Mazibuko, for the supply of clothing and cleaning supplies. It was only the best for Tembisa Hospital: lounge shirts at R1 350 each, cargo trousers for R1 500 a pair and four pairs of hiking boots (two black and two brown) for R3 700 each.[288] On 8 February 2021, two payments to Apollo of R19 600 were processed for four plastic buckets. Walk into any shop today, and you can leave with one of these for less than R150. The hospital bought two in red and two in blue and, at R9 800 a piece, the taxpayer funded a 5 000 per cent price hike.[289]

With the family network now in full view, I found 152 individual transactions amounting to R54 743 221, and I could start to map a trend. While Tembisa was led by Dr Lekopane Mogaladi – the dentist-cum-hospital-administrator who was suspended after Shonisani Lethole was starved to death on a Covid-19 ward – the Mazibuko family was barely a blip on the procurement radar. Their constellation of companies attracted only R2.5 million in contracts, including those for the expensive buckets and what should have been luxury clothing at that price.[290]

Dogged by scandal, Mogaladi was suspended in January 2021. After he was consigned to obscurity, the hospital was rudderless for a period before Dr Ashley Mthunzi was installed in April and made permanent two months later. Mthunzi, who had led other hospitals in Gauteng prior to this deployment, was styled as a progressive. On his LinkedIn profile, he said he was someone who strove for excellence. 'I am self-driven and motivated, and I am a team player. I'm a problem solver, a critical thinker and a good communicator. I believe in developing people,' he wrote.[291] Lofty.

The Mazibuko business empire had hardly been a money spinner until Mthunzi took over at Tembisa. Of the R54 million the companies were paid by the Gauteng Health Department, deals worth R52 million were actioned by Mthunzi. The same trend appeared when I examined Sekhokho's hospital boom.[292] As hospital CEO, Mthunzi could authorise procurement beneath R500 000, and he was the final signatory. Many companies saw a distinct change in their fortunes after he took the helm; here, the lightning-fast enrichment of the Mazibukos was the bellwether.

By the time I drove to Geluksoord in search of Ntshangase and 'his' Minzorex, I had been sifting through Babita's emails and cellphone for four months. I had built my own map of connections between what I believed to be tender cartels. I knew that I could dig into these syndicates for years without publishing, going ever further in search of the complete picture. But I was already exposed. I had confronted Sekhokho, the Mazibukos and others as I tried to piece things together. I had also issued questions to the Gauteng Health Department on the report, and I knew these would circulate and possibly reach the same person who had betrayed Babita. After I published, I would have some cover.

This was a story that we could break wide open. The records, documents and conversations that came from our own forensic examination could not be gainsaid. And we had a lot. The groundwork had been done, and we could start publishing what we had found.

The first story was about the existence of the report, a document that was the first tenable motive for Babita's murder. We set out how and when she had raised her fears of the guys from Tembisa, and how she had frozen payments and called for forensic investigation. The Gauteng Health Department was forced to concede that her entreaty was dismissed. Instead, a compliance audit was undertaken. Internal auditors visited hospitals and clinics at random and rifled through the respective procurement departments.

Babita had told them where to look, but instead of implementing her recommendations, her boss, Madyo, decided to launch the unguided compliance audit. That's like a trauma surgeon who sees that his patient has been shot in the face but starts by examining another patient's feet. It was clear that very little within Babita's report was taken seriously – and then payments were unfrozen.

At Tembisa Hospital, auditors found weaknesses in supply-chain management systems and controls. Mthunzi appointed a bid adjudication committee and a section that monitored demand for goods and services, and he was told to discipline hospital officials. After all, his hospital was buying more than any other facility, even more than Chris Hani Baragwanath Hospital in Soweto, the largest medical complex on the continent. There were strong indications that the demand at Tembisa was contrived.[293]

The Sekhokho story came next: 'Babita Deokaran tried to stop "secret" Tembisa Hospital payments to ANC leader', the headline screamed.[294] Then Madyo's deceit was exposed. 'No investigation, no protection: Inside department head's big lie to Babita Deokaran'.[295] Both the CFO and her department went to ground and refused to engage with me. And no, they would not hand over the Tembisa Hospital audit findings. I would need to find another way to get those. I had barely scratched the surface. The Mazibuko clan was unmasked, and the story set out how I had linked the family members, their open fronting and their massive payday from Tembisa Hospital.[296]

This was only the beginning of the series we would publish. There were bigger fish swimming in Tembisa Hospital's supplier pool.

CHAPTER 18

Tembisa Hospital, the contract factory

The Gauteng Health Department, an organisation perpetually embroiled in scandals of graft and corruption, faced a new wave of ignominy. The chief accountant had been murdered after reporting indicators of fraud and cash extraction on a near industrial scale, and MEC Nomathemba Mokgethi was wedged firmly between a rock and a hard place. If her department had heeded Babita's warnings and forensically audited Tembisa Hospital, they could not have missed the clear signs of fronting and price inflation. If they had ignored what she had found, they would have a hard time explaining their inaction. As it turned out, Madyo had concealed Babita's findings for reasons unknown, and my investigation was backed by credible evidence and records. The only option left was to circle the wagons, deflect and obscure, and try to ride out the media storm.

In an internal communiqué among the management team, which was leaked to me, the department set out their strategy of silence.[297] 'Can you kindly assist with a response to the sensitive enquiry received. I suggest that the CFO prepares the initial response and legal looks at it before we finalise it for sign-off. Some journalists, in cases like this, will contact multiple people within the institution to source comment. If the journalist makes contact with any of you, explain that any questions must be sent to the media relations team. Avoid the temptation to even try and explain anything to him. This matter, depending on what kind of responses we get and whether there is any progress in the case, is likely to hog the headlines for a long time, more so in light of the recent commitment by the provincial government to root out corruption from its ranks.'[298]

The instruction was copied to the office of Gauteng Premier David Makhura. His public statements in the wake of Babita's death were also likely to be dredged up. There was also an instruction for Tembisa Hospital CEO Ashley Mthunzi. If the bothersome journalist approaches you, say nothing.[299]

While Gauteng health leaders battened down the hatches, I was neck-deep in documents and paperwork. Some tenderpreneurs and their networks were easy to identify. Family members would have fleets of companies registered in their names, and there were familiar patterns in the ownership of some firms.

A person would be the sole director of five companies, all of which had been registered on the same day. In fact, some of these entities were spawned in such quick succession that the registration numbers were nearly sequential. I found the email addresses they had used to correspond with the department. The receiving requests for quotes and issuing invoices were strikingly similar and appeared to follow a stencilled format: 'name.initial.surname@gmail.com'. That was weird, I thought – another red flag that cast doubt over their legitimacy as trading entities.[300] As I had found earlier, none had websites or social media accounts. Moreover, none had been licensed by the South African Health Products Regulatory Authority to trade in medical equipment. And again, the names of these companies were ludicrous.

Take one Antoinette le Roux. The 55-year-old was the sole director of Brielle Rumi, Luna Imogen, Mae Freya, Magnus Rhett and Nora Eloise, which supplied Tembisa Hospital with surgical equipment and medical consumables – leading to a R10 million business boom.[301]

How these entities were named followed no rhyme or reason, at least none I could fathom. I thought they had been generated randomly, and in a way that was beyond lazy. Le Roux had not even tacked 'medical supply' or 'hospital goods' on to the company names to make them appear credible. Probably the only commonality between her and other directors was that their hospital supply businesses were not their only source of income. All were employed permanently in regular jobs. Le Roux was a bank teller at a Standard Bank branch on the East Rand.[302]

I was looking at clusters of letterbox companies that existed only on paper. I was confident that at least 45 of these template entities could be grouped together. Controlled by nine people, the paper companies landed contracts worth more than R110 million in just two months.[303] That's what the evidence suggested, but if I was going to expose these networks as fake, I needed more.

Companies that were doing so well – bidding for and delivering orders of hospital beds, ventilators, needles, syringes, gloves and other furniture at a volume that would fill shipping containers – would surely be easy to find. If they were real, they would have offices, staff and storage space. Day after day, I travelled the length and breadth of the province, and sometimes beyond the borders of Gauteng, to look for these companies. What my search turned up was critical. Some addresses did not exist. Others were for churches, facilities for the mentally challenged, guesthouses and vacant stretches of veld. I traced some addresses to suburban homes, where the owners or tenants knew nothing of any business activity. To me, it seemed that these locations had been chosen at random – a veritable 'close your eyes and stab a pin on Google Maps'.

When someone registers a company, the law requires a fixed address. But the Companies and Intellectual Property Commission relies on good faith, and these companies' addresses were not verified. I had found an apparent pattern of fraud.

Sydney Thindelo, via his cluster of companies, secured 43 individual contracts with a total take of R20.1 million – again in less than two months. At one point he worked for a Johannesburg accoun-tancy firm, but I could find no links to any of the other proprietors. All his addresses were false; one led me to an exotic pet shop that sold snakes. I thought that was apt. My efforts to get him on the phone also came to naught. I left a message to say I knew he formed part of an extraction network, and I provided a long list of questions so that he could defend himself. He refused to answer.[304] All that I got out of him was this, via WhatsApp: 'I just want to confirm that I have nothing to do with the unfortunate thing that happened to Mrs Babita.'[305]

One order that Thindelo filled was a splurge on 100 bonded-leather wingback chairs at a total cost of R495 000. The hospital was billed through one of his companies, Sogaki.[306] This is the type of furniture one would expect to find in a cigar lounge, not in a hos-pital. I imagined Mthunzi sitting in a massive room with mahogany wall panels, surrounded by 100 chairs and puffing on a Cohiba. How else would you explain an impoverished hospital dropping half a million rand on luxury furniture?

Shortly after he had taken the reins at Tembisa and before this scandal broke, Mthunzi welcomed a delegation of visiting politi-cians from the parliamentary portfolio committee on public service and administration. They were conducting a spot check on service delivery. He spoke to a trailing group of journalists and laid bare the challenges his facility faced. He was new in the job, but Tembisa could be turned around. The hospital had to double its staff complement, and it was operating 1 200 beds, way above its stated capacity of 840. Mthunzi said that the hospital had been allocated the budget of a regional hospital, even though it had been considered a tertiary facility for a decade at that point and still lacked critical equipment that would enable it to serve patients more efficiently.[307] How would bespoke leather furniture benefit the infirm? I wondered. This was just one dubious purchase among thousands.

I found a husband-and-wife pair, Avikash and Christine Signarian, whose ten companies banked R30 million in four weeks. This was an incredible entrepreneurial success for a couple who rented a backroom in the Pretoria suburb of Lotus Park.[308] When I showed up at the house, their landlords, an elderly couple, told me that the couple were at work. It was my folly to arrive during business hours. I tried to get the Signarians and others on the phone with no success. I would call them throughout the day and into the evening. Calls were ignored. However, WhatsApp messages returned two blue ticks, so they knew that I was on their heels. And they must have known why.

One day I set out to visit companies steered by a man named Samendran Chin. Surprise, surprise – all were fake. Chin had been ignoring my calls, but I gave him another try. I dialled. Avikash Signarian answered. I was taken aback. Had I mixed up their contact numbers in the swirl of research and tracing? As it turned out, Signarian and Chin were colleagues, and the number was a work line that they shared. Both were sound engineers for recording label David Gresham Records. When Signarian realised who he was talking to, he cut the call. Now I could put the Signarians and Chin together. Links were starting to reveal themselves.[309]

On the phone, they remained at arm's length and could evade me in perpetuity. But I knew where they worked, and I decided to pay them a visit. I walked into the glitzy reception area of the record label at their Melrose Arch headquarters and announced myself. I was an investigative journalist looking into public health corruption, and I wanted to speak to Chin or Signarian – but first prize would be both. I was told that they were out of the office on a job. 'In that case, then, I'll speak to someone in authority here. It's important. I'll wait,' I said. The words 'investigative journalist' and 'corruption' drew the managing director out of a meeting. In a boardroom, I spread out company reports for him. I told him that his employees had been moonlighting and were making millions after hours, and here was the proof. He was shocked when I told him that together, their companies had been paid nearly R25 million by Tembisa Hospital.[310] I added a bit of mustard: 'That's R35 million if you include Avikash's wife.'

He knew nothing of this, and I agreed that he could not answer questions on behalf of employees. He got Chin on the phone and put him on speaker. 'I have a journalist here with me, Samendran. He is asking about your companies. He said he has been trying to talk to you?'

The elusive Mr Chin was caught off guard. 'No man, that is private. Why is he coming to the office? I was told not to speak to him.' He would not discuss it. He was done.

I wondered who had told Chin to shut up. Both he and Signarian tendered their resignations the next day with immediate effect.

Clearly both the Gauteng Health Department and its suppliers were going to ground.

Skinny jeans and
a soccer star

Neeshan Balton has a stern countenance with a piercing gaze. There is a quiet, resolute air to his presence. At the age of 63, he sports a mop of greying hair and a white beard.

He is a man who helped shape South Africa's move from oppression and racial segregation under apartheid to an epoch of democracy and equality, when the ANC stormed to victory in the first democratic elections in 1994. His family hails from Sophiatown but were forced to move to Lenasia under the repressive Group Areas Act. He studied education at the University of the Witwatersrand, where he threw his weight into political activity.

In 1982, Balton joined the Lenasia Youth League. When it was banned under a national state of emergency, he was sent to train with the ANC in Botswana. On his return, he led a double life. He worked as a teacher to mask his clandestine activity: setting up underground structures for the ANC. He was a secret actor in the armed resistance – uMkhonto weSizwe – and established and led an MK cell named after anti-apartheid activist Ahmed Timol, who had been murdered by the Security Branch. With others, Balton had a hand in more than 35 sabotage and bombing operations.

After the tide turned, he served on the City of Johannesburg's transitionary council, helped organise the ANC's election campaigns and served as director-general in then-Gauteng premier Mbhazima Shilowa's government.

In 2008, following the election of Jacob Zuma, he resigned from the government and the ANC. He then began a new life of activism, as a voice to help keep misgovernance in check. When I met him at an East Rand shopping mall in early August 2022, he was the chair of the Ahmed Kathrada Foundation. For Babita, he had been a confidant.[311]

By then, with story after story, the stench of corruption had broken in waves over the Gauteng Health Department, which was on the defensive. The Democratic Alliance called on the Public Service Commission to investigate Madyo and her role in the saga.

Before being parachuted into a top job at the department, she had been seconded from another department – Infrastructure Development. She then applied for the permanent position and was appointed even though she did not obtain the highest score among those shortlisted for interviews. The highest-scoring candidate was supposedly disqualified for not meeting the job requirements. Madyo didn't deserve the job either but was appointed with the agreement of Gauteng Premier David Makhura.[312]

'I have a terrible feeling that history has repeated itself with another CFO embroiled in corruption allegations that show the deep rot remains in this department despite all promises to clean it up,' the DA's Jack Bloom said at the time.[313] The inference was that Madyo's appointment had been manipulated for a political imperative.

Speaking to SAFM's Stephen Grootes, Makhura said that his office had taken note of my reportage – specifically, the allegations that Tembisa Hospital had been turned into a contract factory allowing shadowy syndicates to bank hundreds of millions of rand – and was appointing an independent forensic investigator to probe the hospital's buying practices.

His head of department would consider 'labour matters' related to Madyo and Mthunzi, and, he cautioned, 'issues related to the tragic death and murder of Babita Deokaran are still under investigation by law-enforcement agencies and therefore law-enforcement agencies must be allowed space to do their work'.[314] There it was: the default position of silence.

When Makhura fired his previous health MEC, Dr Bandile Masuku, for his ties to Covid-19 corruption and the enrichment of politicians, the premier told a press conference that it had been the most consequential financial scandal of his tenure.[315] I beg to disagree. He had been forced to take an inward look at the Health Department, but it was still a site of extraction.

The Ahmed Kathrada Foundation was planning a memorial service on the anniversary of Babita's death, and Balton called me to a meeting that day. He was the person Babita had turned to after her trumped-up suspension. He asked me if I would speak at the event, and I told him I couldn't. It was too dangerous. It would make it clear that I was working to force accountability in the Gauteng Health Department and to finish what she had started.

He asked me if I was worried, considering the work I was doing and Babita's murder. It was a pointed approach, and I told him that fear was what 'they' wanted. I would not be cowed. I assured Balton that we had taken steps to manage my safety, and that the people behind Babita's murder, should they come for me, would not have the element of surprise on their side. In truth, worry had taken hold. I had CCTV cameras and an alarm system installed at my house. When I arrived for our meeting, I sat at the back of the restaurant so I could watch the door. I knew that if people wanted me dead, the attack would come where I was most vulnerable: in a car. Every drive administered a new dose of paranoia and fear. I changed my schedule and drove to and from work at odd hours. I developed different routes in case I was being watched by those who wanted to plot my routine.

It's hard to describe what being alert constantly feels like. My eyes hurt from obsessively scanning mirrors when I drove. Had I seen that car before? How many people were in it? Were the windows down? It was unyielding and exhausting. The reality was that if they wanted me dead, they were likely to succeed. A spray of automatic gunfire, and the bothersome journalist would be dealt with. But I decided that if that day came, I would not make it easy.

To mark a year since Babita was killed, I published another instalment in the series: 'Tembisa Hospital's R500 000 skinny-jean spending spree . . . and the soccer star who scored'.[316]

The hospital had approved a R500 000 payment for a shipment of skinny jeans in the middle of the third wave of the coronavirus while the facility battled overcrowding, dire staff shortages and death. The contract to supply 200 pairs of denims – for girls aged six to seven – went to a company named Inez Chaste, one of ten separate business entities controlled by retired soccer star Themba Shabalala and his wife, Evelyn.[317] When I visited the business address of this company, I found a creche that had been operating for years. The ten shell companies had only existed for a month before Tembisa Hospital's procurement office tapped them for work, and they fell within a network of 45 entities that I believed were a single R110 million syndicate.

On the eve of his retirement from professional football, Shabalala, a former Jomo Cosmos and Bidvest Wits defender, founded his clutch of five companies. Speaking to *Soccer Laduma* at the time, he said he would become a sports agent and hoped to develop young talent. He said nothing of his work in the public health sector.[318]

At the memorial service, standing at the lectern, Balton held up a handful of pages. They were copies of my reports that he had printed out, and one after the other, he read the headlines. How could it be, he asked, that a journalist had exposed the corruption that Babita had first warned about? Where was the leadership of the Gauteng Health Department, and what exactly had they done? Makhura had been invited but stayed away. He hid behind a statement with all the usual talking points: we take it seriously; there will be an investigation. The man didn't want to be questioned.

The single transaction for the skinny jeans was one among thousands, but it was such an outrageous thing to spend money on. Radio stations picked up the story. Civil society organisations issued statements decrying financial mismanagement. TV news broadcasters latched onto it, and Tembisa Hospital's skinny jeans dominated public discourse. It even lured Mthunzi into the open. In defiance of a directive to keep his mouth shut, he was interviewed by 702 talk-show host Clement Manyathela.[319]

'Good morning, Clement, and good morning to the listeners. I need to clarify this and give some education on supply-chain processes before I get to the skinny jeans.'[320]

Ah. Edification beckoned.

'The issue of skinny jeans. I signed for suture material. We have the invoice, and the suture material is what we received at the hospital.'[321]

Mthunzi explained that in the procurement process, an incorrect code was used to capture the purchase. It should have been for sutures, and there had been an innocent error. There were no jeans. He embarked on a long soliloquy explaining how procurement works. There must be a need, and an order starts with a hospital official. There are several steps in the process, and he, as the CEO, merely signed off on it. The splurge did not start with him. He was busy throwing his employees under the bus.

Manyathela gave him a long leash, but Mthunzi was rattled and incoherent. His staunch defence of his probity excluded the syndicate in which I had positioned Inez Chaste and the other contract barons. Vetting companies, he said, was outside his competence. But the buck stopped with him, not just for the skinny-jeans splurge but also for the R850 million in hospital spending. Every single transaction would be picked apart, whether he liked it or not.[322]

Bullets in the post box

Early on a winter's morning in June 2022, a police officer, part of a protection detail assigned to guard Director-General in the Presidency Phindile Baleni, discovered an envelope in the post box at her home. Folded within the single, crumpled sheet of paper was a single 5.56-calibre bullet, ammunition for assault rifles.[323] Both the note and the bullet were intended to send a message. The note read:

Dear Miss Baleni.

Please take the following into consideration.

1. Advise the Justice [Department] to release the suspects of Babita Deokaran – no case against them.

2. Advise the President not to proceed with state capture findings.

We don't want you to be like Thabo Masebe, Babita, Mpho Moerane. We know where you drive and all your visiting points. The plan is complete. Only if you consider our proposal, then the deal will be struck off. The President listens to you more than any other person. Those two cars you always travel with . . . we have a good plan for them. We are not scared of the soldiers that are escorting you.

Something special is on for you. We have our eyes on the ground in any province you travel in. Time is ticking.[324]

By then, Babita had been dead for nearly a year. Thabo Masebe, who was acting as director-general in Gauteng Premier David Ma-khura's office, had died two months before after suddenly falling ill at his Kempton Park home.[325] Mpho Moerane was a reference to Johannesburg Mayor Mpho Moerane, who had died in May 2022 as a result of injuries sustained in a car accident near his Mondeor home.[326] There was no indication that Masebe and Moerane had been eliminated, but this letter cast a shadow over their deaths. Had they been silenced, as Babita was?

The threat to Baleni was manifest. Those who had sent the letter had been watching her. They knew the cars she travelled in and the strength of her security detail, and they made a point of spelling this out. If this high-ranking state official did not convince President Cyril Ramaphosa to abandon the recommendations of the Commission of Inquiry into State Capture and somehow set free the six *izinkabi* charged in relation to Babita's assassination, she would get other bullets.

The findings of the commission and Babita's murder were dispa-rate. The only commonality was that both could be tied to deep-rooted corruption. State capture, in the sense that it was understood then, was a subversion of democracy, where ANC leaders and their officials enriched privateers in exchange for payoffs, and it was done at the highest level. The assassination of Babita could be set within this scheme. This letter signalled an assault on the rule of law.

Phakamani Hadebe and the other five *izinkabi* had been denied bail and were imprisoned while awaiting trial. The threat to Baleni was instructive. Dropping a bullet in the post box of a government leader is not a tactic innocent men would employ. It positioned the *izinkabi* as guns for hire in the political arena, protecting illicit revenue streams. Three days after the first anniversary of Babita's death, Madyo and Mthunzi were placed on precautionary suspension. Public pressure had exacted a toll, and Makhura was compelled to act.[327]

'Given the seriousness of the allegations and the possible link to the murder case of Babita Deokaran – [the] former chief director of finance, exemplary public servant and courageous whistleblower, who was brutally killed a year ago – the Special Investigating Unit has been appointed to investigate these allegations with urgency,' he said in a statement.[328]

Madyo and Mthunzi were suspended 'to ensure that their presence in the office does not impede the investigation of the serious allegations pertaining to the improper procurement and payment of service providers at Tembisa Hospital'.[329]

This was a promising development. I had feared that Makhura would appoint a pliant audit firm that would whitewash the investigation, but the premier had set the SIU on Tembisa Hospital and its suppliers. Getting both Mthunzi and Madyo out of the department while this investigation was underway was a logical move. By virtue of their positions, they both had a duty to safeguard the public purse – yet, under their watch, shell-company syndicates with ties to the ANC had taken root.

Moreover, Makhura had waxed lyrical about the need – and want – of his administration to root out corruption. This would be a public show of words becoming action. But the premier's stated vision and pragmatism were not shared by those in positions of influence in the Gauteng Health Department. In the background, far from public view, Mthunzi and Madyo were being protected.[330]

Dr Nomonde Nolutshungu was appointed as head of the Gauteng Health Department just four months before I started to expose Tembisa Hospital's spending spree and the spending anomalies Babita had reported just three weeks before her murder. Nolutshungu had a pedigree in the public health service. She had occupied the same post in 2012 and later departed for the position of health attaché in Washington, DC. She represented South Africa on the global stage, leading diplomatic efforts on global public health with the US government, its agencies, academic institutions, the private sector and large philanthropic organisations. She had also worked as a chief director within the national Health Department, with a focus on HIV/Aids, tuberculosis and sexually transmitted diseases.[331] She was well-qualified with the experience needed for this challenging role, but not everyone was pleased by her presence.[332]

The new head of department was in an invidious position, caught between the need to do her job well – by ensuring that millions of people received the best possible care in government hospitals and clinics – and the political imperatives of those to whom she reported. In the swirling maelstrom of the Tembisa Hospital fallout, Makhura pushed for Mthunzi and Madyo to be suspended. If this was to happen, Nolutshungu had to be the one to do it.

Nolutshungu set about drafting the letters of precautionary suspension. Late on 24 August 2022, she received an anonymous email with a subject line in capitals:

UNPROFESSIONAL, IRRATIONAL AND
ILLOGICAL CONDUCT[333]

Dear HOD,

Your hate toward the sitting CFO Lerato [Madyo] is noticeable. We are watching how you are using your office to eliminate dissenting voices at a senior management level. Your collaborative effort with the DA will blow up in your face and we will expose it soon.

At the right time, the public will be taken into confidence about the real reasons why you have decided to kill the professional career of Madyo. We are sending you a message that you ought to do your job diligently and respect the office you are occupying, and separate personal issues.

You should also notice that your predecessors never finished their five-year contracts because of personal issues. Kindly focus on your job.

From: A concerned member of society.[334]

This was the day before Nolutshungu was to place Madyo and Mthunzi on suspension. The timing was key. The email also made reference to Nolutshungu's daughter, her movements and her relationships. It was patently a threat to derail investigations into and disciplinary action of Madyo and Mthunzi.[335] The power and influence the pair wielded within the Health Department had already been on display, and now darker, more insidious methods were being employed to safeguard their tenure.

It seemed to me that those who moved to counter Tembisa Hospital corruption were threatened with death as political deployees tried to cover their tracks.

CHAPTER 21

The hidden hand

My focus was on unmasking the controlling minds behind 217 companies that had driven a near R1 billion buying spree at Tembisa Hospital.[336] Some days were spent sifting through publicly available documents to link suppliers to upmarket property purchases and eye-watering spending on luxury cars. Other days were spent on the road, hounding down those I believed to be proxy directors.

I had a trove of evidence that allowed me to move beyond the realm of allegations to hard fact. I was able to push out a story every week. Drip-feeding this damning information into the public domain meant that it was impossible for the Gauteng Health Department to ignore the scandal. It would have to take action. An unintended consequence, however, was that every story heightened the risk to my safety. I had initially been asked if I wanted bodyguards, but I had declined. I was warned that mine was a risky path, but no one had directly threatened me. But since then, a bullet was left in Presidency Director-General Phindile Baleni's post box, while the newly installed department head, Nomonde Nolutshungu, had been threatened when she started her investigation into Tembisa Hospital and its officials. It would be naive to believe I couldn't be in the firing line.

I was on edge and firmly in the grip of distrust and suspicion. Every time I pulled out of my driveway, I worried that gunmen could be waiting for me. Fear was ever-present, and I became a recluse. I felt that when I left my home, I would be exposed. This shift in lifestyle took a toll on my wife, Bernadette. Also a journalist, she was employed at the time as a court reporter for broadcaster Eyewitness News. While we work in the same industry, the subject matter we deal with couldn't be more different. Court reporting relies on documents in a process designed to be open and public. The plaintiff has their say, and the defendant responds. The legal wrangle plays out in open court, and then there is a ruling. It's all relatively black and white. Every time I told Bernadette about the shadow state and what I had found, I could see the colour drain from her face. My pursuit of the story rattled her, and one night she broke.

I remember the evening well. We were sitting on the edge of our bed, and she was weeping. She asked me if I knew what would happen to her if I died. It was something I had thought about often, but her response chilled me. She told me that her life would be over. It would not be worth living if I wasn't in it.

I was nowhere near finished with my dalliance with danger and death, but she wanted me to know what was on the line. I had to be careful, she stressed. She had become collateral damage in this saga, and it was not something she had signed up for. She was not the one taking on this investigation.

For the first time, the true impact of my work on my marriage hit home. I felt enormous guilt. She never asked me to stop, though. I knew that, as terrifying as it was, I had her backing to do the right thing.

That night, I called my boss, Pieter. I laid everything out for him. I had not received a direct threat, but that in itself was almost counterintuitive. If someone wanted me dead, they would not warn me beforehand – and the real risk I faced was, in fact, heightened. Pieter didn't hesitate. He would protect me as much as he could. The next day, a tall man with a pistol tucked into his waistband arrived at my gate. He had been in the military and served in South Africa's special forces. Now he would be fixed to my hip whenever I ventured out in public.

Our first assignment was visiting a home in the suburb of Kibler Park along the eastern expanses of Johannesburg. I had found an address linked to Antoinette le Roux, the humble bank teller whose five oddball companies had seen a R10 million boon from Tembisa Hospital. I was convinced that, on the balance of probabilities, she was a proxy director, part of a much larger syndicate, and I was keen to confront her face to face. When I arrived at the house with my bodyguard, her sister spoke to me through the fence. She was taken aback when I told her that her 55-year-old sibling was a secret millionaire. She insisted that they no longer lived together, and Antoinette was not home. My bodyguard was standing behind me, his eyes fixed on the road.

I asked the woman to pass on a message: I knew Antoinette was not the mastermind of this scheme, and I believed she was being used. 'Your sister has big shit coming her way. If I have found her, the SIU and the police are going to be on my heels. Please tell her this: if she talks to me and is honest, I can protect her from public exposure as a source. I can do nothing to get her out of trouble with the authorities, but if she declines, I will make it my personal mission to ensure that her face and name are everywhere.

'She is going to need to retire soon, and when the bank fires her for this, she's going to lose her pension and she's coming to live with you.'

My offer had a clock. She could contact me in the next 24 hours if she wanted to talk.

I waited, but the elusive Ms le Roux never called.

In the days that followed, I was forced to shift my focus from Antoinette le Roux and others I suspected were proxy directors to a new figure: Stefan Joel Govindraju. In only 48 hours between 31 August and 1 September 2022, he had been appointed as a director of 45 entities that had been trading with the hospital.[337] That all these successful businesspeople would abandon their cash cows, all at the same time, was beyond comprehension. To cede their control of the entities to Govindraju, each would have had to complete paperwork. A CoR 39 form to amend a company directorship would need to be submitted to the Companies and Intellectual Property Commission via an online portal.

The way these companies were abandoned, and the fact that they all simultaneously changed hands within two days, pointed to central coordination. I was certain that Govindraju had been the hidden hand all along, and in the face of our reports that singled out these clusters of entities, he let his proxies off the hook. I suspected that he had been the one filling out all the CoR 39 forms and was at the zenith of the network. Was he the one who told sound engineer Samendran Chin not to talk to me? If he was not the puppeteer, why else would he take over these firms that had already been blackened by my reporting and now faced an SIU probe?

Govindraju's acquisition of these entities was helpful to me, because, looking at his CIPC director profile, I was able to see the extent of his web of influence. Other companies, not flagged by Babita, had also transferred control to him – and they had also been trading with the hospital. All in all, Govindraju had taken the reins of an empire and was now the sole director of 54 medical supply companies. Now he was on my radar.

After this development, I started looking into Govindraju's life. He is something of a ghost online, with no profiles on Twitter, Facebook or Instagram. I didn't even have a picture of him. All I could find was that he had submitted a doctoral thesis in chemistry at the University of the Witwatersrand. It was submitted in 2017 under the title 'Synthesis and characterisation of hybrid nanocomposites using polyvinylcarbazole and metal selenides to demonstrate photovoltaic properties'[338]. After that, Govindraju dropped off the map – at least online.

I put in repeated phone calls to him, none of which were answered. Using messaging applications WhatsApp, Signal and Telegram, I asked him to meet me. I told him that, by virtue of the takeover, he was now a central figure in my investigation, and I wanted to give him an opportunity to explain himself. He would not sit for an interview or take my calls, and he asked that I submit my questions in writing. I sent them, and he claimed they hadn't come through. When I pressed him again, he said he needed to talk to his lawyer. Then he missed a deadline because of a religious holiday. I am no idiot; I know when someone is avoiding me. Next, he blocked me. So, I made his corporate coup public.[339]

The headline read: 'How Tembisa Hospital's R500k skinny jean supplier and shell corporation bosses flew the coop'.[340]

'Dr Stefan Joel Govindraju now directs the group of companies which saw R116 million in dubious trade from the hospital, his conglomerate accounting for nearly a quarter of the 217 "possibly fraudulent" entities unearthed by the whistleblower.[341]

'In two days, company directors resigned en masse, and ceded control to him. The companies – shell corporations that used false addresses and exist only on paper – form part of an extraction network that scored hundreds of contracts from the East Rand health facility, providing everything from luxury leather furniture to ventilators.'[342]

Of the 217 entities flagged by Babita, almost a quarter were now controlled by Govindraju. I gave him every opportunity to comment, to explain why the companies had changed hands and to defend his probity. But I was iced out.[343]

Once the story was published, I began receiving strange phone calls. The number was hidden, and the man on the other side said I was right to be suspicious of Govindraju. I asked for a meeting, but the caller refused. However, he was happy to share information with me over the phone. One night he guided me through several interlinked Facebook profiles to an album of Govindraju's wedding pictures. There was a family portrait of the couple and their in-laws. Govindraju had obviously cleansed his online presence, but this gem was missed. It was clear that whoever was on the other end of the phone was close to him. On another call, the man told me that Govindraju's wife, Dhereshni, was a pharmacist working at a

Johannesburg-based pharmaceutical factory, and he gave me the name. I decided to pay her a visit.

One day I rocked up at the company unannounced. I told the receptionist who I was and that I wanted to speak to Dhereshni. But I was out of luck; she wasn't there that day. If I was going to make myself a nuisance and get under Govindraju's skin, I wagered that Dhereshni would be a pressure point.

On a Friday afternoon, I typed out a long letter with questions about her husband's tender activities and dropped it off at her office. I enjoyed making first approaches like this close to a weekend. I imagined that, after reading my questions, Saturday and Sunday would be two days of stress. This overture clearly riled the couple, and I got a heated email from Govindraju.[344]

> You have dropped off a letter at Dhe's [Dhereshni's] work-place. I am unsure as to what your motive is. I hazard a guess that you are perhaps looking to extort information from me on the premise of intimidating her. I have nothing to hide and am available for questioning by the relevant authorities. Not you. You have already approached her employer. I find that very invasive considering she has nothing to do with my business dealings. According to legal advice received I was told that I have the right against self-incrimination, which includes the right to refuse to answer an incriminatory question.[345]

But Dhereshni was involved, and she couldn't deny it. She had arranged a job for one of the proxy directors at her company. It was a low-paying gig, packing medicine into boxes.

I had got under Govindraju's skin, and he had resorted to his right to silence to avoid 'self-incrimination'. I suspect that as soon as that letter landed on Dhereshni's desk, he caught an earful from her.

Govindraju presided over a network of shell companies led by proxy directors picked from his family members and friends. I was able to link most of them back to him through personal relationships that had, previously, remained hidden. How lax were procurement prescripts at Tembisa Hospital that a group of nearly 60 companies – so obviously illegitimate, and most likely controlled by one man all along – could inveigle their way into the supplier pool and operate undetected for years? For Govindraju and others to capture Tembisa Hospital's procurement office, they needed help from the inside.

Tembisa Hospital's
tender don

In a seedy restaurant deep in the bowels of the Johannesburg inner city, I sat in a dimly lit booth pushed into a back corner. I watched the door, waiting. It was not a popular haunt. I was the only patron when it should have been the lunchtime rush. My only company was a pair of somnolent waiters behind the bar.

I was there to meet someone who had worked with Babita. He was panicky and nervous, understandably. If he spoke out, he said, the ubiquitous 'they' would kill him and his family. He would agree to meet but then fail to arrive or just stop taking my calls. I knew I had to handle him carefully. If I could get him to trust me, I could cultivate a source at the Gauteng Health Department. Having a set of eyes on the inside would be invaluable.

It was a slow burn. After being stood up twice, I let him cool off for a couple of weeks. Then I sent him a voice note.

'I know you are scared, and I know things are dangerous, but I give you my word that, if we do this right, no one will ever know that we have spoken. I am in this, too. I get it. All I am trying to do is tell Babita's story, and I have blind spots, and I need your help. Please let me know.'

The entreaty seemed to win him over. Maybe it was my invocation of Babita or the common ground of our fears. We arranged to delete our messages to each other once they had been read. He sent me a location and time and asked me to make sure I wasn't being followed. And then the messages disappeared.

I had turned my phone off when I left the office and advised him to do the same. I wanted to take every precaution to keep him safe, and I had to eliminate the possibility of nefarious people comparing our cellphone location data and putting us together. He was late, and I considered that I might well be leaving another non-meeting with nothing. But, just then, he hurriedly entered and scanned the room, his shoulders dipped low and a hoodie pulled over his brow. When he sat down, there was a crack in his voice. I shook his hand and I could feel the tremor. This guy was shitting himself.

He asked me to promise that no one would ever find out that we had spoken. He made it clear that if something happened to him or his family, I would have blood on my hands. There was also a risk that he could lose his job. Gauteng Health Department management had placed a chokehold on sharing information and was hunting for leaks, he said. I told him I knew the stakes and that I would go to a prison cell or my grave before outing a source. I then set out what I had found in Babita's report. He had been following the news.

'Everyone knows Tembisa Hospital is a problem. That's a trough, that place. People know it's the hospital where people eat,' he said.

'If you look at anyone, you need to look at a guy named Morgan. He is the don of that place, and he controls everything. He is always at the hospital, and he knows everyone by name and everyone knows him. Sometimes, if you go to the [supply-chain management] office, you will find him inside,' my Deep Throat added.[346] Now, this was something. I recognised Morgan.

Hangwani Morgan Maumela was the sole director of nine companies[347] trading with the hospital. His businesses were prolific. I had also found another director who controlled three entities – Aluwani Maumela.[348] A contact in the Department of Home Affairs confirmed that they were cousins. The pair – via an armada of companies – were due R35 965 699 when Babita froze payments to them. Of the entire R104 million in Tembisa transactions that she halted, one-third had a single destination: the Maumelas.[349] Records I found indicated their companies had supplied the hospital as far back as 2018.[350] They were major players.

From what I could see, most of Morgan's companies shared an address – a posh flatlet on a Fourways housing estate. It was an indication that many supposedly independent entities were run out of the same place. The three companies controlled by his cousin were based on another lifestyle estate, 300 kilometres away in Polokwane, Limpopo. While these firms all appeared separate and distinct from one another, their owners had been sloppy. I could group most together because they shared the same post-box number.[351]

When I first contacted Aluwani by phone, I must have caught him at an inopportune time because he was in a foul mood. Maybe the bile was the effect I had on him. I wanted to know how exactly he was related to Morgan and how the businesses operated. In response, I got an expletive-laden dressing-down.[352]

'Who the fuck are you? I don't have to tell you fucking anything,' Aluwani said. I pushed harder, insisting that we already knew they shared DNA, and the links I had found – the addresses and the overlooked post-box – made me certain I was right.[353]

'Why are you lying?' he said.

That's when the call was cut. Aluwani didn't want to talk about his companies or their work.[354]

Morgan was even more elusive. As hard as I tried, I couldn't pin him down on the phone. I resorted to dispatching emails to those linked to his companies that I had found in Babita's ledgers. No response was forthcoming.[355] To me, it was significant that neither Maumela wanted to talk. It was a commonality among all the suppliers I had approached. If these companies were legitimate and their dealings were above board, surely I would face pushback? Instead, most closed ranks.

It was likely, I reasoned, that Morgan was the more dominant force among the two. He had more irons in the supplier fire, and it was he who had been fingered as the don of the hospital by my source.

As for the man himself, there was very little to go on. Tenderpreneurs often have a handy tendency to splash their wealth online, flaunting pictures of mansions, supercars and Dubai holidays. Morgan was not one to boast on social media. I could see from the accounts that his companies were being paid huge amounts of money, but I needed to prove this. When I found the deed for the MHR Maumela Family Trust, I had an answer, in large part.[356]

He was a trustee, along with his sister, Rumani, and his mother, Mboneni. The trust had been named using the first letters of their first names, and it held a property portfolio that most billionaires would covet.[357] Founded in 2016, the trust had within two years acquired a lush Camps Bay property for R32 million. The four-bedroom house was described by a real-estate agent as a 'one-of-a-kind architectural accomplishment' with panoramic vistas of Table Mountain and the bay.[358]

'The house oozes class, style and refinement. The property takes in unimpaired sea vistas and majestic mountain views through the multiple glass floating roof sections,' an advert for the mansion read. It was replete with an entertainment area and a deck surrounding a glass-rimmed pool on the top floor.[359]

Two years later, Morgan's trust snatched up a palatial property on Victoria Road in Bantry Bay, one of the most sought-after locations in the country, where a square metre has an average price of R80 000. According to a LinkedIn article posted by Lance Real Estate CEO Lance Cohen, the property boasts untrammelled sea views 'as far as the Karbonkelberg, which towers above Llandudno and Sandy Bay'.[360]

'There are simply no buildings in front of it,' he wrote. '[This property] was recently sold by Lance Real Estate for R75 million to an upcountry South African businessman. This is the single most expensive residential purchase in South Africa in 2020.' That businessman was Maumela.[361]

Then there was the R13.5 million home at Pecanwood Estate Golf and Country Club in Hartbeespoort in the North West. The property sits on the banks of the Hartbeespoort Dam, flanked by South Africa's first Jack Nicklaus signature golf course. In 2021, a R13 million home in Hurlingham was added to the portfolio. Ever expanding, the trust also paid R16 million for a ritzy, 6 547-square-metre stand on Oxford Avenue, Sandton.[362]

Within four years, Morgan and his relatives amassed an impressive property portfolio with over 10 000 square metres of some of the most upscale real estate on the continent. I couldn't be sure if the trust had other revenue streams, and Morgan wasn't talking. But I could see that the don of Tembisa had tapped into a rich cash vein at the hospital.[363]

I visited one of his Sandton properties and found a construction site. The multistorey house was clearly going to be massive – I could see as much from satellite imagery. From the roadway, most of the structure was hidden behind four-metre-high walls, and the verge was lined with cars as builders and tilers beat a path in and out. I parked a distance away and watched. A black BMW X5 slipped into an available berth. Two men in suits got out and walked into the property; ten minutes later, they returned to the car and left. I hastily scribbled down the registration and sent it to someone who could access eNatis, the national traffic database. Turned out the black BMW was registered to the police and allocated to the presidential protection detail.

CHAPTER 23

Friends in high places

The long-running TV staple *Top Billing* was a weekly showcase of opulence and excess. Hosts toured the homes of local and international celebrities, including the likes of Springbok rugby player Bryan Habana and US President Donald Trump's ex-wife, Ivana. Beauty, fashion, food, home decor, travel and weddings were its mainstay, and *Top Billing* gave viewers a glimpse of how the other half lived.

In 2019, a decor insert showcased a villa in Hyde Park, one of the most sought-after locales in the country. Presenter Jonathan Boynton-Lee was dazzled by the vaulted ceilings in the foyer and the custom-made chandeliers that lit up curated artwork and sculptures.[364]

'This is more of an artwork than a house,' he quipped, with his guide, the interior designer, nodding in stage-managed affirmation. 'Our client wanted to add his own personality to the environment,' the interior designer said.[365] That client was Hangwani Morgan Maumela.

Only the finest would serve for the don of Tembisa Hospital. I trawled deeds-office records and found that his family trust had bought the designer villa in 2018 for a cool R25 million.[366] Within a year, the interior designer was leading camera crews through the property and boasting that it had been renovated floor to ceiling, with no expense spared. From the tiles to the knives and forks, everything had been carefully selected for a high-end client. Bespoke and custom-made furniture was on display in the lounge, and a lift took you to a basement home cinema, a whisky bar stocked with handpicked malts and a 300-square-metre parking lot. Clearly, millions had been ploughed into the refurbishment, far beyond the purchase price.[367]

By the time the Hyde Park remodelling was complete, companies controlled by Morgan and his cousin, Aluwani, had been registered as suppliers of the Gauteng Health Department. Morgan would still not talk to me about how he made his money, but it was clear that most of his wealth originated from Tembisa Hospital, where patients had starved to death and the sick and infirm slept on the floor because of perennial overcrowding. It was likely that this hospital had bankrolled Morgan's luxury pad.[368]

The villa was Morgan's primary residence. When I did my first accounting of his property holdings, I pegged the total value at R150 million, just based on the purchase prices.[369] After the first story about Morgan was published, outing him as Tembisa's tender don, my phone rang constantly. I was tipped off that there were more properties and that he had deep political connections. With the first story, I managed to shake the tree; now, the fruit came tumbling down. There were other properties acquired by the trust which I had missed.[370]

There were two beachfront homes at Ballito's exclusive Zimbali Country Club, with a cumulative value of R35 million. Morgan's trust paid R70 million for another stand in Sandton and R30 million for two adjoining flats in Cape Town's Sea Point. All in all, the trust held real estate valued north of R310 million.[371] It was a remarkable parade of extravagance.

Once Morgan's role in the Tembisa saga was out in the open, many people – including some who were close to his inner circle – came to me with information. One man was from Vhufuli, the Limpopo village where Morgan had grown up. Others had been in his orbit when he hit his tender heyday. All insisted on anonymity and feared his reprisal should they be named. I can't frame each in any more detail than I already have. Doing so would risk exposing them. But the value of what they told me, and what I was able to corroborate, created an image of a wealthy man with friends in high places.

I understood Morgan to be a quiet figure who valued his privacy. I was told that he was a frequent patron of the Bryanston nightclub Rockets. There he would lavish high-end booze and cash on women. He had a penchant for sports cars – vehicles that he had custom-painted in a particular shade of azure frost blue. These low-slung Italian supercars would literally stop traffic in the Rockets parking lot. When the *Top Billing* camera crew showed up at his villa, all the cars had been moved out to avoid attracting unwanted attention. Slowly, I was starting to get a sense of the man and what he spent his money on.

When I tracked down Morgan's father, Basil Mudau, to his home in Vhufuli, the elderly man helped me establish Morgan's family tree. This revealed ties to President Cyril Ramaphosa. The links stretched back to Ramaphosa's first marriage, to Hope Mudau, in 1978.

Basil is Hope's brother. Morgan's mother, Mboneni, was a director in the Limpopo Health Department before she retired in 2021.[372] This was nuclear. Ramaphosa had his image blighted when his official spokeswoman, Khusela Diko, stepped down from her post after she was tainted by the Covid-19 procurement graft. That scandal now seemed paltry compared with being related – albeit distantly – to a central figure in the procurement scandal at Tembisa Hospital and the assassination of a whistleblower.

'He grew up as a nice boy, very quiet, and when he started working ... he started in Pietersburg [Polokwane] doing these tender things. Whenever I asked him [about this work], he would say I am doing tenders,' Mudau told me while we sat in the shade of a tree in the village.[373] 'I hardly knew what tenders he was talking about until the story came out. I felt very bad. I couldn't even eat. I tried to contact him, but he was nowhere to be found.'

The father-and-son relationship was obviously rekindled shortly after my visit. I got a sternly worded reproach from Morgan's lawyer.

I was not to speak to members of his family, and they considered me unethical. (Oh no!) They threatened to complain to the press ombudsman about my conduct.[374]

When I could confirm that Morgan was a relative of Ramaphosa's, I immediately sent questions to the president's office. His spokesman, Vincent Magwenya, tried to deflect. Yes, they knew of Morgan and they were aware that he traded on his presidential link, but there was no relationship with the president. You know what African families are like, I was told.[375]

'To the extent that Maumela is the son of the president's ex-brother-in-law, the president has no further knowledge of Maumela, nor has he ever had any relationship with him,' Magwenya said. 'The president does not have any knowledge of Maumela's business dealings, nor was he aware of his involvement with the Tembisa Hospital or any other state entity. As stated, he has no relationship with Maumela.'[376]

That Morgan and Ramaphosa are related had stunning implications. The SIU had, by then, launched a preliminary investigation at the behest of Gauteng Premier David Makhura. A full probe has to be authorised and proclaimed by the president. The probability existed that Ramaphosa would have to set the SIU on his own family. 'The president considers every application by the SIU on its merits, and he will certainly sign such a proclamation should the SIU, as it so often does, motivate for the need for such an investigation. It would be extraordinary for President Ramaphosa not to sign a proclamation,' Magwenya added.[377]

It was clear to me then that Magwenya was trying to distance his principal from Morgan. For a tenderpreneur to have ties to the Union Buildings and those at the levers of power and political influence was scandalous. The spin doctor could distance Ramaphosa from Morgan, but he could not gainsay the latter's friendship with Bejani Chauke, the president's principal political advisor.

Chauke is a man who holds immense political sway. He ran for political office at the ANC's elective conference in 2022 and played a critical role in the CR17 campaign that saw Ramaphosa take the party's presidency. He was regularly dispatched as a special envoy to countries such as Saudi Arabia, and in political circles he is referred to as the president's 'fixer'. His company, Acute Strategies, is often involved in election campaigns in Africa.[378]

Morgan and Chauke both had homes in the Hyde Park complex featured on *Top Billing*. With Maumela at Stand 3 and Chauke at Stand 6, the pair were neighbours.[379] When I sent questions to Chauke about his friendship with Morgan, his response did not come to me. Instead, he went to *News24* political editor Qaanitah Hunter. Chauke told her that my information was so outlandish, I must be addicted to cocaine.

I am not sure what his approach to my colleague was intended to achieve. If he wanted her to help him and try to convince me to abandon this story, he had obviously misjudged her. She is better than that. When another newspaper reported on separate claims about Chauke, he included my questions and responses to them in what he sent back. He claimed that he had only ever met Morgan twice, both instances being meetings of the body corporate. The trouble was that I had people who could place Chauke in Morgan's home – constantly. One person told me how the president's fixer appeared for breakfast at the villa one morning in a robe and slippers. And then there was the car registered to Ramaphosa's police protection detail that had showed up at Morgan's home. Now I had a plausible explanation for its presence. The fact was that Morgan had allies in the uppermost echelons of power, in both the ANC and the state.

I was also reliably informed that Morgan would regularly holiday with state-capture beneficiary Edwin Sodi – the quintessential tenderpreneur, who has geared his business empire to secure government work. The main arm of his network is Blackhead Consulting.

In 2014, through a joint venture, Sodi and his partner, Ignatius Mpambani, were awarded a R255 million tender by the Free State Department of Human Settlements to audit the prevalence of asbestos in low-cost housing projects. In 2015, the auditor-general issued a report finding the contract irregular and advised the department to stop paying – but the money continued to flow. Here is the rub: Sodi and his ilk outsourced the work to another firm, paid them R21 million and banked the profit.

Mpambani was later assassinated – a murder that remains unsolved. His Bentley was riddled with bullets as he travelled through Sandton, and police found a sizable amount of money in the boot. Blackhead went on to win a contract to conduct similar audits on asbestos roofing in low-cost housing in Gauteng.[380]

Sodi is also one who enjoys the highlife. His home is an R85 million mansion in Bryanston. Viral Instagram footage from within shows his garage filled with a selection of limited-edition Ferraris, Lamborghinis, Rolls-Royces and Bentleys. Were these all funded by the taxpayer?

When the gauche businessman appeared before the State Capture Commission, he received a grilling over Blackhead's R1 billion annual turnover and shady payments to ANC cabinet members Zizi Kodwa, Pinky Kekana and Thulas Nxesi, as well as millions of rand in donations he had made to the party. Sodi had also processed a payment of R3.6 million to the ANC for T-shirts, and the commission heard that he had dispatched R370 000 into Paul Mashatile's personal bank account. In Sodi's version, this was money destined for party work. Mashatile was never called on to explain this windfall.[381]

The long and short of it was that Sodi sported political access and state work flowed his way – much like Morgan.

Sodi's access to Mashatile, at least on the face of it, was beneficial. Between 2014 and 2017, the Gauteng Department of Human Settlements paid Blackhead R134 million for a housing project in Diepsloot East – but not a single structure was built. When the provincial government started paying Sodi in 2014, Mashatile was the chairperson of the ANC in the province. While cash flowed to Blackhead, Mashatile was given the run of Sodi's luxury mansion on Cape Town's Atlantic seaboard.[382] To all intents and purposes, the pair were close. Mashatile and Morgan held court, and the latter's access to political power brokers was firmly cemented, in my mind at least. That Mashatile had these people in his orbit undercut the ANC's public posture on the need to clean up corruption.

Morgan's supercar collection, I was told, was the stuff of lore. My source, ensconced in his village, told me of his visits and how the sports cars – built for speed – travelled at a snail's pace along potholed roads. At one of his palatial properties in Sandton, a garage large enough to house 27 vehicles had been purpose-built. Morgan was known in niche car circles and rumoured to customise his azure frost-blue rides with yellow brake callipers. In some instances, cars would be purchased and returned immediately to their European factories for retrofitting to specification, my sources alleged. But there was a problem. There was no such fleet registered in Morgan's name. If he owned them, they were registered to proxies – people, companies or trusts. Maybe the automotive collection was merely a myth.

At one point, I was tipped off that Morgan was stashing a Lamborghini at a dealership outside the province. I drove off to find it. When I arrived, I was greeted by two lots. They had obviously drawn a line between the high-end cars and the more economic options. The former was in an enclosed showroom with velvet ropes and polished floors. The latter was outside, exposed to the elements with a fibreglass overhang that caught the wind. I am a journalist, and I look like one. I knew I would stick out like a sore thumb in the glitzy showroom, so I started by feigning interest and kicking the tires of the cheap cars outside. Slowly, I inched toward the building and then entered. An enormous man in a suit let me pass, and I started ambling along. I could feel his eyes burning into the back of my head. I didn't have the bank balance to be in this room, and I was dressed that way too.

For me to link this car to Morgan, I would need to take down its vehicle identification number, (VIN), a painfully small series of numbers and letters embossed on the car's frame beneath the windscreen. With this number, I could find a trail of everyone who had bought and sold the car.

There were footsteps at my heels – a salesperson. I spun a tale of how I was only browsing. I had a meeting later and was killing time; I really didn't need any help. It was policy, she said, that all customers were escorted. Fine. I had a chaperone. I would have to steal a picture of the VIN, somehow, without alerting my minder and the large man at the door. I spotted the Lamborghini at the front of the showroom, encircled by velvet ropes. When I got close to it, I realised that, of nearly 100 cars in the room, it was the only one that had a sticker placed over the VIN.

I called Pieter and told him I had been bested by a piece of paper. He told me to go back and rip it off. I opted for the safer course. I was never able to find out if that Lamborghini, in a shade of blue with yellow brake callipers, was linked to the Tembisa tender don. His rumoured collection of cars was untraceable.

When the hospital saga broke publicly and Morgan and his network of companies were named in my reporting, he put his villa on the market. It was originally listed at the princely sum of R38 million. His family trust eventually let it go for R30 million. Other properties held by the trust were placed on the market too.

Until now, the trust had been buying stands across the country, and I wondered what had triggered the decision to sell. The Hawks' Babita murder investigation was dead in the water, but a unit seized with economic crimes had been tasked with probing the hospital and its suppliers. The SIU had started its own investigation in earnest. To me, Morgan was acting like a cat on a hot tin roof.[383]

The tip of the iceberg

In October 2022, Gauteng Premier David Makhura tendered his resignation to the speaker of the provincial legislature, bringing down the curtain on an eight-year reign over South Africa's economic centre. During this time, his provincial health department had hobbled from one scandal to another. On his watch, 141 vulnerable patients from Life Esidimeni were scattered across hapless NGOs and died in aid of saving costs.[384] Shonisani Lethole starved for days because nurses at Tembisa Hospital didn't feed him and doctors abandoned him, consigning him to death.[385] Makhura had to fire a health MEC at the height of a pandemic for his ties to a dubious splurge on PPE,[386] and then there was the killing of Babita Deokaran and the shadowy extraction web she uncovered.

It is a legacy few would be proud of, especially when failure can be measured in lives lost. Makhura was replaced by his former education MEC, Panyaza Lesufi, whose ascension came after the bombastic and populist leader had won a closely contested provincial elective conference several months earlier. The party held a slim majority thanks to coalition agreements, and Lesufi took the position.[387]

During the transition period, as one of his last acts, Makhura asked the SIU to probe Tembisa Hospital and the syndicates feeding off it.

The SIU embarked on a preliminary investigation using a second-ment arrangement. At the height of the graft and looting through Covid-19 PPE tenders, the unit had signed a memorandum of under-standing with the provincial government. This gave its operatives access to documents and payment records held by the Gauteng Health Department, and they operated with Makhura's authority and backing. They had to assess if my stories had any factual basis, and if they did, ascertain if they needed a proclamation to fully investi-gate the facility. If the shadow economy of the hospital fell within the ambit of an already ongoing national PPE investigation, several bureaucratic steps could be excised from the process. Madyo and Mthunzi, for their part, had already been placed on precautionary suspension, and the SIU would determine if they had a case to answer.

The Hawks had also moved on the hospital by now, in the wake of what we revealed. As Babita's story unfolded publicly, the Demo-cratic Alliance (DA) posed a question to the police minister.[388] 'What are the reasons for the delay in investigating members of senior management who are allegedly involved in corruption relating to public funds to the tune of R850 million within the Gauteng Department of Health?'[389]

The minister responded that the matter had not been reported and instead emanated from media reports. An inquiry docket had been opened, and the investigation was 'still at an early stage. No suspects have been identified yet.'[390]

The DA posed its question on 9 September, and the national police commissioner proffered this answer exactly 13 days later.

'Provincial serious corruption inquiry number 5/9/2022' was the fifth docket to be registered that September, and the Hawks refused to divulge the exact date when the investigation began.

Perhaps the Hawks investigation only came about because they had been asked for progress on something that did not yet exist? Yes, the investigation was no doubt at an early stage – it was just days old and probably all but an empty file at that juncture. They managed to skirt accountability with answers that were economic with the truth. But that it had come to this was a damning indictment of their ability, and inclination, to dismantle serious networks of corruption.

When Makhura stepped down, his health MEC, Nomathemba Mokgethi, was shuffled out of leadership. In the legislature, under withering questions from the DA's Jack Bloom, Mokgethi tried to shield both Madyo and Mthunzi, insisting that Babita had never 'formally' raised her concerns about the hospital. During Mokgethi's transition period, her department frustrated SIU investigators. Of the thousands of transactions flagged by Babita, they would only furnish the SIU with documentation for 27, and it took three months to extract just those. It was a mere sliver of what they had asked for, but it was enough. Their findings were devastating.

On 13 December 2022, new Gauteng Premier Panyaza Lesufi gathered his executive and issued a media notice that he would make the report public at a press conference.[391]

The SIU report set out the hindering stance Mokgethi's managers had taken when payment records and documentation were requested. When the SIU was given a list of the suppliers Babita identified, the registration numbers had been left out. Investigators then had to conduct hundreds of company searches to fill in the gaps. A spreadsheet drawn from the department's accounting system was called for. It never arrived. Investigators had to use back channels to get the payment records they needed.[392]

The SIU had used my stories as a guide when it looked to validate claims that company bosses had formed syndicates that were then inserted into the hospital's supplier pool, and they settled on the same three names I had: Hangwani Morgan Maumela, Stefan Joel Govindraju and Rudolf Mduduzi Mazibuko.

Govindraju, via 56 individual companies, had been paid R436 million from deals, mostly through Tembisa Hospital. The nine entities tied to Morgan Maumela and his cousin had banked R336 million, and the Mazibuko family patriarch saw R249 million come his way. The three men behind the hospital's anomalous spending pattern were the ultimate beneficiaries of more than R1 billion in less than two years. The figures were astonishing. My suspicions had been confirmed by the SIU, which, with its access, had delved deeper than I could. And that was just while following the money.[393]

When the SIU investigators took a hard look at exactly how the suppliers were appointed, they were confronted with a litany of irregularities: fake, forged and outdated documents, and forms that had been tampered with. The winning bidders should never have been considered for adjudication, and the same was true of the losing ones. But there were also other curious signs. The handwriting of supposedly rival bidders was suspiciously similar. The transactions the SIU examined should all have been disqualified.[394] There was no evidence that the prospective bidders were selected from the central supplier database.

When a contract goes out for quotation, suppliers are chosen at random from this database. At Tembisa Hospital, officials in the supply-chain management office were cherry-picking companies to bid against each other, which prevented fair competition and helped engineer an outcome. If three companies in Morgan's network were bidding collusively, there would only be one winner.

When the SIU apportioned blame and responsibility, they looked to the ultimate signatory: Tembisa Hospital's CEO. Both Ashley Mthunzi and the man he replaced, Lekopane Mogaladi, had made their mark on these documents.[395]

'The individuals responsible for authorising the purchase request form would have been in a position to have sight of quotations and supporting documents submitted by the winning bidders. Irrespective of the numerous irregularities identified by the SIU, Drs Mthunzi and Mogaladi authorised these purchase forms,' the report read.[396]

The buck stopped with the boss. Mogaladi was long gone, and the SIU recommended that Mthunzi face a disciplinary process for failing in his duties as the accounting authority at the hospital. Clearly, Tembisa's shadow economy had boomed under Mthunzi, even if it had first taken root under his predecessor. Purchase-order documents that Mthunzi signed would have first passed the quotation adjudication committee – intended as a safeguard against fraud and irregular expenditure and comprising five hospital staffers. They, too, had missed or ignored these anomalies. Eleven hospital staff would face disciplinary action. While Madyo and Mthunzi were on paid suspension awaiting their hearings, some of these hospital officials were allowed to resign. Those who stayed were not moved or suspended but continued working, including those in the supply-chain management section that had a hand in directing thousands of contracts to three men.[397]

The office of the premier – driving the disciplinary process against Mthunzi, Madyo and the Tembisa Hospital officials – used the SIU's findings as a stick. Mthunzi and Madyo were charged with thirteen counts of misconduct based on the anti-graft squad's findings. Both were charged with failure to exercise oversight. I think that piggybacking on the SIU's investigation was the easiest way to get the pair axed and moved out of the public service. Conspicuously absent were charges for Madyo's failure to act on Babita's report. That, in my view, amounted to gross dereliction of duty.

Mthunzi would not take his suspension lying down. He launched two – ultimately unsuccessful – Labour Court applications to lift his suspension and have him returned to office.

While the Gauteng Health Department fought him off in the courtroom, trade unions were sowing discord at the hospital. When Mthunzi and Madyo were placed on paid suspension, the unions had threatened to render the hospital inoperable. The Institutional Labour Caucus – representing trade unions including Denosa, Nehawu and Ynitu, the little-known Young Nurses Indaba Trade Union – called the suspensions irrational and disgusting.

The unions held that both Madyo and Mthunzi were being attacked and their characters assassinated. Then came the thinly veiled threat.[398] 'We continue to call on the department to engage labour in the issue for the sake of labour peace and also to ensure that the hospital continues to run smoothly.'[399]

This was significant. The pair obviously had the support of unionised hospital staff who appeared to rally around them. If nurses refused to work, the patients they cared for would be at risk. But for all the bluster, the caucus was something of a paper tiger. Denosa and Nehawu retracted the statement when it was released, and it turned out that it had been authored and issued by Ynitu president Lerato Mthunzi – wife of the hospital boss.[400] In the end, there were no disruptions. It was merely a failed public relations ploy.

Mthunzi's signature was on all the documents gathered by the SIU, and his general oversight was obvious. But Madyo had a plausible defence. She could argue that in her role, she could not possibly have called for and read the documents that underpinned every transaction. There were systems in place that were supposed to ensure that, by the time she authorised monthly payment runs, everything had been checked. But I thought she was culpable. Babita had sent her report on Tembisa Hospital's suspicious transactions directly to Madyo, and the pair had discussed it in text exchanges. Madyo lied and concealed the existence of the report after Babita was assassinated. When Babita was out of the way, she unfroze R104 million due to suppliers. Instead of the forensic audit Babita had called for, Madyo had internal auditors visit the hospital to assess its compliance with procurement procedures.

The report generated by that team was also suppressed and unlikely to ever see the light of day. I certainly would not have got my hands on it without the DA's Jack Bloom. At the age of 64, Bloom is a stalwart of the opposition benches and has been a member of the Gauteng legislature for three decades. He is known for his dogged scrutiny of the health portfolio. He would take what I revealed in the press and ask questions, and he had the law on his side. If he posed questions to the Health Department or asked for documents through the legislature, they could not deny him.[401]

It was little wonder that this report had also been a closely guarded secret. After testing a sample of just eighteen transactions, auditors found that hospital officials had corrupted the procurement system and tampered with documents. One purchase order that fell within their purview was for 200 pairs of forceps. They did not assess pricing. If they had, they would have found that Tembisa Hospital paid nearly R2 500 for a product that could be ordered online for R70.

Critical documents had been withheld by the hospital, but the auditors were still able to draw damning conclusions.[402] There were no control mechanisms to scrutinise the companies winning these contracts, which would normally prevent or detect fictitious suppliers. Companies quoted the same price for completely different products. Within the hospital, procurement staff knowingly used expired broad-based black economic empowerment and tax certificates in an attempt to legitimise the orders.[403]

'It clearly indicates that supply chain management officials are using outdated [documents] from the companies as they know that the bidding committee and accounting officer will approve without checking the validity,' the confidential report read. 'Note that all quotations approved are just below R500 000, and it is recommended that this be investigated urgently. In view of the seriousness of the findings, [an] investigation into the supply chain management processes is recommended.'[404]

There it was, in black and white. The confidential report was proof that auditors had drawn the same conclusions as Babita. Yet, both documents were cast aside and Madyo did nothing. Instead of taking action, the report was sent to Mthunzi, who was tasked with disciplining his staff for processing purchases he himself had approved. The fox was guarding the henhouse.[405]

The SIU, even while hamstrung by the Gauteng Health Department, was able to trace more than R1 billion in payments secretly steered to a trio hidden behind a latticework of shell companies. Its inquiry, without the unit's powers of intrusion to examine cellphone records and bank statements, revealed the major players and the officials within the system who had enabled them.[406] Based on its findings, the SIU would need to motivate for a presidential proclamation to investigate Tembisa Hospital. This was way beyond opportunistic looting through crooked PPE deals. These were networks seemingly established for a singular purpose, with a thin veneer of legitimacy.[407]

'The irregularities uncovered in this investigation are merely the tip of the iceberg. It points to serious maladministration at Tembisa Hospital as it relates to irregular procurement processes,' the SIU report read.[408] The true scale of this shadow operation was not yet known.

CHAPTER 25

Kill the story

Dr Ashley Mthunzi was a man under fire. His hospital had been exposed as an epicentre for shell-company syndicates, and he had been shut out.[409] While he was on suspension, Makhura's office hit him with misconduct charges, and he would face an inquiry to defend his probity.[410] When the Gauteng Health Department told him to stay silent while he was at the centre of a very public scandal, he broke ranks and spoke to 702 radio host Clement Manyathela.[411] The threatened industrial action – in response to his suspension, and which I strongly suspected he staged through a minnow trade union controlled by his wife – had little impact.[412] He was trying to put his thumb on the scale.

By the time he was suspended, I had been on his heels for months. With every story I published, I made sure to harry him. He was copied on every request for comment sent to department spin doctors. The data on Babita's laptop was revealing – I could show that Mthunzi had been the central catalyst for the success of three tender barons and their constellation of companies. He knew exactly who I was, and because he blocked me on WhatsApp, I know he had my number saved.

On the eve of his suspension, and before the SIU issued its damning findings, Mthunzi called on his connections in the ANC. It was a Tuesday morning, and I was still at home when I received a

WhatsApp message from Amos Phago.[413] 'Morning . . . Pls let me [know] when you have 5 minutes for a conversation. Amos Phago from ANC Communications.'[414]

I called him back. I didn't know this person, and I was curious about what he wanted to discuss. On the phone, Phago was affable, I presumed because he wanted something. He told me that he had been following my stories about Babita's assassination and the Tembisa Hospital contracts she flagged, and he offered to broker a meeting with Mthunzi.[415]

'You know, my brother, sometimes we miss each other. If you two can talk, then maybe there can be understanding,' he said.[416]

I questioned Phago on his approach and why the ANC was trying to set up this meeting. Phago then started to retract. It was nothing official from the party, and he was merely a back channel, acting on behalf of the Progressive Business Forum. I don't think I was as receptive as he had hoped.[417] I figured that it was an attempt to kill the story.

'The [forum] guy requested that I assist in contacting you, by making use of the media contacts. He asked me to help on a personal level as someone who has a lot of media contacts. Again, it's not a request for the ANC to assist. I have never met the CEO nor spoken to him in the past.'[418]

I told Phago to inform both his masters and Mthunzi that I was not amenable to a meeting, not least one that had been fixed by political players. I was going to write about this overture, I said, and Phago protested. When he realised that I was not going to be convinced otherwise, I got a call from the head of the forum, Sipho Mbele.[419]

The Progressive Business Forum was established by the ANC in 2007 to raise funds for the party from the business community. Forum members are normally corporates that pay a membership fee to get access to ANC leaders and seating at ANC events, such as dinners before conferences.[420] Mbele was also quick to add that he had made contact in his personal capacity, not as convenor of the forum. He said that he was a childhood friend of Mthunzi's, and the pair had recently met at a funeral.[421]

'He said to me that he was struggling with *News24* and, as a friend, I suggested that he meet with you and have a cup of coffee so everyone can get on the same page,' Mbele said.[422] 'This was in my personal capacity because he is a friend, and [it] has nothing to do with the [forum]. I didn't even intend on being present; I just said I would help reach out.'[423]

It was an unexpected approach, but one that was telling. Mthunzi clearly had friends in the ANC.

It was widely believed that in the Gauteng Health Department, hospital administrators and senior managers were appointed by virtue of their political ties and not necessarily based on their qualifications and experience. These officials were, unofficially, deployees of the ANC, it was said.

I got a call one day from a woman who claimed to be Mthunzi's girlfriend. She told me how he had wined and dined her in a whirl-wind romance before she found out that he was married. She also told me that her trip to work each day took her past the ANC's headquarters at Luthuli House and that his car was often parked there. She knew it because it was a common location for their trysts and because he had a personalised number plate.

As a public official, Mthunzi had presided over the ordered extraction of funds from his hospital, and there was no way he could deny it. If it had been a single transaction, he could have used ignorance as a defence. But he approved thousands of orders, and there is no way he could not have known about the tender boom at Tembisa Hospital. He was accountable, but his allies in the then-ruling party were rallying around him.

A trial and
its tribulations

By July 2023, nearly two years after Babita's assassination, the men charged with her murder were still being held in prison without bail. They had spent this time in the remand section of Johannesburg Prison, a jailhouse notorious for gang activity, a thriving drug trade and inmate-on-inmate rape.[424] The facility is known as 'Sun City', a cruelly ironic nod to the holiday resort on the borders of the Pilanesberg Nature Reserve several hours' drive from Johannesburg. There are no lush green golf courses and gleaming blue swimming pools within the prison's looming barbed-wire fence. Instead, the cells are so cramped that inmates sleep on grimy foam mattresses on the floor, in a building permeated by the acrid stench of urine and sweat. Men are traded as sex objects, and violence is endemic.

Prisoners awaiting trial and those who have been convicted are separated into different sections, both of which are overcrowded. The men in the remand section are all awaiting trial and, in the eyes of the law at least, remain innocent until proven guilty. They live in packed communal cells with those accused of the most heinous crimes. Detainees can languish in this hell for years waiting for a court date. Prison gangs rule by fear and intimidation.[425] It is a hard place where innocent men suffer.

Despite this, Phakamani Hadebe, the man who supposedly coordinated the deadly attack on Babita, and Zitha Radebe, Phinda Ndlovu, Sanele Mbhele, Siphiwe Mazibuko and Siphakanyiswa Dladla looked better than when they went in. They would soon have their day in court.

I believed Captain Masenxani Chauke and his commanders in the Hawks had no appetite to investigate beyond the hitmen. If so, the mastermind of this crime could have slept soundly even after his triggermen were arrested. In the world of targeted killings, the shooters are inevitably disposable. They are often seasoned criminals who will do their time quietly, knowing that their paymaster will financially support their family members on the outside. That is the quid pro quo for their silence.

After a few months, Chauke had withdrawn from the investigation and the docket was passed on to another, more junior officer, Warrant Officer Wiseman Mavundla. Chauke was, I was told by my sources in the Hawks, threatened by persons unknown. I could never pin down the exact circumstances of this supposed threat, but if true, it was enough for him to step aside.

Mavundla seemed like a solid cop who had been handed a lemon. Two weeks before the trial was to start, analysis of the six men's cellphones was still ongoing. As an investigative tool, this should have been prioritised and rushed. It would have decoded messages and calls between the hitmen, proving that they were coordinating surveillance and the murder. One of the six had taken a picture of Babita's front gate, but who did he send it to? On the eve of the trial, both the investigating officer and the state prosecutor could not have known, and the case was shaky at best.

The strongest piece of evidence in the entire investigation was Phakamani Hadebe's confession. It provided a narrative of the plotting and execution of the murder and linked all the other men to the crime. At trial, the Hawks could submit the analysis of the camera network, which was circumstantial but useful. But the crime scene had been a mess, and the Hawks had failed to find the white BMW used in the attack or the murder weapons.

Advocate Steven Rubin was the state prosecutor in the case. In his early forties, Rubin has a mop of hair that sweeps over his brow and is beginning to grey. I had watched him handle, in black robes, the bail application of Hadebe and the other *izinkabi*, and he clearly knew what he was doing. The six had made a strong bid for bail, but he had managed to fend them off. The evidence was wobbly, and when the case went to trial, it would hinge on Hadebe's confession.

On 22 August 2023, one day before the second anniversary of Babita's murder, the six hitmen shuffled into the dock at the Johannesburg High Court. The denials of criminality and claims of torture and innocence in Hadebe's bail statement had all been a lie. All six would now enter a plea and sentencing agreement with the state to avoid an open trial. There would be justice, at least for this coterie of killers.

Initially, they had pleaded guilty to planning and seeing through the murder. But two years later they gave another version.[426] The six had all acknowledged their role in the assassination and understood that under the doctrine of common purpose, they could be charged with murder, even if they had not been the ones doing the shooting. They had admitted being part of the group that stalked and surveilled the accountant and was in Winchester Hills on the day of the killing. In the new version, they named Khanyisani Mpungose as the man who recruited them and did the shooting in the company of another, Siphiwe Mpilo Sithole. They also explained why Babita had to die. She had been 'creating problems at her place of employment'. The spectre of Zweli Mkhize as the mastermind was nowhere to be seen.[427]

The six received sentences ranging from six to 22 years. In ultimately accepting their plea, Judge Motsamai Makume said that the court was dissatisfied because the person who pulled the trigger had not been arrested. The plea deal laid bare exactly how little investigative work had been done, leaving the real orchestrator of the killing free. When Makume handed down the sentence, and before the six were to be led back to the cells, they celebrated. Their relatives had packed the gallery, and they crowded the dock and hugged and kissed the killers as court orderlies tried to herd the men into the underbelly of the court building. The air was jovial.[428] On a distant bench in the corner of the room, Rakesh sat and cried.

The six men were poor. They came from harsh, rural backgrounds, and none had the financial means to pay for legal representation. They would have qualified for legal aid. Yet these indigent men had a legal team so high-profile that the mismatch was glaring. Their three-advocate team included former National Prosecuting Authority head Menzi Simelane, ex-KwaZulu-Natal director of public prosecutions Simphiwe Mlotshwa and Sanele Sibisi. Lawyers such as these come with a hefty bill, and I wondered how the families from Nhlawe had marshalled such money. We will never know.

Outside the court, prosecuting authority spokeswoman Phindi Mjonondwane said that what the six had divulged would now guide the murder investigation.[429] 'In our quest to deliver justice to the family of Deokaran, we will continue with the information the accused gave us.'

She added that the authorities were looking into 'certain people of interest' named during the plea and sentence negotiations. 'They provided us with information that will get us the mastermind,' she claimed, confidently.[430]

In terms of the law, entering into a plea agreement is a rigorous process. Rubin needed the concurrence of the investigating officer, and he had to consult Babita's family and get the nod from his higher-ups. I think he was right to broker this deal. He did not have a watertight case and, truth be told, his chances of securing a conviction were 50/50 at best. Guilty men would have walked free. The ultimate outcome – with the *izinkabi* behind bars – was the best possible under the circumstances.

At court, Rubin was flanked by two burly men, one shadowing him constantly and the other standing at the door. I know bodyguards when I see them; they are easy to spot. They wear loose-fitting shirts and overcoats to conceal their weapons. An even more obvious 'tell' is that their eyes dart around the room because they're worried about being shot. The prosecutor had obviously been assigned a protection detail.

While avoiding a trial had been the best decision, it was influenced, at least in part, by a sinister force. Mavundla had made a WhatsApp group including the witnesses in the case, from Hicks and the police officers who made the arrests to the investigating officer, Babita's helper and others. In the days leading up to the court appearance, many received phone calls. Those who did said the caller was a white man, and his message was uniform. Stay away from the trial; don't testify. We will kill you should you choose to defy us.

This man also called the investigating officer and threatened him. Mavundla was told that if Rubin tried to prosecute this trial, he would be killed and his wife raped. That explained the presence of the minders. Under these circumstances, if witnesses started to balk out of fear and refused to testify, a deal with the killers was Rubin's only option. The man on the other end of the threatening calls had made certain of that.

This only served to benefit the *izinkabi* and the person who had paid them. There would be no probing cross-examination, and no evidence would be led. The plea kept things quiet. Rubin had done the best he could with the touch-and-go case and ensured a modicum of justice and accountability.

The Hawks now had new leads: the naming of Mpungose as a central figure in the assassination, and the unnamed accomplice. But these proved dead ends. Mpungose had been shot and killed at a taxi rank in Kempton Park three months after Babita was murdered. Cops investigating the case chalked it up to taxi violence and, predictably, it had not been solved. I suspect there might have been a deeper reason for the murder – perhaps someone was getting rid of a loose end. It was certainly a convenient killing. Sithole, the accomplice, could not be traced.

The Hawks' investigation into Babita's killing stalled in the days after it began, and Chauke must be made to account for that. Most damning for him is this: Mpungose was one of the two other men who were arrested by Hicks and his team and then summarily released. The Hawks had Babita's killer, and they let him go.

The memory of Babita Deokaran

In court that day, Rakesh looked on as the men who had killed his sister – surrounded by their relatives and their well-heeled legal team – celebrated what should never have been a victory for them. The state accepted a plea and sentencing deal that staved off a touch-and-go trial, and the *izinkabi* offered up the name of their recruiter and lead triggerman. Their deal also saw them offer an apology to Babita's family:[431] 'All six accused wish to tender an apology to the family of the deceased.'[432]

Their contrition was hollow and obviously for show. They had been handed sentences that would remove them from society for large parts of their lives, but they were smiling and laughing. They felt they had won.

The importance of placing these men behind bars cannot be understated. Murder is regarded as the most heinous of crimes, and the seriousness of taking a life can never be downplayed. Babita had highlighted irregularities in the Gauteng Health Department's spending – she was 'creating problems at her workplace' – and, for this, someone decided she had to die. Her murder was a step backward at a time when the need for accountability was being advanced.[433]

Their imprisonment might have represented justice, but only in part. Rakesh felt empty.

'Yes, justice has been served, but I see no remorse in any of them,' he said. Tears welled in his eyes, and he struggled to mask his pain. 'This marks the end of a harrowing chapter in our lives, and we hope and believe there'll be another chapter where the mastermind will also be arrested.'[434]

For the Deokaran family, the justice meted out against the *izinkabi* was cold comfort. The men had been paid to eliminate Babita, but those who had commissioned them remained free.

In our weekly investigations team meeting, we used this development to take stock. Pieter asked me if now was perhaps the time to move on. Corruption in South Africa had reached endemic levels. Money earmarked for worthy recipients and pivotally important service delivery was being diverted to the politically connected. When I started this project, I had planned to publish a series of eight stories telling the story of Babita's last investigation. But I had been guided by evidence, and my body of work had burgeoned with over 30 separate instalments.

Should I now stop this project and turn my attention to some other new malfeasance? I was in two minds. Yes, my work had given the Deokaran family insight into why they had to lose a mother, sister and aunt, but they were still denied justice. Was finding the mastermind behind the murder beyond my abilities?

The corruption probes by the SIU and the Hawks had only just begun, and progress was slow. I felt we had more to expose, and I had the opportunity to keep Babita's memory alive. We had named the architects of the scheme but not explained how they managed to do it. I thought that if these syndicates were to be dismantled, we would need to expose exactly how they preyed on the public purse.

When Madyo and Mthunzi were charged with misconduct, a state advocate was appointed to prosecute the disciplinary case against them on thirteen separate counts. Each charge arose from a transaction that both had a hand in authorising.

As the pair were senior managers, their disciplinary hearing was a quasi-judicial process, in which the state attorney collated 900 pages of evidence and handed it over to their counsel in discovery. I got my hands on this cache of documents, which provided invaluable insight into how the Tembisa Hospital contracts were directed to specific shell companies – all of which were controlled by just three kingpins – and how the entire chain of procurement was captured.[435]

Given the small number of people controlling the companies, I had always suspected the practice of 'cover quoting' but could never prove it. Cover quoting is a scheme in which entities collude to structure their prices so that the contract award has a predetermined outcome. With the evidence I had, I could only see which companies had won bids because they were paid, but I had no visibility of the two losing bidders. The disciplinary process against Mthunzi and Madyo changed this.[436]

In January 2022, Tembisa Hospital supply-chain management officials contacted three companies to quote on a contract to provide sutures. These companies were Preliboo, Samoplex and Etnarin Corp.[437] They would go up against one another, a competitive process that was supposed to ensure value for money, and they quoted the following figures: Preliboo – R485 200; Samoplex – R495 600; Etnarin Corp – R500 000.[438]

In theory, these companies should have been randomly chosen from the central supplier database. But in reality, they had been handpicked for this bid. They were all controlled by kingpin Stefan Govindraju. Something else that pointed to collusion was the price of the sutures, with all three firms quoting at a rate more than 300 per cent above the industry standard. A comparative examination of the documents – both those of the rival bidders and those awarded the contracts – revealed similarities in handwriting, raising the possibility that they were all filled out by the same person.[439]

Morgan Maumela had used a similar modus operandi to extract money, all while obscuring his role as puppet master. In May 2021, two companies, Magnolia Trading Enterprise and Black AK Trading

& Suppliers, were competing for the same bid to supply the hospital with surgical equipment. The bid documents listed two women as the respective directors of these entities. I tracked both women down in Limpopo. One is an unemployed security guard and the other works for the municipal parks department, cleaning public swimming pools. Their identities had been stolen, they insisted. The Companies and Intellectual Property Commission certificates submitted with the bid were forgeries meant to obscure the real person benefiting from the deal. Magnolia – in fact controlled by Maumela – won the bid, while Black AK lost. The latter company is owned by Vusimusi Matlala, Morgan's much-feared consiglieri.[440]

Once I had examined the pricing of these deals, I could prove that Tembisa Hospital suppliers were charging a premium for everything they sold. In just one example, Mthunzi authorised the purchase of 100 surgical drapes for R475 000 from a company called Olimocraft. This company was part of Rudolf Mazibuko's seventeen-company conglomerate. The payment for what equated to R4 750 per drape had been approved by Madyo. If purchased by private hospitals, the drapes would cost less than R240 each. And this was supposed to be the cheapest option![441]

The quantity of products the hospital bought suggested that the need or demand was contrived. One company I linked to Govindraju sold 1 200 neonatal blood-pressure cuffs to the hospital. All well and good – sick babies deserve the best possible care, and if equipment is needed, there should be no compunction in buying it. But the size of this consignment was nonsensical. These are not single-use items; they can be used for years if properly maintained. No one can tell me that a hospital with an 840-bed capacity has more than 1 000 sick newborns admitted at any given time.

This is how Tembisa Hospital's shadow economy flourished. For it to be successful, it required the connivance of hospital staff at every step of the buying process. First, there had to be a need, and then a doctor or nurse would initiate the procurement. From there, it moved to a demand committee to determine if the hospital should spend money on the item. The matter then went to the supply-chain management office, where suppliers were chosen at random to bid against one another. If no irregularities were found in the paperwork, it was escalated to the quotation adjudication committee, which recommended the purchase. It was then ultimately signed off by the hospital CEO.

Next, the transaction went to the provincial office, and a purchase order was issued. The supplier delivered the goods, and a hospital official signed a goods-received note. Only then could the company be paid. Key people all along this lengthy chain must have been captured.

Nearly every stage of the process was managed by a medical professional. Quantity inflation should have been picked up and stopped by the demand committee. Fake companies should have been weeded out by the supply-chain management office and, if they had missed something, by the quotation committee. But all these individuals rubber-stamped each contract as part of a R1 billion buying splurge.

Examining the base paperwork of the thirteen contracts Mthunzi and Madyo approved, there were so many red flags and irregularities that all the bidders, both the winners and the losers, should have been disqualified. In one deal awarded to a company in the Govindraju syndicate, seventeen separate irregularities were allowed to pass through the checks and balances when even just one should have led to its elimination. Yet no one raised any objection. But the master key in this scheme were the supply-chain officials. They decided which companies should bid and compiled the supporting documents, overlooking obvious forgeries and strikingly similar handwriting. They formed the bedrock of these networks.[442]

When I was confronting company bosses linked to this tranche of thirteen deals, I phoned a woman who was the sole director of an entity that had been a losing bidder. I asked her about the business and the quote she had submitted. She struggled to answer my questions. When I pressed her, she said that she had a friend who was helping her 'get tenders'. I gave her the name of the winning bidder, and she confirmed that he was the friend. She had, in effect, admitted to being a proxy and playing an ancillary role in bid rigging. I could see she had other legitimate businesses. I told her that when I made her role public, her world would come crashing down around her. She was distraught. I could hear her crying on the other end of the phone. I must say I felt nothing. She begged to meet me as she wanted to tell me everything.

When we met, she was shaking like a leaf. She told me how the man for whom she was acting was using her. She admitted to laundering money for him and showed me the bank statements. Her company bid for and won one contract, and as soon as the money landed in her account, she was ordered to transfer it to another entity. She was allowed to keep a small cut. I told her she was in serious trouble.

'What should I do?' she asked through tears. I told her that I was no lawyer, but I knew that those who confessed first often got the best deal. If she was a fringe figure, as she claimed, I suggested she talk to the SIU. That was how I passed a credible witness on to both the SIU and the Hawks. She wanted to tell the truth. Several days later, she deposed an affidavit in a meeting with both agencies.

I could never use what she told me. If I did, it would out her as the source of the information, and she feared that her life would be in danger. I had a journalistic duty to protect her, even if she had been a participant in a corruption operation that had long remained hidden. But what she revealed would be of value to SIU investigators. I had been picking apart these networks for years and gathered intelligence on nearly every company Babita flagged in her initial report. Much of what I found was probably true, but because it couldn't be independently corroborated by sources and documents, it would never see the light of day. I thought this was an incredible waste.

That was when I decided to approach the SIU investigators. I made it clear that I was neither a witness nor a whistleblower, and I would not depose affidavits or statements. I would simply tell them what I knew, without compromising my sources. In our first four-hour meeting, I laid out all my suspected connections and links. This was done in secret. I already felt that my life was under threat. My cooperation with the authorities would only heighten the danger, but I felt it had to be done. Some journalism purists would believe that my actions crossed an ethical boundary. There is – and should be – space between the arms of the state and a free press. But I had information that could aid an investigation, and I believed – as I still do – that I acted in the public interest.

In September 2023, an SIU proclamation that would unleash investigators on the hospital and its suppliers was signed by the president. Proclamation number 136 of 2023 untethered the anti-graft squad. In their preliminary investigation, they had set out how fraud and syndicate activity had beset the hospital, and they were able to prove it without their powers of intrusion. Now, backed by presidential authority, they could issue subpoenas for cellphone records, bank statements and bid documents. I had pushed the Tembisa contract scammers into the open, and now the noose was tightening.[443]

Tembisa and other feeding troughs

In her report, Babita had examined buying patterns in the health department, and her focus had been drawn to Tembisa hospital. While she warned that 'possibly fraudulent' activity was most prevalent at the East Rand facility, the illegitimate suppliers she identified were also making money from other hospitals in the province's public health network.[444]

Although I had long since unmasked the main actors in the tender scandal, I was inclined to believe that their syndicates had a far broader reach.

When Govindraju executed his shell-company takeover and all the proxy directors flagged by Babita ceded control of their paper entities to him, I noticed something interesting. From the Companies and Intellectual Property Commission database, I could see that other individuals who had not yet featured in my investigation had also handed over their companies to this enigmatic character at the same time.[445]

One such person was Loteesha Signarian, a call-centre agent from Durban. Her brother and sister-in-law had also been proxy directors acting on behalf of Govindraju, and when they flew the coop, Loteesha followed suit. Her companies had been trading with the Gauteng Department of Health.[446] Govindraju had built a sprawling front empire of 60 companies that had infiltrated Tembisa Hospital and others. From this network, 35 individual payments were traced to the Ekurhuleni Health District, Pholosong Hospital and Heidelberg Hospital.[447]

Morgan Maumela also had a network far larger than the twelve entities linked to him by name, either through his own directorships or those held by his cousin. Three companies, Barnjo Trading and Supplies, Tebogo Medical Suppliers and Atang Medical Suppliers, had the same address as Morgan's firms. One Lucinda Barriel was the controlling mind behind Carrington Trading Enterprise, Fourteen O Nine Trading Enterprise and Twenty-Six O Four Trading Enterprise – entities flagged in Babita's initial report. Barriel is mother to Morgan's children out of wedlock and a trustee of the Oda Ori Family Trust, along with Morgan's sister, Rumani.[448]

Companies formed by Morgan and his cousin had received R336 million in payments from Tembisa Hospital in two years. But their total take from the Gauteng Health Department was R381 million. Other hospitals were also funding his luxury lifestyle.[449]

Another man I could link to Morgan was Vusimusi Matlala, known in some circles as 'Cat'. Matlala's three companies, Black AK Trading and Suppliers, Cor Kabeng Trading and Suppliers, and Falcon Cat Trading and Suppliers, saw hospital deals channelled their way. Outwardly, Matlala's only link to Morgan was a once shared directorship in CAT VIP Security.[450] In their private lives, Morgan and Matlala were much closer. My sources with insight into Morgan's relationships had styled Matlala as his muscle.

Matlala himself was a wealthy man. He lived with his wife, Cordelia Kabeng, in the upmarket suburb of Waterkloof Ridge in Pretoria. He had a proclivity for the finer things in life, and his mansion had a room for his designer shoes. A professional shoe cleaner would visit every other month to make sure the footwear gleamed. A personal chef prepared his meals, and a personal tailor did suit fittings at his home.

He had a driver on staff, along with a security force and a platoon of housekeepers and assistants who kept his palace running smoothly.

When I first identified Matlala as part of Morgan's network, I shook loose a new source. One day, this source arrived at our Randburg office carrying a stack of bid documents. There were quotations and purchase orders from companies in business with Mamelodi Hospital. The source had pilfered as much paperwork as they could secretly carry away. I was worried that the documents would be missed and offered to make copies so that they could be quietly returned. Don't stress, I was told. The house is full of these documents. They sit in piles on tables and on the floor and erupt out of drawers. The bundle I held in my hands would not be missed.

The cache of paperwork was revealing. Matlala had access to internal documents, quotes and bid submissions for an array of companies that had no obvious connection to him. Were these entities acting as proxies for his interests? His true reach and influence may have been more extensive than I had thought. Matlala would now be a central figure in the whole saga.

Clearly, Tembisa Hospital was not the only feeding trough. Beyond the 217 possibly fraudulent entities on Babita's list, there were companies that she had missed. The scheme of extraction was bigger than anyone could have imagined and signalled systemic procurement issues in Gauteng's public hospitals. How else could companies that existed only on paper and operated from fake addresses slip past the checks and balances to infiltrate the system?

Stealing fast

The Special Investigating Unit (SIU) is an organ of the justice ministry with the sole purpose of safeguarding the public purse.[451] The South African government spends about R1 trillion per year – and this buying power at municipal, provincial and national level is backed by the taxpayer.[452] State procurement – which keeps schools and libraries open, social assistance grants paid and parastatals and utilities in operation – is a site of malignant extraction. Through fraudulent and crooked public spending, billions of rand are stolen at a rate faster than it can be clawed back. The SIU is designed to chase down and recover the money.

The unit's investigations can only be set in motion by presidential proclamation. Since taking office in 2018, President Cyril Ramaphosa has issued 135 such decrees, letting loose the watchdog on state agencies and departments accused of mismanaging cash. Thirty-three proclamations were issued between January and October 2024.[453] With forensic investigations often spanning months and years, the SIU's complement of 700 investigators is spread thin.[454]

Advocate Andy Mothibi is a tall man with a quiet, stolid affect. When I spoke to him in 2024, he had led the SIU for nine years. During his tenure, nearly R137 billion was returned to the fiscus. Moreover, R54 billion in potential future losses were prevented when syndicates were dismantled and their dubious tenders set aside.[455]

'While we continue to come up with results, you know, it [graft and corruption] just doesn't seem to stop. At times it is frustrating, yes, but we are not going to tire because of that,' he told me.[456]

Corruption in the South African context has become inherent, at least in part because of the disjointed response of law-enforcement agencies. A dearth of convictions means criminals operate with a sense of impunity. Recovering the money is only one aspect of justice. It would be folly if the hidden actors were never brought to book.[457]

'[While] these perpetrators continue to be of the impression that they can act with impunity, we will not see the end of this,' said Mothibi. 'There's this belief that the [law-enforcement] machinery is not consistent in consequence management. If the whole justice system is not working appropriately, you can recover money and assets they've stolen, but they will walk the streets free. That's not justice.'[458]

Extraction schemes, often well-hidden with the collusion of government officials, are difficult to unravel, requiring cyber investigations, forensic accounting and data analytics – all of which take time.[459] 'These days, criminals or the corrupt have perfected their methods, including the way they hide their assets. We have seen them get very creative.'[460]

One aspect of the procurement system that allows it to be corrupted is that it is largely paper-based. Officials are also reluctant to modernise the system. In this technological void, the corruption at Tembisa Hospital flourished.[461]

In Mothibi's words: 'There's pushback when you want to automate and make the supply-chain management process transparent. And this becomes understandable because those people, both inside and outside of the state, are taking advantage of a broken system.'[462]

When crooked hospital staff needed to engineer the outcome in the procurement process, all they had to do was doctor old bid submissions. They knew that hospital officials on the quotation adjudication committee didn't care to even read the documents and ensure compliance.[463]

Officials working in the hospital's supply-chain management office occupied positions for years and never sought promotion because they stood to make millions from the facility's shadow economy through backhand payments. As I have shown, they controlled the entire system. The key frailty in Tembisa Hospital's spending, near impossible to mitigate, was collusion from within.

Mothibi knew the cost of acting against corruption. He could not travel without armed men accompanying him. Procurement corruption is no longer exclusively defined as white-collar crime. When the SIU threatens those in the shadow state, it faces an onslaught of attacks and death threats.

'When they realise that we are uncovering what they have done, things become dangerous and often lethal,' Mothibi told me. 'Living this way is difficult – but, you know, it's the call that we responded to. We continue to do our best while, of course, being ever watchful of any threat on our lives. Sometimes when I speak to my mother, she says to me that maybe I have done my service. I can't even walk to the shop by myself. She knows about the risky terrain . . . it's scary sometimes. But, for me, it's a calling, and our work is not yet done.'

CHAPTER 30

Matlala, the money man

Pretoria's Waterkloof Ridge is the preserve of the capital city's prime property market, home to embassies, foreign diplomats and politicians. The suburb is situated against a hillside and residents live in palatial homes with unencumbered views of the Union Buildings and the vibrant inner city. One of these people is Vusimusi 'Cat' Matlala.

Late one December evening in 2024, a 100-strong complement of police officers surrounded his Plough Avenue mansion. As dusk settled over the ridge, tactical elements from the elite Special Task Force and the National Intervention Unit scaled walls and ran over the tennis courts and manicured green lawns of Cat's home. Police burst through the front gate of the property and disarmed private security guards stationed along the perimeter before converging on the house and forcing their way inside. When the dust had settled, Cat was in handcuffs, face down on his bedroom floor and surrounded by men with rifles.[464]

The police operation was led by the Crime Intelligence Division and, specifically, an anti-kidnapping task team assembled within it. In the past decade, kidnappings have soared by 264 per cent from 4 692 in 2014–15 to 17 061 in 2023–24, and the rate of increase has not abated. In the third quarter of 2024 alone, police were dealing with 50 reports of kidnapping a day.[465] It had become a lucrative industry in the underworld, with businessmen or their family members taken and held for ransoms amounting to millions of rand. Behind this booming trade are organised crime cartels that stretch across the country and deep into neighbouring Mozambique. The raid on Cat came after Pretoria businessman Abey Dikgale's wife and nine-year-old son were abducted while leaving Centurion's exclusive Copperleaf Golf and Country Estate a month before. The Bentley in which the mother and child were travelling was forcefully stopped after they departed from their security enclave. When cops descended on Cat, the pair had been missing for more than a month.

Jerry Boshoga, Dikgale's business partner, was also kidnapped in Centurion while heading to a meeting with an associate. A R60 million ransom was demanded for his safe release. In videos sent to his family, a shirtless Boshoga was filmed kneeling with his hands tied behind his back. A hooded man assaulted him repeatedly, punching him and kicking him in the face. Boshoga's muffled moans could be heard as the blows landed. In another video, he was allowed to speak. With one eye swollen shut and blood streaming from his nose and mouth, he begged his family to pay. He was being tortured.

In court papers, Cat said, 'The officers asked me if I [know] anything [of] the kidnapping of Mr Abey Dikgale's wife and son and why I would help someone I don't know and aid in the kidnapping. I answered and confirmed that I was requested to assist the Dikgale family to locate [the] whereabouts of Mrs Dikgale and their minor son. This is due to the fact that I am the owner of [a] security company.'[466]

Cat had inveigled his way into a police investigation in which he had no business. Obviously, this raised suspicion within the anti-kidnapping task team.

When his home and business premises were raided, police seized cellphones, computers and an arsenal of guns, along with a Rolex Oyster Perpetual watch valued at more than R200 000. Cat had bought the watch in Hong Kong while on holiday, and he wanted it and the rest of the confiscated items returned to him. He approached the Gauteng High Court in Pretoria and listed Police Minister Senzo

Mchunu and National Police Commissioner Fannie Masemola as respondents.[467]

Cat is a man with a diverse and colourful portfolio of business interests. Through three companies, he became a tender player as the ultimate beneficiary of Tembisa Hospital contracts worth R5 million – with the orders processed and payments made within a month. That is how he first appeared on my radar. I placed him in Morgan's network. But it was his private security company, Cat Protection and Security, that had drawn the anti-kidnapping task team to his doorstep. The firm was founded on 25 May 2017 by Cat's wife, Cordelia Kabeng. Morgan Maumela was appointed as a director in September that year but resigned six days later, handing over to his friend, consiglieri and confidant.

Cat is the sole director of the company, which provides a range of high-end services, including close protection and bodyguarding, secure asset transport and 'information gathering', both locally and abroad. The entity's website provides a glowing profile of the 'Group President'.[468]

Vusimusi Matlala is the founder and President of CAT VIP Protection services, with over 30 years' experience in law enforcement, he founded CAT VIP as there was a need for elite human and asset protection in South Africa. He has invested in setting the standard of competence and professionalism in the security industry at an unattainable high, and also ensuring that CAT VIP is sitting at the top of the VIP security hierarchy. His unique insights and consulting capabilities are highly regarded by many organisations and governments around the world in providing protection solutions that meet their requirements. He is an expert advisor in the law enforcement industry in South Africa, and forms a crucial part in contributing to fighting crime in the country. Vusi's presence, combined with his situational awareness and agile approach to high-risk situations are the essential components for correct execution of delicate and confidential operations at every level. He is passionate about proper protocols, quality instructions and giving every client a customised high level CAT VIP experience. He commands the etiquette, discretion, proficiency and professionalism to work as an effective operative – physically and mentally.[469]

To cut through the hubris and self-aggrandisement, if Cat truly had over 30 years' experience in law enforcement, he would have begun this work when he was still a teenager at school.

There are many rumours about how Cat got his moniker. One story holds that it came from an incident in which he nearly died. He had been shot, and his injuries looked like they might be fatal. But he survived, and from that point on he was known as the cat with nine lives. When I asked him where his nickname came from, he laughed off my question.

A look at his criminal profile – a database held by police that logs a person's every detention, arrest and prosecution – revealed that he had been the subject of police investigations on no less than thirteen different occasions. These involved allegations of theft, possession of stolen property, housebreaking, robbery and attempted murder. All these cases were withdrawn, among them a matter relating to his alleged possession of illegal guns.

In 2016, Cat and three other men were arrested in a police sting operation in the basement of Sandton's The Core shopping mall. Security guards at their station in the basement had become suspicious of a car and called the cops. Inside they found three R5 assault rifles, reflective police vests and a police radio. Among those detained that day was Kagiso Ledwaba, a fugitive from justice. He was a hitman for Czech crime boss Radovan Krejčíř, and he was handed a 25-year jail term for his role in the assassination of German businessman Uwe Gemballa. Ledwaba had staged a daring escape from the Palm Ridge Magistrate's Court after his sentence was handed down, but the law caught up with him at the shopping mall. He was charged, convicted and sentenced, but the charges against Cat were withdrawn. Nine lives indeed.[470]

When Cat emerged as a focal point in my investigation, I homed in on his medical supply businesses that had seen a multimillion-rand boon from Tembisa Hospital. This led me to his wife, Cordelia Kabeng. She was the founder of his security company, and one of Cat's shell companies, Cor Kabeng Trading and Suppliers, was named after her.[471] I could see how money was flowing into the Matlala household, and Kabeng's prolific Instagram presence provided answers on how it was spent. She had 12 000 followers and showcased her luxury lifestyle in daily posts. I downloaded reams of pictures from her profile and priced her handbags, shoes and clothing.[472]

> Louis Vuitton Speedy Bandoulière Monogram Empreinte handbag – R59 000
> Large Dior Toile de Jouy book tote – R68 800
> Dolce & Gabbana daily medium leather tote – R27 500
> Balmain B-Court monogram jacquard sneakers – R10 000
> Gucci Horsebit leather pumps – R16 000
> Gucci Horsebit 1955 small shoulder bag – R29 000[473]

One image had the Gucci bag and shoes paired in an ensemble. Kabeng, wearing a pristine white two-piece, was seated in a helicopter. This was how the wife of a tenderpreneur flaunted her wealth.

Kabeng would also chronicle her daily life with videos filmed in a cavalcade of her husband's private security vehicles, either as she was shuttled to and from the airport or on the daily school run with her kids. These cars had been illegally fitted with blue lights. There was no emergency – just a rich woman trying to keep to her schedule. In captions she posted with these videos, she called herself 'Mama Cat' and boasted of her high-speed, armed and (illegally) equipped escorts taking her to 'drop off her cubs'. After all, her husband was an influential man whose tentacles stretched into the highest ranks of both the South African Police Service and the Ekurhuleni Metro Police Department (EMPD).[474]

I found that, in 2021, Cat had been given a memorandum signed by acting EMPD chief Julius Mkhwanazi. In it, he spoke of the 'endless' working relationship between Cat's security company and his force, and he listed the descriptions and registration numbers of six cars. These cars were owned by the security company, and the single-page letter was Cat's supposed authorisation for using blue lights, which were strictly reserved for cops. Mkhwanazi and Cat were close – so close, in fact, that the former registered Cat's security vehicles in a clandestine scheme as part of the EMPD fleet. Cat would never have to pay fines or licensing fees ever again. The municipality's ratepayers would foot that bill.

But then I got involved. The cars were quietly reregistered in the name of the security firm. My questions roiled EMPD management, and Mkhwanazi was suspended and subjected to an investigation. This probe found prima facie evidence of fraud and uttering, and it led to a disciplinary hearing and criminal charges. But nothing was done. Mkhwanazi's three-month suspension lapsed without a hearing, and he returned to work. Then he was promoted. The man so close to Cat is the police chief of a metropolitan municipality. Officers who investigated Mkhwanazi have been demoted, disciplined and purged.

Cat's links to high-ranking cops run even deeper. When he rushed to court to get his watch, guns and cellphone back, he revealed that he enjoyed access to the police's national head of detectives, Lieutenant-General Shadrack Sibiya.[475] Cat was also the controlling mind of a company called Medicare 24 Tswane [sic] District, registered in 2019. I don't know if misspelling Tshwane was intentional. This company, according to its website, provides occupational health services to corporates and is based at a strip mall in Bardene, Boksburg, on Johannesburg's East Rand.

'We are changing the future of the Medical Service Industry in South Africa and the continent. We have the best-trained and most efficient teams in the industry. Our teams provide affordable, world-class health and wellness solutions and facilities to corporates and individuals alike,' runs the company's online description.

This is where Sibiya can be placed in close proximity to the one-time-thief-turned-businessman. In June 2024, Medicare bid for and won a three-year tender to provide health services to the SAPS for R360 million. At the time, Cat had been publicly implicated in the Tembisa Hospital procurement saga that Babita uncovered. He could face at least one fraud charge for allegedly falsifying bid documents and was a feature in active investigations by the SIU, the South African Revenue Service, the National Prosecuting Authority and the Hawks. So, a man under suspicion of public procurement malfeasance was given a massive tender by the very organisation investigating him. Did any of this arise during the due-diligence process? Was another bid-adjudication committee asleep at the wheel? It beggars belief.[476]

Even just a cursory look at this deal shows the red flags were everywhere. Medicare was to provide a vast array of health services for the police's 180 000-strong workforce spread across nine provinces. The medical arm of Cat's empire would need to be significant if they were to deliver. The recurring tender was previously held, in successive awards, by insurer Metropolitan, a firm large enough to be listed on the JSE. Now it had been awarded to a fledgling entity run from a shopping mall – a company that, just a year before, was on the verge of being deregistered for failing to submit annual returns to the Companies and Intellectual Property Commission.

When the tender was awarded, Cat had to set up shop at SAPS' Pretoria College, and he was struggling to get access. When he was barred, Cat said, he turned to Sibiya to intercede.[477] I found it astounding that a businessman with a criminal past and links to procurement fraud could call for a meeting with one of the country's top policemen, and it would happen. Sibiya's conflict in this scenario was patent, clearly revealing Cat's reach in law enforcement. When I asked the SAPS to provide me with the full file of documents relating to this deal, I was spurned. The official line was that the award was above board, but I was not allowed to look at the paperwork. My inquiry concerned how a taxpayer-funded organisation spent public money, and there were constitutional imperatives about transparency. But they denied me access. That, in itself, was dubious.

When I revealed that a Tembisa Hospital tender tycoon, flagged by Babita before her assassination, had another state-sponsored windfall, Cat did something I did not expect. On the day that our story was published, he resigned his directorship in Medicare. This business providing health services for South Africa's police force is now run by a 29-year-old woman whose only business experience is in the cleaning company she founded – a company that has never traded.

Death at every turn

In 2021, the year Babita was assassinated, 25 181 South Africans were murdered. During the Covid-19 pandemic and the various levels of lockdown that came with it, the total tally of killings had dropped. But, after the return to everyday life, there was a surge.[478] Violent crime has flourished in the void left by directionless policing initiatives, the denuding of capacity and human capital during the state-capture epoch, and internecine power struggles in police leadership, often defined by political intrusion and meddling.

South Africa now also ranks as the twentieth-worst country in the world in terms of safety and security.[479] This can be ascribed to the failures of the police. In 2023, our murder rate was at its highest level in two decades. At the same time, the detection rate for murder cases dipped to just above fourteen per cent. This rate is a measure of the successful investigation, positive identification, arrest and charging of perpetrators. The detection process covers the period from the opening of a police docket until a suspect is arrested and charged, or until the docket is closed as unfounded or withdrawn in court.[480] Before the ink was even dry on the docket opened after Babita's murder, there was only a one-in-ten chance the case would be solved.

For the Hawks, which spearheaded the investigation nigh from the start, solving the murder was always going to be a challenge. Targeted assassinations are, by their nature, complex crimes. Evidence would need to link the *izinkabi* to those who had ordered and paid for the contract on Babita's life, stitching in countless layers of hidden fixers, intermediaries and proxies. Solving these crimes requires acumen across fields of expertise: traditional police methods of investigation alongside innovative techniques, using technology to build a complete narrative of a crime, and dismantling the entire murder value chain in a digital age. This requires forensic capability to stitch together cellphone location data, bank statements, vehicle tracking logs and phone interactions such as messages and calls. Catching evolved criminals requires a new breed of cop. When Chauke was in charge of Babita's murder probe, he seemingly ignored crucial digital evidence and put in the bare minimum in terms of effort and will. Because of what he and his team failed to do, the mastermind was allowed to walk free. Chauke, from what I could prove, showed no intention of investigating the case fully.

I know some good police officers remain in the Hawks. But these men are hamstrung and overloaded with work, carrying more active investigations than any one person can possibly handle. I have been told harrowing stories that paint the crime-fighting organisation as hapless and limping. Units that should have a head count of 150 officers are operating with fewer than 30 members. These men are forced to take turns using state vehicles because there are so few, and some cars are pulled out of service for months because of paperwork for something as simple as replacing tyres. Many officers buy their own stationery, pay for the printing of documents and purchase airtime from their own funds. Officers with rank have laptops with software from 2008, and even then, being assigned a computer that you can pick up and take home with you is a privilege. The Hawks are stuck in the dark ages.

That the police can only solve one in ten murders is alarming, more so when incidents of targeted assassinations – involving whistle-blowers, government officials, police officers and lawyers – have become more prevalent. What has also become more pronounced is the brazen manner in which these individuals are targeted. I believe this audacity is because those involved know there is a 90 per cent chance they will get away with it. These should be considered attacks on democracy and the rule of law.

Izinkabi are disposable in this game of death. They are recruited as part of cash-in-transit heist gangs, kidnappings for ransom, armed robberies and hits. Their skills are in high demand. If they are arrested, they enforce a code of silence, and while their families are secretly supported on the outside, they serve their time. The masterminds remain comfortable, knowing that the chance they will be pursued is statistically low.

For instance, on Saturday, 19 March 2023, father-and-son liquidators Cloete and Thomas Murray were assassinated in broad daylight. A car had pulled up alongside them as they travelled on the N1 from Johannesburg toward Pretoria and riddled the vehicle and its occupants with bullets. Thomas succumbed at the scene, and his father died hours later in hospital. My colleague Kyle Cowan launched his own investigation into the murder. He found that the cops had abandoned files and documents when the Murrays' car was towed away from the crime scene. Kyle found a file titled 'I2 Infinite Innovations'.[481]

The Murrays were securing properties registered in the name of I2, a company belonging to brother and sister Rushil and Nishani Singh. The father and son were familiar with the siblings, who were also directors of BIG Business Innovations. The two companies were at the centre of a R200 million fraud case opened by Investec Bank. Cloete Murray had been appointed joint liquidator of BIG, and later Thomas was appointed liquidator of I2. The Murrays had seized luxury vehicles including a McLaren sports car and several Mercedes-Benzes. On that Saturday, they were securing a nearly R30 million property portfolio owned by I2. Kyle placed his own life at risk chasing down this story and revealed critical information, including the detailed movements of the car used in the attack. He even named the man driving it.[482]

Another instance: on Sunday, 6 August 2023, Hawks detective Frans Mathipa was gunned down on the freeway outside Pretoria.

While travelling at 120 kilometres per hour, he was shot twice in the head. He died instantaneously, and his car left the roadway and crashed. At the time, he was investigating apparently rogue elements of the South African Defence Force's special reconnaissance unit, men who were highly trained weapons of war. This cohort had allegedly kidnapped and disappeared an international terror suspect, and their snatching of the suspect at a Johannesburg shopping mall was caught on camera.[483]

Yet another instance: on Wednesday, 12 July 2024, Zenzele Benedict Sithole was sitting in his car, stuck in traffic in the afternoon malaise of central Johannesburg, when a man walked up to his window and stuck a revolver in his face before emptying the cylinder. A bloodied Sithole slumped over his steering wheel, and the car lurched forward before his foot slipped off the accelerator. The hitman, caught by CCTV cameras at an adjacent building, simply walked away. Sithole's wife kept the shirt he was wearing when he was shot, and she has never washed it. They had been married just months before his death. Sithole was a veteran detective who had cut his teeth with the Hawks before taking up a job at the City of Johannesburg. In this role, he led investigations into powerful political people behind municipal corruption cases.[484]

These three assassinations have two distinct features in common. First, the victims were part of, or adjacent to, law enforcement, tasked with dismantling criminal and corrupt networks. Second, none of these cases has been solved. For years, those left behind by these men have been denied justice. The Deokaran family knows this reality all too well.

On 17 April 2024, Armand Swart, a father of two who worked at an engineering firm in Vereeniging, was shot to death while on his way to work. He had pulled up to the company's gate and was waiting for it to open when a car screeched to a halt alongside him and unleashed a salvo of gunfire. He was shot 23 times and died in his seat. I investigated this murder and found that Swart was collateral damage – an innocent killed in a case of mistaken identity. Two weeks before the attack, his company had filed a confidential whistleblower report with rail parastatal Transnet. The company made components for use on railway infrastructure, obscure steel implements, and was considered an original equipment manufacturer. But it did not trade directly with Transnet. Shell companies tendered for and won deals. They simply bought the equipment and then applied a healthy markup.

The engineering firm's bosses discovered that an innocuous component – a simple spring no larger than a finger – they produced and sold for R3.20 had then been sold to Transnet with a price tag per unit of R152. With the state-owned freight and logistics company buying a consignment of 8 000 of these springs, what should have been a R25 000 purchase morphed into one worth more than R1.2 million. Hitmen had been given a picture of their target, and despite days of surveillance and reconnaissance before the killing, they ended up murdering the wrong man. Swart's only crime was that he looked similar to their mark – one of the managers at his firm who had filed the report. This elimination, much like Babita's murder, had been motivated by a need to mask corruption and extraction from the public purse.[485]

What sets these two cases apart is the way they were investigated. Within 24 hours, three members of the Vereeniging hit squad were traced and arrested. Detectives used licence-plate recognition cameras to plot their movements before and after the killing. Their cellphone location data, obtained under subpoena, underpinned this. Ballistic analysis of the guns they carried when they were arrested linked them to a spate of assassinations. WhatsApp discussions found during a forensic analysis of seized cellphones led to Sandton businessman Katiso Molefe being identified as a central figure. His nephew, Lucky Molefe, had been the buyer with Transnet who engineered the inflated deal, and when his uncle was arrested, he went on the run. The leader of the killing crew was believed to be veteran Johannesburg detective Michael Pule Tau.[486]

Tau had unfettered access to police profiling tools, containing all aspects of personal information, as well as the police's internal case system. For a rogue police officer, this provided invaluable intelligence both before and after the crime. He was – allegedly – the inside man, helping his hitters evade arrest and cover their tracks. There is a warrant of arrest for Lucky, but I doubt the police will ever find him. In court, his uncle worked hard to paint him as the controlling mind of the extraction scheme.[487] But Lucky did not sport the trappings of wealth one would expect from a mastermind figure. His uncle, however, has a mansion and a collection of sports cars, suggesting that if cash was pulled from Transnet's coffers, it found its way to him. Lucky is probably dead already, and I would be surprised if police ever manage to bring him to court to contradict his uncle's narrative. That notwithstanding, police were able to decode a targeted assassination, arrest and charge most of the actors – from the *izinkabi* to the alleged masterminds – in under a year. They were indicted in the same period. Police have built a solid case and used digital forensic methods to bolster it. Looking at the way this whistleblower murder was investigated and moved through the court system, Swart's family may just see justice. But they are among the lucky few.

The team of cops pushing the Swart murder investigation to finality were threatened with death and, on one occasion when they were returning from a court appearance, nearly run off the road. There are indications that high-ranking officers have tried to derail the investigation. They are the enemy within and a testament to why good police officers keep their circles small. The detectives now live in safehouses and are guarded by tactical cops around the clock.[488]

In South Africa, anyone who acts against corruption, no matter who they are, does so knowing that while it is the right thing to do, it could see them killed. And they do so with the knowledge that if they are eliminated, their murders have only a one in ten chance of being solved.

Accountability lost

While he languished on suspension, disgraced Tembisa Hospital boss Ashley Mthunzi collected R2.5 million from the state through his salary. He faced a disciplinary inquiry, alongside Gauteng Health Department CFO Lerato Madyo, and the pair fought for their jobs and their probity. It would seem both had been installed in critical positions because of their political connections to the ANC and, under their watch, had either enabled or overlooked payments worth R2.3 billion to extraction syndicates.

When he ended up in hot water, Mthunzi used his connections in the party's communications structures and business arm to try to intercede with me, a move that backfired badly.

The pair faced just thirteen charges of misconduct and, even though a near 1 000-page bundle of incontrovertible evidence made their misconduct manifest, the process was drawn out over two years. Before their guilt or innocence could be determined, Mthunzi died. The Deokaran family was denied justice and accountability once more.[489]

On receiving the news of his death, the family issued a statement: 'Mthunzi may have not paid his dues here on earth, but he will pay for it in the afterlife, and he is hopefully burning in hell. Almost three years after our sister was murdered and our anger has not subsided.'[490]

Alex van den Heever is an adjunct professor and the chair of social security systems administration and management studies at the University of the Witwatersrand. Bespectacled and bracingly intelligent, he had been quietly aiding me in my investigation for years. When I started, I knew next to nothing about the protocols and rules of public health procurement, and he graciously guided me behind the scenes. He had acted as a senior advisor at the Council for Medical Schemes, the health-insurance regulator in South Africa, and worked as a senior researcher at the Centre for Health Policy at Wits. Beyond that, he knew the Gauteng Health Department inside out, as he was a former director of finance at the department.[491]

In his opinion, 'The millions in blatant and poorly hidden irregular expenditure were so obvious that a normal organisation would have acted decisively to apply consequences. Plainly, the Gauteng Department of Health is no ordinary organisation. Importantly, this misconduct is exactly what Babita Deokaran flagged and why she was murdered. The evidence was all over the place, in black and white. All persons in positions that controlled this expenditure were either complicit or so incompetent that reasonable grounds should exist for their immediate removal from their positions, and not just a mere suspension.

'The incredible delays in carrying out the disciplinary processes cannot reasonably be explained. No properly functioning organisation would tolerate this. The treatment of these officials is in stark contrast to the immediate discipline meted out to whistleblowers or those who defy illegal orders. It is hard not to conclude that these individuals are being treated differently, either for their connections or for what they know. One need look no further than this to explain the general dysfunction of the Gauteng Department of Health.'[492]

The disciplinary process was managed by Gauteng Premier Panyaza Lesufi's office and, given that Madyo and Mthunzi were allowed to further drain the state of R5.5 million through their combined salaries – paid to them for sitting at home and doing nothing – it all played out for their financial benefit. When I attended the first sitting of this procedure, six months after they were suspended, the state attorney, acting for Lesufi and the state, had not yet been able to compile two charge sheets, an exercise that should take days, not months.

Mthunzi's death meant that he would never have to account for his actions and, because he was not found guilty and dismissed, he was still considered to be in the service of the province when he died. Thus, his estate – and his unionist wife, who connived to destabilise the hospital as revenge for his suspension – is entitled to a legacy of payments from the Government Employees Pension Fund. The money drain will continue.[493]

What's more, Mthunzi should never have landed Tembisa Hospital's top job in the first place. The impudent, arrogant character was parachuted into the plum position despite red flags on his own declaration form. Yet, the top brass of the Gauteng Health Department cast aside their own rules to ensure he was placed at the helm. An investigation by the public protector, set in motion by a complaint by Jack Bloom, the dogged Democratic Alliance member in the provincial legislature, revealed that giving Mthunzi the Tembisa job was grossly irregular.[494]

On a form submitted as part of his application, Mthunzi had declared that he was not a South African national and that he remained under a cloud of misconduct allegations relating to his previous posting at Pholosong Hospital. The former claim was false; the latter was confirmed to be true. Investigators discovered that the panel that endorsed his appointment did not challenge him on these statements and neglected to perform even fundamental background checks before slotting him into the role.[495]

This highlighted the flawed manner in which senior managers in the department were hired and exposed a glaring lack of thorough background checks. The politically connected hospital administrator, a key enabler of corrupt activity and price gouging, was promoted.[496]

The public protector found: 'They did not conduct financial stability checks, citizenship or identity screening and criminal records checks as the GDoH [Gauteng Department of Health] does not have a service provider to do such checks because of budgetary constraints and it was during the Covid-19 pandemic restrictions. There is no evidence to show that the functionaries enquired from Dr Mthunzi about the declarations that may have affected his suitability for the post during the recruitment and selection process.'[497]

I thought that this was an affront to Babita's memory, until I figured out how Madyo was let off the hook. The woman in whom Babita confided about her safety concerns was allowed to quietly resign and slither away. She was never questioned on why she had covered up multiple audit reports about procurement issues at the hospital. She, too, kept her pension.

Even now, with her out of the system, if Madyo thinks she can evade me she is misinformed. She now goes by Daniella Molapo. I am waiting for her to try to worm her way into another state department.

The man who had overlooked Mthunzi's dubious past and the discrepancies on this job application was Arnold Malotana, acting head of the Gauteng Health Department. He rose through the ranks of the public service but may have skeletons of his own.[498] In 2023, the AmaBhungane Centre for Investigative Journalism published a damning report setting out how a former service provider at the Gauteng Health Department implicated Malotana and two other senior officials in a tender-rigging scheme in which they allegedly scored R10 million in kickbacks.[499]

AmaBhungane got their hands on the whistleblower's explosive affidavit filed with the Hawks, which included email communication, contracts, invoices and bank statements as evidence of the corruption allegations. When they published, Malotana was still acting in the role. He denied the allegations but declined further comment, citing the pending investigation. Despite an active Hawks corruption investigation and an independent SIU probe into a R31 million tender Malotana had allegedly fixed, he was permanently installed in the position by Lesufi midway through 2024.[500]

Under his tenure, the Gauteng Health Department is as it was prior to Babita's death: cash-strapped and plagued by scandal. At the close of 2024, Malotana and his department were hauled to court by NGOs Section 27 and the Cancer Alliance for failing to use a R748 million budget allocation for the treatment of cancer patients. The department announced through the media that R250 million would be used to procure planning services for the outsourcing of radiation and oncology services for one year. The remaining R534 million would be used for equipment, including radiation bunkers. This hapless maladministration of nearly R1 billion placed in jeopardy the lives of more than 3 000 cancer patients who depended on state medical care.[501]

On 19 December 2024, Malotana issued a communiqué to all hospital CEOs. It laid out the fragile state of the department's finances: 'GDOH has been experiencing serious cash-flow challenges which affects [sic] its liquidity and the ability to render effective, quality and seamless services to all its clients. The cash flow risks require all departmental officials, including clinicians, to search for more efficient ways to deliver health services.'

Hospital bosses were instructed to shift cash from underused programmes to more strategic priorities. The province's public health network appeared to be on life support, and hospitals were falling apart. At the time, former radio DJ Tom London was admitted to Helen Joseph Hospital and, in a social media broadcast, revealed the sorry state of the facility. There was no running water from basin taps, only two dirty toilets with no toilet paper, and, when he complained to nurses and staff, he was met with scorn. At one point in his stay, there was no toilet for him to use. He soiled himself and was left to lie in that state for nearly a full day.[502]

Since Madyo was placed on suspension in August 2022, the Gauteng Health Department still has not found a permanent replacement for her. The fallout from the Tembisa scandal has also further hobbled the hospital itself. Almost the entire cohort of supply-chain management officials was either fired or resigned, and these posts have been left vacant. Those who suffer most are the patients.

The businessmen behind the extraction syndicates – Morgan Maumela, Stefan Govindraju and Rudolf Mazibuko – are also yet to experience any consequences as a result of their schemes. The investigations started in 2022 by the SIU and the Hawks remain ongoing and are so vast and complex that they are only likely to be completed in 2026. Despite Babita's warnings and the weaknesses in the way goods and services are procured, very little has changed. The systems that were so easily perverted and corrupted have been left in situ. The only alteration is this: the threshold for hospital buying that can be approved by the CEO was raised from R500 000 to R1 million. Extraction syndicates, remade and reconstituted with new networks of shell companies and proxy directors, now have even more latitude to steal.

Conclusion

In death, Babita has become a symbol of bravery and courage. She exemplified honesty and integrity and was an example of a civil servant who actually served. She opposed corrupt forces that had been given access by virtue of their positions and political influence. She faced disciplinary action on trumped-up charges. Her good name was smeared among her colleagues, and she was demoted.

Babita was well aware that the Gauteng Health Department was a captured, thriving den of iniquity. When she stumbled across dubious buying patterns at Tembisa Hospital and issued her report, she had an inkling that this was a dangerous pursuit, yet she forged ahead anyway. She paid for it with her life.

In December 2024, an event to mark International Anti-Corruption Day was held in her honour. It was called 'Babita's long walk for justice', and in attendance on the day was the head of the Hawks, General Godfrey Lebeya. The night before the commemoration, Tony Haripersadh called me. The Phoenix chapter of Babita's family would also lend their support to the initiative, he said, and he knew Lebeya would be there. He asked me what he should say to him. I told him not to pull his punches. 'Walk up to him and tell him to his face how the Hawks have failed you. I am sure he is well aware of this already, but he deserves the shame of hearing it directly from you.' Tony did just that.

The Hawks had hardly covered themselves in glory during their long investigation of Babita's murder. The primary detective on the case, Chauke, by this point promoted to the rank of lieutenant-colonel, was central to this failure. From what I had established, he did little to pursue the paymaster of this crime, turned a blind eye to potentially valuable evidence and jeopardised the prosecution of six *izinkabi*. It was he who ordered the release of Khanyisani Mpungose, the alleged gunman, who himself was murdered months after he was set free.

But Chauke should not shoulder the blame alone. As a detective, he fits into a command structure. His dockets and investigation diary would be checked and scrutinised regularly by his commanders, who seemingly also did nothing when they should have intervened. Babita's murder inquiry is a case study that reveals the systemic failure of the police to deliver on their constitutional mandate: investigate crime, rid society of dark elements and ensure a safe and prosperous South Africa.

For her family, only memories of Babita remain. Her fortitude, a torch that illuminated vast corruption in the shadows, is beginning to flicker and fade. For Thiara, each day dawns with the weight of her mother's absence, a cold reminder of a life cut short for a noble cause. Every day, on a Facebook group, Babita's sisters publish a picture of her with a tally of the number of days the person or people who paid for her death have remained free. Every day they implore President Cyril Ramaphosa to take action and give them closure. The number of days has now reached the thousands, and I am not sure if Ramaphosa has even seen their daily appeals.

The uncomfortable reality they must confront is that Babita's murder is unlikely to be solved. Evidence has been destroyed. Memories have faded. The Hawks have lost the impetus they had in the days after the hitmen were arrested. In writing this book, I asked Gauteng Hawks boss General Ebrahim Kadwa to speak to me. Chauke's reporting line ended with him, and he was there at Turffontein Racecourse when Phakamani Hadebe and his taxi hitmen were nabbed. I wanted to know if he shared my view that his subordinates had botched a high-profile assassination investigation.

If there was no justice for Babita, did he ever consider what message this transmitted to other whistleblowers? How many would choose to stay quiet because law enforcement had failed? Would there be consequences for Chauke and others? Did he still feel he had to boldly claim that every possible avenue was explored during their probe?

His response:

> Good morning, Jeff.
>
> Apologies for delay in responding to your request.
>
> The investigation into Babita Deokaran is still ongoing and our policies do not allow us to authorise lateral interviews for any other purpose outside investigation, as this may have an effect on ongoing investigation and trial. This request can be revisited once the case has been finalised.
>
> Hope you find this in order.

Well, no, I don't find that in order. Once again, those who should face a grilling for their bumbling missteps will hide behind the refrain of 'an open investigation' that will drag on for years. If history has taught me anything, this investigation is likely to amount to naught. By definition, it is now a cold case.

Babita's final internal investigation threatened vast networks of extraction led by a trio of men, some with deep-rooted political ties and the protections that no doubt come with them. She had dutifully gathered documents and built her case. She had described rampant procurement corruption as a genocide, and I think she was right. It requires a special kind of psychopath to steal from a hospital, but any mote of morality was overwhelmed by greed.

For doing her job, Babita was betrayed. A person or group within the Gauteng Health Department must have tipped off powerful actors who turned to the criminal underworld to protect their interests. Directly or indirectly, the *izinkabi* were probably paid by taxpayers' money intended for the benefit of patients at Tembisa Hospital.

Babita was a casualty of the shadow state, a parallel criminal world designed to prey on public funds. This realm and its secret economy flourish unseen. Crooked health officials ensured that R2.3 billion was channelled to extraction syndicates, and money meant for the hospital was diverted to privateers. This is not where the felonious economy starts and ends. These garish businessmen still need to spend their loot, which they did through splurges on property, expensive cars and billionaire lifestyles. They are enabled by car dealers, estate agents and lawyers, all funded indirectly by the taxpayer. They are also protected by hapless or corrupt police officers and an endless army of hitmen who take their deadly stock in trade to the highest bidder. This is why Babita had to die.

What was spawned from within Tembisa Hospital is an evolved form of state capture. When Ajay, Rajesh and Atul Gupta compromised President Jacob Zuma and his acolytes, it was part of a shady scheme to pull money from state-owned enterprises. The amounts tallied in the billions, and the Guptas were empowered by pliant ANC ministers who were willing to auction off their morals to the highest bidder. While the effects of the scheme were devastating, they were also easy to find. High-value tenders attract a lot of scrutiny, and the benefactors were easy to define. State capture is not over. It is just blossoming in a different form. Real extraction happens every day through small, insignificant payments that often go unnoticed. It happened at Tembisa Hospital and at least five other facilities in the provincial health network. The captors have infiltrated municipalities, provincial administrations and parastatals. It is through small, innocuous transactions executed at scale that the capture endures.

A scheme with an almost identical modus operandi was dismantled at state power company Eskom. Dozens of employees received at least R180 million in kickbacks from low-value contracts at some of South Africa's largest power stations. These deals, valued at up to R1 million, have less rigorous oversight and approval processes than formal contracts. While this is meant to facilitate quicker decision-making, the SIU found that the small contracts were being misused for corrupt activities. The unit's investigation identified 45 vendors at fifteen power stations – including Kusile, Kriel and Duvha – that paid kickbacks for years.[503]

In another example, former University of Fort Hare student leader Sicelo Mbulawa was allegedly the hidden hand behind a web of shell companies that banked millions from corrupt supplier contracts at the institution – while he was studying toward a degree. Seemingly with the help of university official Eleanor 'Mumsy' Feni, Mbulawa allegedly manipulated the university's procurement system in a scheme that stretched back six years and extracted millions before they were stopped by the cops. Mbulawa and four others have been charged in connection with a string of assassinations of university officials at Fort Hare who were investigating this network.[504]

Tender price inflation and deals channelled to shell companies were also the basis of Vereeniging engineer Armand Swart's assassination.[505] It is a hallmark of the shadow state, and this method of operation is easily replicated. The upright few who refuse to stay silent when confronted with rampant graft, like Babita, are taken out. Eliminated. Silenced. Corruption is far from a victimless crime. The cost, for the whistleblowers at least, can be counted in bodies.

Syndicates taking root at Tembisa Hospital and other facilities have enjoyed significant access and influence, wittingly or unwittingly enabled by the politicians. They determine how senior managers are appointed, and it would appear that qualifications, experience and interview scores are not the most important metrics. Their qualifications are secondary to their political ties, and the result is a dysfunctional health system, bordering on broke, that roundly fails its patients.

Long before Babita's warning, Tembisa Hospital was widely regarded as a feeding trough empowered by officials in both the supply-chain management office and the executive suite. That no one took action could be seen as a tacit endorsement, or they could simply claim that they were blissfully unaware. After Shonisani Lethole, riven by Covid-19 and clinging to life, was starved and mistreated at Tembisa Hospital in June 2020, the Office of the Health Ombudsman started a far-reaching inquiry. Among the hundreds of nurses, doctors and other officials the ombudsman interviewed, one witness remained hidden: nursing services manager Wilfred Mothwane.

Mothwane told the ombudsman that he tried to warn his management that designating the facility as a Covid-19 reception facility was a bad idea. At the heart of his concerns was the shortage of PPE. While smocks, masks and gloves were purchased and donated to the hospital, a shortage remained. Protocols were not being followed, and the infection was spreading. Only those frontline workers dealing with pandemic patients were issued with protective gear. Those who weren't simply refused to work. This prompted strike action. Hospital kitchen staff, nurses and others flatly refused to enter wards lest they contract the virus. Shonisani starved to death while meals were left at the hospital unit's door and never actually delivered.

On the day Shonisani was admitted, Mothwane was nursing patients on the ward. He left his office because his staff had revolted and people were dying. When the ombudsman's investigation began, Mothwane was off sick, as he had tested positive for the virus. However, he sought out the ombudsman on his own despite Tembisa Hospital CEO Lekopane Mogaladi trying to prevent him from giving testimony.

Mothwane had a story to tell, and it was devastating. His warnings had been ignored by hospital management, and Shonisani wasn't the only one to die in inhumane conditions. There were many others, he said.

In August, two months after Shonisani died, Mothwane wrote a letter to then-Gauteng Health Department MEC Bandile Masuku, pleading for an urgent investigation into the hospital. He also asked Masuku to verify the true Covid-19 death toll at the facility.

'I, as the nursing manager, was instructed to underreport Covid-related deaths. I want the deaths investigated to see if the actual death numbers were reported. I feel an investigation into this matter may yield useful information in identifying discrepancies in the reporting. I think they are trying to hide something.'

He also raised the issue of corruption around how PPE was purchased. He had discovered that donated PPE was being passed off as purchased. 'This indicates that actual stock ordered was never received but paid for.'

Tembisa Hospital was chosen to face the brunt of the pandemic, but its leadership was hapless – and people died as a result. It should never have been designated as a centre of care, but the management of the hospital was resolute and firmly on this path. Mothwane had an explanation. With Tembisa seeing Covid-19 patients, the procurement budget swelled and there was more money to steal. He had seen the warning signs and called for an urgent investigation, but he was ignored.

Had someone in authority acted and directed that the hospital's procurement office be audited, those trawling through the payments would likely have found the shell company networks, price gouging and irregular contract manipulation, as Babita did. At that stage, they were already in the system.

Perhaps if Mothwane's allegations had been probed, Babita might have been alive today. It is yet another failure that allowed syndicates to thrive. There is an anecdote of a PPE supplier who had a key to the departmental warehouse. When he received orders, he would simply slink into the store and lift stock, repackage it and sell it back to the same people from whom it had been stolen.

Corruption and graft have become a disquieting mainstay in the Gauteng Health Department. It is everywhere and, to me, it is little wonder that the department's R65 billion annual budget runs dry. If procurement was fair, transparent, accountable and based on a real need, with a drive for value for money, Gauteng's public hospitals would not be in this dire state.

What do we learn from the resistance and lack of political will to modernise the procurement system with an electronic portal? It's astounding that in 2025, bid submissions for Gauteng Health Department work are entirely paper-based. Tembisa Hospital staff perfected the exploitation of loopholes in this system, and an electronic alternative would flag problematic transactions in real time.

The frailty of this paper-based system was exposed when, in April 2025, Tembisa Hospital was targeted by arsonists. Two fires were set in archive rooms, using petrol and paper. The blaze threatened to consume the finance office – an uninspiring room decked with stacks of files on every available surface.

Fire is the ultimate destructor of evidence, and someone at that hospital wanted to erase something from the record.

What Babita found were the first hints of syndicate activity. It was a fraction of what the SIU unravelled: billions bleeding from a delicate health system and a money-laundering operation the likes and scale of which they had never encountered. It was sophisticated, and it was a well-kept secret.

And where are those company owners and enterprising 'business-people' first outed by Babita? Most have disappeared, but others have remained in the headlines. From what I can track, they are thriving.

Sello Sekhokho, an ANC office-bearer, has his eye on higher office. While there was a lull in his business, in 2024 he returned as a supplier to the Gauteng Department of Health, this time flogging toilet paper.

Stefan Govindraju was criminally charged for failing to keep up with his tax obligations related to another little-known entity. When

I had a look, I found another five companies making money from Tembisa Hospital – shell companies that Babita never found.

For most, it seems accountability is a ways off.

When I was handed Babita's cellphone and laptop, I had the slim hope that I might be able to get some sense of justice for her and for those she left behind. I think that I failed. What I gave to them were answers, and the reason why Babita had to die. None of which will bring her back.

When I first met Rakesh and other members of the Deokaran family, I swore to them that I would follow this story to the end. But there were times, many in fact, when I questioned my resolve. I was waiting for my bullets, and the constant fear threatened my relationships. Crippling apprehension permeated my life. I hoped that, if I had to die at the hands of the *izinkabi*, it would at least be quick. It would be better than living as someone maimed and crippled by gunfire, whom my wife and family would have to care for.

I figure that if those behind Babita's killing wanted me dead, I would already be in my grave. But pursuing this assignment has left indelible marks on my life. I remain, to this day, in a heightened sense of awareness. It is not something that one can simply switch off. I still vary my routes when I travel, change up my schedule and constantly watch people, looking for erratic behaviour or the telltale bulge of a gun concealed in a waistband. At restaurants, I sit as far to the back as possible and watch the door.

All this is because my work on this story has not yet finished. Those behind the Tembisa Hospital syndicates have yet to feel the sting of consequence and justice. Extraction from state entities is likely to continue through hastily assembled new fronting webs. I will keep a watchful eye on them. And on the SIU, the Hawks and the Gauteng Department of Health. I will make sure that what Babita found in the ledgers of the hospital can never be covered up again, and that those pulling the strings of murder pay for their crimes in some way.

Notes

Introduction

1. Milazzo, M. 21 August 2024. 'Deadly Journeys: Thabo Jijana's Nobody's Business, the Minibus Taxi Industry, and the Racial Politics of Mobility in Post-Apartheid South Africa'. Taylor & Francis Online. https://www.tandfonline.com/doi/full/10.1080/00138398.2024.2370181#abstract

2. Thomas, K., Netshikulwe, A., & Mngqibisa, N. 2018. 'The rule of the gun: Hits and assassinations in South Africa'. https://globalinitiative.net/wp-content/uploads/2018/03/The-rule-of-the-gun_Assassination-Witness.pdf

3. Phakamani Hadebe confession. 27 August 2021.

4. Ibid.

PART 1

Chapter 1

5. Author's interview with Rakesh Deokaran, 16 January 2025.

6. Ibid.

7. Ibid.

8. Ibid.

9. Al Jazeera. 26 August 2021. 'WHO: Covid-19 vaccination triples in Africa but still low'. https://www.aljazeera.com/news/2021/8/26/who-covid-19-vaccination-triples-in-africa-but-still-low

10. South African government. 'Covid-19/Coronavirus'. Accessed 2 January 2025.

11. National Institute for Communicable Diseases. 'Latest confirmed cases of Covid-19 in South Africa – 26 August 2021'. Accessed 2 January 2025.

12. Ibid.

13. Author's interview with Rakesh Deokaran, 16 January 2025.

14. Ibid.

15. Author's interview with Karishma Mangali, 24 August 2024.

16. Author's interview with Rakesh Deokaran, 16 January 2025.

17. Ibid.

18. Ibid.

19. Ibid.

20. Author's interview with Karishma Mangali, 24 August 2024.

21. eNCA live stream. 26 August 2021. 'Slain whistleblower's funeral service in Phoenix'. YouTube. https://www.youtube.com/watch?v=wbCA2dFTOOo

22. Ibid.

23. Author's interview with Neeshan Balton, 8 September 2021.

24. Cruywagen, V. 24 August 2021. 'Murder of Gauteng health official Babita Deokaran: Investigators probe link to her PPE whistle-blowing'. Daily Maverick. https://www.dailymaverick.co.za/article/2021-08-24-murder-of-gauteng-health-official-babita-deokaran-investigators-probe-link-to-her-ppe-whistle-blowing/

25 Ibid.

26 News24. 24 August 2021. 'Editorial | Why did Babita Deokaran have to die?'. https://www.news24.com/news24/opinions/editorial/editorial-why-did-babita-deokaran-have-to-die-20210824

27 Letter from Pravin Gordhan, 26 August 2021.

28 Gauteng Provincial Government. 'Nomathemba Emily Mokgethi – MEC for Social Development'. Accessed 13 September 2024.

29 eNCA live stream. 26 August 2021. 'Slain whistleblower's funeral service in Phoenix'. YouTube. https://www.youtube.com/watch?v=wbCA2dFTOOo

Chapter 2

30 Author's interview with Rakesh Deokaran, 16 January 2025.

31 Interview with Thiara Deokaran, 22 September 2022.

32 Author's interview with Rakesh Deokaran, 16 January 2025.

33 Ibid.

34 Ibid.

35 Ibid.

36 Giokos, H. 28 August 2022. 'Crime in SA | Six men charged with Deokaran killing'. eNCA. https://www.youtube.com/watch?v=ejm4E4m0pXA

37 Ibid.

38 Interview with Thiara Deokaran, 22 September 2023.

39 Ibid.

40 Ibid.

41 Ibid.

42 Ibid.

Chapter 3

43 Author's interview with Karishma Mangali, 24 August 2024.

44 Ibid.

45 Ibid.

46 Author's interview with Renu Williams, 12 January 2025.

47 SA History Online. 'List of employers to whom Indentured Indians were assigned'. Accessed 20 January 2025.

48 Tongaat Hulett. 'Our business'. Accessed 20 January 2025. https://www.tongaat.com/our-business/sugar/south-africa/

49 Author's interview with Renu Williams, 12 January 2025.

50 Ibid.

51 Ibid.

52 Author's interview with Tony Haripersadh, 17 January 2025.

53 Ibid.

54 Author's interview with Renu Williams, 12 January 2025.

55 Ibid.

56 Ibid.

Chapter 4

57 Author's interview with Karishma Mangali, 24 August 2024.

58 Forensic image of Babita Deokaran's cellphone.

59 Ibid.

60 Ibid.
61 Ibid.
62 Confidential source documents.
63 Author's interview with Rakesh Deokaran, 16 January 2025.
64 Ibid.
65 Ibid.
66 Ibid.
67 Postmortem report, Babita Deokaran. 24 August 2021.
68 Ibid.
69 Ibid.
70 Ibid.
71 Author's interview with Renu Williams, 12 January 2025.
72 Forensic image of Babita Deokaran's cellphone.
73 Ibid.
74 Ibid.
75 Ibid.
76 Ibid.
77 Ibid.

PART 2

Chapter 5

78 Author's interview with Captain (retired) Freddie Hicks, 28 August 2024.
79 Ibid.
80 Ibid.
81 Ibid.
82 Ibid.
83 Ibid.
84 Ibid.
85 Ibid.
86 Ibid.
87 Ibid.
88 Ibid.
89 Confidential source documents.
90 Ibid.
91 Author's interview with Captain (retired) Freddie Hicks, 28 August 2024.
92 Ibid.
93 Ibid.
94 Ibid.
95 Ibid.
96 Ibid.
97 Ibid.

Chapter 6

98 Author's interview with Captain (retired) Freddie Hicks, 28 August 2024.
99 Ibid.

100 Ibid.
101 Ibid.
102 Ibid.
103 Ibid.
104 Ibid.
105 Ibid.
106 Ibid.
107 Ibid.
108 Ibid.
109 Ibid.
110 Ibid.
111 Ibid.
112 Ibid.
113 Ibid.
114 Ibid.
115 Ibid.
116 Bhengu, L. 2 September 2021. 'Babita Deokaran murder: 2 more people, found in possession of large sums of cash, arrested'. News24. https://www.news24.com/news24/babita-deokaran-murder-two-more-arrested-caught-in-possession-of-large-sums-of-cash-20210902
117 Ibid.

Chapter 7

118 Author's interview with Captain (retired) Freddie Hicks, 28 August 2024.
119 Phakamani Hadebe confession. 27 August 2021.
120 Ibid.
121 Ibid.
122 Phakamani Hadebe bail affidavit. 21 September 2021.
123 Ibid.
124 Ibid.
125 Ibid.
126 Phakamani Hadebe confession. 27 August 2021.
127 Phakamani Hadebe bail affidavit. 21 September 2021.
128 Knoetze, D. 3 October 2021. 'Watch: "Tubing" – the apartheid torture method still being used by SAPS today'. Carte Blanche/ViewFinder. https://viewfinder.org.za/watch-tubing-the-apartheid-torture-method-still-being-used-by-saps-today/
129 Wicks, J. 3 September 2021. 'Babita Deokaran: Cops looking at "senior ANC figure" as possible assassination mastermind'. News24. https://www.news24.com/news24/investigations/babita-deokaran-cops-looking-at-senior-anc-figure-as-possible-assassination-mastermind-20210903
130 Phakamani Hadebe confession. 27 August 2021.
131 Cruywagen, V. 3 November 2021. 'Babita Deokaran murder: Zweli Mkhize not off the hook despite murder accused's U-turn'. Daily Maverick. https://www.dailymaverick.co.za/article/2021-11-03-babita-deokaran-murder-zweli-mkhize-not-off-the-hook-despite-murder-accuseds-u-turn/
132 Phakamani Hadebe bail affidavit. 21 September 2021.
133 Ibid.
134 Captain Masenxani Chauke bail affidavit. 4 October 2021.
135 Ibid.

Chapter 8

136 Cruywagen, V. 20 December 2021. 'No bail for Deokaran's alleged killers'. Daily Maverick. https://www.dailymaverick.co.za/article/2021-12-20-no-bail-for-deokarans-alleged-killers/

137 Wicks, J. 3 September 2021. 'Babita Deokaran: Cops looking at "senior ANC figure" as possible assassination mastermind'. News24. https://www.news24.com/news24/investigations/babita-deokaran-cops-looking-at-senior-anc-figure-as-possible-assassination-mastermind-20210903

138 Ntuli, N. 29 July 2019. '"Always raining bullets": Weenen fighting takes its toll, jeopardises 700 citrus jobs'. The Witness. https://www.kwanalu.co.za/always-raining-bullets-weenen-fighting-takes-its-toll-jeopardises-700-citrus-jobs/

139 Wicks, J. 18 December 2021. 'Babita Deokaran "killer" still a government employee after 120 days in a cell'. News24. https://www.news24.com/news24/investigations/babita-deokaran-killer-still-a-government-employee-after-120-days-in-a-cell-20211218

Chapter 9

140 Ibid.

141 Matlala, G. 13 September 2021. 'Slain whistleblower Deokaran's chilling message to colleague days before hit'. Sunday World. https://sundayworld.co.za/politics/slain-whistleblower-deokarans-chilling-message-to-colleague-days-before-hit/

142 Ibid.

143 Ibid.

144 Bhengu, L. 27 August 2021. 'There is a relationship – Makhura on link between Babita Deokaran murder and PPE corruption'. News24. https://www.news24.com/news24/there-is-a-relationship-makhura-on-link-between-babita-deokaran-murder-and-ppe-corruption-20210827

Chapter 10

145 'Report on possible fraudulent transactions identified', authored by Babita Deokaran. 4 August 2021.

146 Ibid.

147 Ibid.

148 Ibid.

149 Ibid.

150 Ibid.

Chapter 11

151 Directorate for Priority Crime Investigation. 'Mandate, mission, vision'. Accessed 12 January 2025. https://www.saps.gov.za/dpci/vision_mission_mandate.php

152 Dlamini, K. 10 October 2018. 'Scorpions' downfall due to political interference'. Corruption Watch. https://www.corruptionwatch.org.za/political-interference-in-south-africas-elite-anti-corruption-unit-leads-to-impunity/

153 Directorate for Priority Crime Investigation. 'Mandate, mission, vision'. Accessed 12 January 2025. https://www.saps.gov.za/dpci/vision_mission_mandate.php

154 Dlamini, K. 10 October 2018. 'Scorpions' downfall due to political interference'. Corruption Watch. https://www.corruptionwatch.org.za/political-interference-in-south-africas-elite-anti-corruption-unit-leads-to-impunity/

155 Ibid.

156 Mitchley, A. 29 November 2022. 'Hawks appoint new deputy chief, but 48% of posts still remain unfilled'. News24. https://www.news24.com/news24/southafrica/news/hawks-appoint-new-deputy-chief-but-48-of-posts-still-remain-unfilled-20221129

157 Directorate for Priority Crime Investigation. 'Mandate, mission, vision'. Accessed 12 January 2025. https://www.saps.gov.za/dpci/vision_mission_mandate.php

158 Ibid.

159 Ibid.

160 Ibid.

PART 3

Chapter 12

161 'Report on possible fraudulent transactions identified', authored by Babita Deokaran. 4 August 2021.

162 Forensic image of Babita Deokaran's cellphone.

163 Ibid.

164 Ibid.

165 Ibid.

166 E-mail database, Babita Deokaran.

167 Ibid.

168 Forensic image of Babita Deokaran's cellphone.

169 Ibid.

170 Email database, Babita Deokaran.

171 Ibid.

172 News24 Investigations. 1 August 2022. 'Silenced | No investigation, no protection: Inside department head's big lie to Babita Deokaran'. News24. https://www.news24.com/news24/investigations/silenced-no-investigation-no-protection-inside-department-heads-big-lie-to-babita-deokaran-20220801

173 'Report on possible fraudulent transactions identified', authored by Babita Deokaran. 4 August 2021.

Chapter 13

174 Press statement. 5 March 2020. 'First case of Covid-19 coronavirus reported in SA'. National Institute of Communicable Diseases.

175 Eyewitness News. 23 March 2020. 'President Ramaphosa: South Africa in 21-day lockdown'. YouTube. https://www.youtube.com/watch?v=LegaUR1A0Jg

176 Ibid.

177 Ibid.

178 Tooley, R. & Mohoai, K. 1 August 2007. 'The impact of corruption on service delivery in South Africa'. Journal of Public Administration. https://journals.co.za/doi/abs/10.10520/EJC51507

179 Eyewitness News. 23 March 2020. 'President Ramaphosa: South Africa in 21-day lockdown'. YouTube. https://www.youtube.com/watch?v=LegaUR1A0Jg

180 Khumalo, J. 2 February 2019. 'Ramaphosa backtracks on "nine wasted years" under Zuma'. City Press. https://www.news24.com/citypress/news/ramaphosa-backtracks-on-nine-wasted-years-under-zuma-20190202

181 BusinessTech. 19 March 2020. 'Massive border fence between South Africa and Zimbabwe to combat coronavirus spread'. https://businesstech.co.za/news/government/383143/massive-border-fence-between-south-africa-and-zimbabwe-to-combat-coronavirus-spread/

182 Hosken, G. 26 April 2020. 'SA's R37m Covid fence "joke"'. Sunday Times. https://www.timeslive.co.za/sunday-times/news/2020-04-26-sas-r37m-covid-fence-joke/

183 Parliamentary Monitoring Group. 25 August 2020. 'Beitbridge border fence findings; with Minister, SIU, Treasury'. Public Accounts Committee. https://pmg.org.za/committee-meeting/30925/

184 Heywood, M. 20 September 2021. 'La Vie en Rose: A single Mpumalanga company robbed SAPS of hundreds of millions in Covid-19 PPE tender'. Daily Maverick. https://www.dailymaverick.co.za/article/2021-09-20-la-vie-en-rose-a-single-mpumalanga-company-robbed-saps-of-hundreds-of-millions-in-covid-19-ppe-tender/

185 Mashego, A. 21 September 2020. 'Businessman's R11m luxury cars boast sparks Hawks' interest'. City Press. https://www.news24.com/citypress/news/businessmans-r11m-luxury-cars-boast-sparks-hawks-interest-20200920-2

186 Mabuza, E. 6 November 2024. 'Hamilton Ndlovu found in contempt of Special Tribunal forfeiture order'. TimesLIVE. https://www.timeslive.co.za/news/south-africa/2024-11-06-hamilton-ndlovu-found-in-contempt-of-special-tribunal-forfeiture-order/

187 Nonyane, M. 14 November 2024. 'Hamilton Ndlovu faces jail time for contempt after failing to surrender R3 million in assets'. City Press. https://www.news24.com/citypress/news/hamilton-ndlovu-faces-jail-time-for-contempt-after-failing-to-surrender-r3-million-in-assets-20241114

188 Press Statement. 1 August 2020. 'President Ramaphosa must immediately account in Parliament for the ANC's Covid feeding frenzy'. Democratic Alliance. https://www.da.org.za/2020/08/president-ramaphosa-must-immediately-account-in-parliament-for-the-ancs-covid-feeding-frenzy

189 Pijoos, I. 27 January 2022. 'Covid-19 corruption: Nomvula Mokonyane implicated in irregularities over R2.7 million soap tender'. News24. https://www.news24.com/news24/southafrica/news/covid-19-corruption-nomvula-mokonyane-implicated-in-irregularities-over-r27-million-soap-tender-20220127

190 Manyane, M. 13 December 2020. 'SIU guns for dodgy PPE tenders'. IOL. https://www.iol.co.za/sundayindependent/news/siu-guns-for-dodgy-ppe-tenders-40b052d8-0dec-4dc6-a830-76e20133426f

191 Rampedi, P. 26 July 2020. 'Under the spotlight: The MEC's wife, Diko and a R125m PPE contract'. IOL. https://www.iol.co.za/sundayindependent/news/under-the-spotlight-the-mecs-wife-diko-and-a-r125m-ppe-contract-06eb0951-4b22-402e-9110-cdd247e29102

192 Madia, T. 30 July 2020. 'Rush to obtain PPE resulted in "abuse" of procurement systems, Makhura concedes'. News24. https://www.news24.com/news24/rush-to-obtain-ppe-resulted-in-abuse-of-procurement-systems-makhura-concedes-20200730

193 Ibid.

194 Section27. Life Esidimeni. Accessed 24 January 2025. https://section27.org.za/campaigns/life-esidimeni/

195 Ibid.

196 Wicks, B. 8 October 2024. 'Gauteng health's R1.2bn scandal: Ex-MEC Hlongwa's alleged corruptor a step closer to extradition'. News24. https://www.news24.com/news24/southafrica/news/gauteng-healths-r12bn-scandal-ex-mec-hlongwas-alleged-corruptor-a-step-closer-to-extradition-20241008

197 Author's interview with Renu Williams, 12 January 2025.

198 Author's interview with Reola Haripersadh, 23 August 2024.

199 Author's interview with Renu Williams, 12 January 2025.

200 Ibid.

201 Ibid.

202 Ibid.

203 Author's interview with Neeshan Balton, 8 September 2021.

204 Ibid.

205 Ibid.

206 Ibid.

207 Ibid.

Chapter 14

208 Makgoba, MW. 27 January 2021. 'The report into the circumstances surrounding the care and death of Mr Shonisani Lethole at Tembisa Provincial Tertiary Hospital'. Office of the Health Ombud. https://healthombud.org.za/wp-content/uploads/2021/01/Final-Report-into-the-Circumstances-Surrounding-the-Death-and-Care-of-Mr-Lethole-at-Tembisa-Hospital-18-January-2021-MONDAY-VERSION-3-FOR-PRINTING.pdf

209 National Institute for Communicable Diseases. 'Latest confirmed cases of Covid-19 in South Africa – 23 June 2020'. Accessed 6 January 2025.

210 BusinessTech. 1 July 2020. 'Gauteng has hit a critical coronavirus milestone – these are the hotspot areas'. https://businesstech.co.za/news/trending/412557/gauteng-has-hit-a-critical-coronavirus-milestone-these-are-the-hotspot-areas/

211 Statistics South Africa. 30 July 2024. 'Mid-year population estimates, 2024'. https://www.statssa.gov.za/?page_id=1854&PPN=P0302&SCH=73952

212 Mitchley, M. 2 July 2020. '"Gauteng health facilities have reached maximum bed capacity" – department'. News24. https://www.news24.com/News24/gauteng-health-facilities-have-reached-maximum-bed-capacity-department-20200702

213 Ibid.

214 National Health Act, 2003. 2 March 2012. 'Regulations relating to the categories of hospitals'. Accessed 12 December 2024.

215 Makgoba, MW. 27 January 2021. 'The report into the circumstances surrounding the care and death of Mr Shonisani Lethole at Tembisa Provincial Tertiary Hospital'. Office of the Health Ombud. https://healthombud.org.za/wp-content/uploads/2021/01/Final-Report-into-the-Circumstances-Surrounding-the-Death-and-Care-of-Mr-Lethole-at-Tembisa-Hospital-18-January-2021-MONDAY-VERSION-3-FOR-PRINTING.pdf

216 Mitchley, M. 2 July 2020. '"Gauteng health facilities have reached maximum bed capacity" – department'. News24. https://www.news24.com/News24/gauteng-health-facilities-have-reached-maximum-bed-capacity-department-20200702

217 Makgoba, MW. 27 January 2021. 'The report into the circumstances surrounding the care and death of Mr Shonisani Lethole at Tembisa Provincial Tertiary Hospital'. Office of the Health Ombud. https://healthombud.org.za/wp-content/uploads/2021/01/Final-Report-into-the-Circumstances-Surrounding-the-Death-and-Care-of-Mr-Lethole-at-Tembisa-Hospital-18-January-2021-MONDAY-VERSION-3-FOR-PRINTING.pdf

218 Ibid.

219 Ibid.

220 Ibid.

221 Ibid.

222 Ibid.

223 Ibid.

224 Ibid.

225 Ibid.

226 Ibid.

227 Ibid.

228 Ibid.

229 Ibid.

230 Ibid.

231 Ibid.

232 National Planning Commission – Commissioner profile. 'Professor Malegapuru William Makgoba'. Accessed 22 January 2025.

233 Makgoba, MW. 27 January 2021. 'The report into the circumstances surrounding the care and death of Mr Shonisani Lethole at Tembisa Provincial Tertiary Hospital'. Office of the Health Ombud. https://healthombud.org.za/wp-content/uploads/2021/01/Final-Report-into-the-Circumstances-Surrounding-the-Death-and-Care-of-Mr-Lethole-at-Tembisa-Hospital-18-January-2021-MONDAY-VERSION-3-FOR-PRINTING.pdf

234 Author's interview with Professor Malegapuru Makgoba, 25 July 2024.

235 Ibid.

236 Ibid.

237 Ibid.

238 Ibid.

239 Author's interview with the Lethole family, 4 August 2024.

240 Ibid.

241 Ibid.

242 Ibid.

243 Ibid.

244 Pijoos, I. 31 January 2021. 'Tembisa Hospital CEO suspended over death of Shonisani Lethole'. SowetanLIVE. https://www.sowetanlive.co.za/news/south-africa/2021-01-31-tembisa-hospital-ceo-suspended-over-death-of-shonisani-lethole/

245 Mahlangu, I. 22 April 2021.

246 Broughton, T. 15 December 2022. 'Tembisa Hospital CEO and senior officials must face disciplinary action over gross negligence, tribunal rules'. GroundUp. https://www.dailymaverick.co.za/article/2022-12-15-tembisa-hospital-ceo-and-senior-officials-must-face-disciplinary-action-over-gross-negligence-tribunal-rules/

247 Author's interview with Lekopane Mogaladi, 24 January 2025.

Chapter 15

248 'Report on possible fraudulent transactions identified', authored by Babita Deokaran. 4 August 2021.

249 Ibid.

250 Ibid.

251 Maughan, K. 11 November 2024. Book extract. '*I Will Not Be Silenced* – Inside Zuma's online harassment campaign to keep journalist Karyn Maughan quiet'. Daily Maverick. https://www.dailymaverick.co.za/article/2024-11-11-zuma-and-supporters-harassment-campaign-to-keep-karyn-maughan-quiet/

252 Posetti, J. & Reid, J. 22 May 2024. ' "Sexualised, Silenced and Labelled Satan" – horrific levels of online violence targeting women journalists'. Daily Maverick. https://www.dailymaverick.co.za/article/2024-05-22-sexualised-silenced-and-labelled-satan-horrific-levels-of-online-violence-targeting-women-journalists/

253 Du Toit, P. 8 March 2021. 'Rogue Crime Intelligence cops "bug" News24 investigative journalist'. News24. https://www.news24.com/news24/investigations/breaking-rogue-crime-intelligence-cops-bug-news24-investigative-journalist-20210308

Chapter 16

254 'Report on possible fraudulent transactions identified', authored by Babita Deokaran. 4 August 2021.

255 Forensic image of Babita Deokaran's cellphone.

256 Ibid.

257 Timse, T. 18 May 2021. 'Questions raised over beneficiaries of City of Ekurhuleni's aid programme for the poor'. amaBhungane Centre for Investigative Journalism. https://www.dailymaverick.co.za/article/2021-05-18-questions-raised-over-beneficiaries-of-city-of-ekurhulenis-aid-programme-for-the-poor/

258 Ibid.

259 Ibid.

260 Author's interview with Sello Philly Sekhokho. 19 July 2022.

261 Ibid.

262 Ibid.

263 Ibid.

264 Ibid.

265 Email database, Babita Deokaran.

266 Ibid.

267 Author's interview with Sello Philly Sekhokho. 19 July 2022.

268 Ibid.

269 Ibid.

270 Ibid.

271 Ibid.

272 Ibid.

273 News24 Investigations. 6 September 2022. 'Silenced | Inside ANC bigwig's R15m Tembisa Hospital payday'. News24. https://www.news24.com/news24/investigations/silenced-inside-anc-bigwigs-r15m-tembisa-hospital-payday-20220906-2

274 News24 Investigations. 30 November 2022. 'Silenced | From boerewors to bandages: Inside ANC leader's R100 million health tender jackpot'. News24. https://www.news24.com/news24/investigations/silenced-from-boerewors-to-bandages-inside-anc-leaders-r100-million-health-tender-jackpot-20221130

275 Ibid.

Chapter 17

276 Minzorex company profile. Companies and Intellectual Property Commission. Accessed 12 May 2022.

277 'Report on possible fraudulent transactions identified', authored by Babita Deokaran. 4 August 2021.

278 Minzorex company profile. Companies and Intellectual Property Commission. Accessed 12 May 2022.

279 'Report on possible fraudulent transactions identified', authored by Babita Deokaran. 4 August 2021.

280 Payment commitment GPDOH 2017 – 2021.xls. Email database, Babita Deokaran. Accessed 12 May 2022.

281 Ibid.

282 Ibid.

283 Ibid.

284 Ibid.

285 Ibid.

286 News24 Investigations. 5 September 2022. 'Silenced | Tembisa Hospital splurge exposed: Leather loungers, skinny jeans and R10 000 for a bucket'. https://www.news24.com/news24/investigations/silenced-tembisa-hospital-splurge-exposed-leather-loungers-skinny-jeans-and-r10-000-for-a-bucket-20220905-2

287 Ibid.

288 Ibid.

289 Ibid.

290 Ibid.

291 Dr Ashley Mthunzi. LinkedIn profile. https://za.linkedin.com/in/ashley-mthunzi-6218815b

292 News24 Investigations. 5 September 2022. 'Silenced | Tembisa Hospital splurge exposed: Leather loungers, skinny jeans and R10 000 for a bucket'. https://www.news24.com/news24/investigations/silenced-tembisa-hospital-splurge-exposed-leather-loungers-skinny-jeans-and-r10-000-for-a-bucket-20220905-2

293 News24 Investigations. 25 July 2022. 'Silenced | "Our lives could be in danger": Inside Babita Deokaran's R850m "fraud" probe'. News24. https://www.news24.com/news24/investigations/silenced-our-lives-could-be-in-danger-inside-babita-deokarans-r850m-fraud-probe-20220725

294 News24 Investigations. 27 July 2022. 'Silenced | Babita Deokaran tried to stop "secret" Tembisa Hospital payments to ANC leader'. News24. https://www.news24.com/news24/investigations/silenced-babita-deokaran-tried-to-stop-secret-tembisa-hospital-payments-to-anc-leader-20220727-2

295 News24 Investigations. 1 August 2022. 'Silenced | No investigation, no protection: Inside department head's big lie to Babita Deokaran'. News24. https://www.news24.com/news24/investigations/silenced-no-investigation-no-protection-inside-department-heads-big-lie-to-babita-deokaran-20220801

296 News24 Investigations. 5 September 2022. 'Silenced | Tembisa Hospital splurge exposed: Leather
loungers, skinny jeans and R10 000 for a bucket'. https://www.news24.com/news24/investigations/
silenced-tembisa-hospital-splurge-exposed-leather-loungers-skinny-jeans-and-r10-000-for-a-
bucket-20220905-2

Chapter 18

297 Internal communiqué, Gauteng Department of Health. 15 July 2022.

298 Ibid.

299 Ibid.

300 News24 Investigations. 5 August 2022. 'Silenced | Tembisa Hospital contract factory: R500k on leather
loungers and letterbox barons unmasked'. News24. https://www.news24.com/news24/investigations/
silenced-tembisa-hospital-contract-factory-r500k-on-leather-loungers-and-letterbox-barons-
unmasked-20220805

301 Ibid.

302 Ibid.

303 News24 Investigations. 23 August 2022. 'Silenced | Tembisa Hospital's R500 000 skinny jean
spending spree . . . and the soccer star who scored'. News24. https://www.news24.com/news24/
investigations/silenced-tembisa-hospitals-r500-000-skinny-jean-spending-spree-and-the-soccer-star-who-
scored-20220823

304 News24 Investigations. 5 August 2022. 'Silenced | Tembisa Hospital contract factory: R500k on leather
loungers and letterbox barons unmasked'. News24. https://www.news24.com/news24/investigations/
silenced-tembisa-hospital-contract-factory-r500k-on-leather-loungers-and-letterbox-barons-
unmasked-20220805

305 Ibid.

306 Ibid.

307 Pheto, B. 12 April 2022. 'Tembisa Hospital CEO lays bare to MPs challenges facing the hospital'.
TimesLIVE. https://www.timeslive.co.za/news/south-africa/2022-04-21-tembisa-hospital-ceo-lays-bare-
to-mps-challenges-facing-the-hospital/

308 News24 Investigations. 15 August 2022. 'Silenced | Love me tender: How husband and wife bagged
R30m in Tembisa Hospital contracts'. News24. https://www.news24.com/news24/investigations/
silenced-love-me-tender-how-husband-and-wife-bagged-r30m-in-tembisa-hospital-contracts-20220815

309 Ibid.

310 Ibid.

Chapter 19

311 De Villiers, J. 26 March 2022. 'Saturday Profile | Kathrada Foundation's Neeshan Balton blames govt for
continuing apartheid legacies'. News24. https://www.news24.com/news24/opinions/analysis/saturday-
profile-kathrada-foundations-neeshan-balton-blames-govt-for-continuing-apartheid-legacies-20220326

312 Press statement, Jack Bloom. 4 August 2022. Democratic Alliance. http://politicsweb.co.za/politics/
gauteng-health-cfo-psc-investigation-requested--ja

313 Ibid.

314 Ncwane, N. 16 August 2022. 'Forensic investigator to be appointed in Babita Deokaran case'. The
South African. https://www.thesouthafrican.com/gauteng/babita-deokaran-murder-case-investigation-
forensic-investigator-latest/

315 Madia, T. 30 July 2020. 'Rush to obtain PPE resulted in "abuse" of procurement systems, Makhura
concedes'. News24. https://www.news24.com/news24/rush-to-obtain-ppe-resulted-in-abuse-of-
procurement-systems-makhura-concedes-20200730

316 News24 Investigations. 23 August 2022. 'Silenced | Tembisa Hospital's R500 000 skinny jean
spending spree . . . and the soccer star who scored'. News24. https://www.news24.com/news24/
investigations/silenced-tembisa-hospitals-r500-000-skinny-jean-spending-spree-and-the-soccer-star-who-
scored-20220823

317 Ibid.

318 Ibid.

319 Podcast – The Clement Manyathela Show. 25 August 2022. https://omny.fm/shows/mid-morning-show-702/tembisa-hospital-s-r500-000-skinny-jeans-contract

320 Ibid.

321 Ibid.

322 Ibid.

Chapter 20

323 Seleka, N. 4 June 2022. '"We know where you drive": Presidency DG receives death threats and a bullet at her home'. News24. https://www.news24.com/news24/southafrica/news/we-know-where-you-drive-presidential-dg-receives-death-threats-and-a-bullet-at-her-home-20220604

324 Ibid.

325 Moagi, C. 23 April 2022. 'Thabo Masebe laid to rest!'. Daily Sun. https://www.snl24.com/dailysun/news/thabo-masebe-laid-to-rest-20220423

326 Khumalo, J. 18 May 2022. 'Former Johannesburg Mayor Mpho Moerane has died – family.' News24. https://www.news24.com/news24/southafrica/news/just-in-former-johannesburg-mayor-mpho-moerane-has-died-his-family-says-20220518

327 News24 Investigations. 26 August 2022. 'Update | Babita Deokaran: Tembisa Hospital CEO, health dept CFO suspended amid R850m scandal'. News24. https://www.news24.com/news24/investigations/babita-deokaran-gauteng-health-boss-lerato-madyo-suspended-amid-r850m-tembisa-hospital-scandal-20220826

328 Ibid.

329 Ibid.

330 Author's interview with Dr Nomonde Nolutshungu, 16 January 2025.

331 Pheto, B. 25 April 2022. 'David Makhura appoints Dr Nomonde Nolutshungu head of health in Gauteng'. SowetanLIVE. https://www.sowetanlive.co.za/news/2022-04-25-david-makhura-appoints-dr-nomonde-nolutshungu-head-of-health-in-gauteng/

332 Author's interview with Dr Nomonde Nolutshungu, 16 January 2025.

333 Ibid.

334 Ibid.

335 Ibid.

Chapter 21

336 'Report on possible fraudulent transactions identified', authored by Babita Deokaran. 4 August 2021.

337 Director report: Stefan Joel Govindraju. Companies and Intellectual Property Commission.

338 Govindraju, SJ. 1 June 2017. 'Synthesis and characterisation of hybrid nanocomposites using polyvinylcarbazole and metal selenides to demonstrate photovoltaic properties'. Faculty of Science, University of the Witwatersrand. https://wiredspace.wits.ac.za/items/eefb4628-8dc6-478a-a6a5-53949b0b7a9e

339 News24 Investigations. 7 November 2022. 'How Tembisa Hospital's R500k skinny jeans supplier and shell corporation bosses flew the coop'. News24. http://news24.com/news24/investigations/silenced-how-tembisa-hospitals-r500k-skinny-jean-supplier-and-shell-corporation-bosses-flew-the-coop-20221107

340 Ibid.

341 Ibid.

342 Ibid.

343 Ibid.

344 News24 Investigations. 5 December 2022. 'Babita Deokaran flagged network of lovers, friends and co-workers "fleecing" public purse'. News24. https://www.news24.com/news24/investigations/silenced-babita-deokaran-flagged-network-of-lovers-friends-and-co-workers-fleecing-public-purse-20221205

345 Ibid.

Chapter 22

346 News24 Investigations. 19 September 2022. '"Don of Tembisa" received millions in payments, bought Bantry Bay and Sandton mansions'. News24. https://www.news24.com/news24/investigations/silenced-don-of-tembisa-received-millions-in-payments-bought-bantry-bay-and-sandton-mansions-20220919

347 Director report: Hangwani Morgan Maumela. Companies and Intellectual Property Commission.

348 Director report: Aluwani Maumela. Companies and Intellectual Property Commission.

349 'Report on possible fraudulent transactions identified', authored by Babita Deokaran. 4 August 2021.

350 Email database, Babita Deokaran.

351 News24 Investigations. 19 September 2022. '"Don of Tembisa" received millions in payments, bought Bantry Bay and Sandton mansions'. News24. https://www.news24.com/news24/investigations/silenced-don-of-tembisa-received-millions-in-payments-bought-bantry-bay-and-sandton-mansions-20220919

352 Ibid.

353 Ibid.

354 Ibid.

355 Ibid.

356 Ibid.

357 Ibid.

358 Ibid.

359 Ibid.

360 Ibid.

361 Ibid.

362 Ibid.

363 Ibid.

Chapter 23

364 Top Billing. 20 May 2019. 'Top Billing visits beautiful Hyde Park home'. YouTube. https://youtu.be/GvJyfhrn9vc

365 Ibid.

366 News24 Investigations. 17 October 2022. 'The Tembisa tender "don" and his ties to Ramaphosa's family, key advisor'. News24. https://www.news24.com/news24/investigations/silenced-the-tembisa-tender-don-and-his-cosy-ties-to-ramaphosa-and-key-advisor-20221017

367 Top Billing. 20 May 2019. 'Top Billing visits beautiful Hyde Park home'. YouTube. https://youtu.be/GvJyfhrn9vc

368 News24 Investigations. 17 October 2022. 'The Tembisa tender "don" and his ties to Ramaphosa's family, key advisor'. News24. https://www.news24.com/news24/investigations/silenced-the-tembisa-tender-don-and-his-cosy-ties-to-ramaphosa-and-key-advisor-20221017

369 News24 Investigations. 19 September 2022. '"Don of Tembisa" received millions in payments, bought Bantry Bay and Sandton mansions'. News24. https://www.news24.com/news24/investigations/silenced-don-of-tembisa-received-millions-in-payments-bought-bantry-bay-and-sandton-mansions-20220919

370 News24 Investigations. 28 November 2022. 'Mother of Tembisa tender "don" scores R30m Sea Point property as tenderpreneur network expands'. News24. https://www.news24.com/news24/investigations/silenced-mother-of-tembisa-tender-don-scores-r30m-sea-point-property-as-tenderpreneur-network-expands-20221128

371 Ibid.

372 News24 Investigations. 17 October 2022. 'The Tembisa tender "don" and his ties to Ramaphosa's family, key advisor'. News24. https://www.news24.com/news24/investigations/silenced-the-tembisa-tender-don-and-his-cosy-ties-to-ramaphosa-and-key-advisor-20221017

373 Ibid.

374 Ibid.

375 Ibid.

376 Ibid.

377 Ibid.

378 Ibid.

379 Ibid.

380 News24 Investigations. 3 October 2020. 'Inside asbestos audit kingpin Edwin Sodi's R85 million mansion – paid for by taxpayers'. News24. https://www.news24.com/news24/investigations/pics-inside-asbestos-audit-kingpin-edwin-sodis-r85-million-mansion-paid-for-by-taxpayers-20201003

381 Ibid.

382 Masondo, S. Karrim, A. & Cowan, K. 25 January 2024. 'Mashatile unmasked | Edwin Sodi paid almost R1bn while donating money to deputy president, ANC'. News24. https://www.news24.com/news24/investigations/mashatileunmasked/mashatile-unmasked-i-edwin-sodi-paid-almost-r1bn-while-donating-money-to-deputy-president-anc-20240125

383 Wicks, J. 24 July 2023. 'Tembisa tender "don's" luxury properties flash sale and the realtors who kept it "secret"'. News24. https://www.news24.com/news24/investigations/silenced-tembisa-tender-dons-luxury-properties-flash-sale-and-the-realtors-who-kept-it-secret-20230724

Chapter 24

384 Section27. Life Esidimeni. Accessed 24 January 2025. https://section27.org.za/campaigns/life-esidimeni/

385 Makgoba, MW. 27 January 2021. 'The report into the circumstances surrounding the care and death of Mr Shonisani Lethole at Tembisa Provincial Tertiary Hospital'. Office of the Health Ombud. https://healthombud.org.za/wp-content/uploads/2021/01/Final-Report-into-the-Circumstances-Surrounding-the-Death-and-Care-of-Mr-Lethole-at-Tembisa-Hospital-18-January-2021-MONDAY-VERSION-3-FOR-PRINTING.pdf

386 Nicolson, G. 9 October 2020. 'Fired MEC Bandile Masuku slams SIU report'. Daily Maverick. https://www.dailymaverick.co.za/article/2020-10-09-fired-mec-bandile-masuku-slams-siu-report/

387 Njilo, N. 5 October 2022. 'Panyaza Lesufi primed for Gauteng premier as David Makhura steps down'. Daily Maverick. https://www.dailymaverick.co.za/article/2022-10-05-scandal-plagued-panyaza-lesufi-primed-for-gauteng-premier-as-david-makhura-steps-down/

388 McGluwa, J. Parliamentary question 36/1/4/1(202200414). The National Assembly.

389 Ibid.

390 Ibid.

391 Final forensic report. November 2022. 'The Office of the Premier/SIU Secondment.Gauteng Health and Tembisa Hospital'. Special Investigating Unit.

392 Ibid.

393 Ibid.

394 Ibid.

395 Ibid.

396 Ibid.

397 Wicks, J. 29 May 2023. 'The big score: Tembisa tender kings "inflated" prices for embattled hospital by up to 2 000%'. News24. https://www.news24.com/news24/investigations/silenced-the-big-score-tembisa-tender-kings-inflated-prices-for-embattled-hospital-by-up-to-2-000-20230529-2

398 Sithole, S. 30 August 2022. 'Tembisa Hospital trade unions call on Makhura to reconsider CEO suspension'. IOL. https://www.iol.co.za/the-star/news/tembisa-hospital-trade-unions-call-on-makhura-to-reconsider-ceo-suspension-fb39a7bb-e497-4825-b716-7944b4b64e87

399 Ibid.

400 Ndlangamandla, M. 22 September 2022. '"Hijacked" nurses' union sides with embattled Tembisa Hospital boss'. amaBhungane Centre for Investigative Journalism. https://www.news24.com/news24/southafrica/news/hijacked-nurses-union-sides-with-embattled-tembisa-hospital-boss-20220923

401 News24 Investigations. 7 October 2022. 'Inside the "confidential" Tembisa Hospital audit which was buried after Deokaran hit'. News24. https://www.news24.com/news24/investigations/silenced-inside-the-confidential-tembisa-hospital-audit-which-was-buried-after-deokaran-hit-20221007-2

402 Ibid.

403 Ibid.

404 Ibid.

405 Ibid.

406 Final forensic report. November 2022. 'The Office of the Premier/SIU Secondment.Gauteng Health and Tembisa Hospital'. Special Investigating Unit.

407 Ibid.

408 Ibid.

Chapter 25

409 Final forensic report. November 2022. 'The Office of the Premier/SIU Secondment.Gauteng Health and Tembisa Hospital'. Special Investigating Unit.

410 Wicks, J. 29 May 2023. 'The big score: Tembisa tender kings "inflated" prices for embattled hospital by up to 2 000%'. News24. https://www.news24.com/news24/investigations/silenced-the-big-score-tembisa-tender-kings-inflated-prices-for-embattled-hospital-by-up-to-2-000-20230529-2

411 Podcast – The Clement Manyathela Show. 25 August 2022. https://omny.fm/shows/mid-morning-show-702/tembisa-hospital-s-r500-000-skinny-jeans-contract

412 Ndlangamandla, M. 22 September 2022. '"Hijacked" nurses' union sides with embattled Tembisa Hospital boss'. amaBhungane Centre for Investigative Journalism. https://www.news24.com/news24/southafrica/news/hijacked-nurses-union-sides-with-embattled-tembisa-hospital-boss-20220923

413 News24 Investigations. 17 August 2022. 'Babita Deokaran: Under fire Tembisa hospital boss calls on ANC connections over News24 investigation'. News24. https://www.news24.com/news24/investigations/babita-deokaran-can-you-meet-under-fire-tembisa-hospital-boss-calls-on-anc-connections-because-he-is-struggling-with-news24-20220817-2

414 Ibid.

415 Ibid.

416 Ibid.

417 Ibid.

418 Ibid.

419 Ibid.

420 Ibid.

421 Ibid.

422 Ibid.

423 Ibid.

Chapter 26

424 Hopkins, R. 29 January 2015. 'Fear, force and sex in Sun City'. Mail & Guardian. https://mg.co.za/article/2015-01-29-fear-force-and-sex-in-sun-city/

425 Ibid.

426 Plea and sentencing agreement in terms of section 105A (1) of the Criminal Procedure Act, 51 of 1977. 22 August 2023.

427 Ibid.

428 Pheto, B. Ismail, A. & Wicks, J. 23 August 2023. 'Babita Deokaran: Killers weave tale of stalking and murder while mastermind remains free'. News24. https://www.news24.com/news24/southafrica/news/babita-deokaran-killers-weave-tale-of-stalking-and-murder-while-mastermind-remains-free-20230823

429 Ibid.

430 Ibid.

Chapter 27

431 Plea and sentencing agreement in terms of section 105A (1) of the Criminal Procedure Act, 51 of 1977. 22 August 2023.

432 Ibid.

433 Ibid.

434 Pheto, B. Ismail, A. & Wicks, J. 23 August 2023. 'Babita Deokaran: Killers weave tale of stalking and murder while mastermind remains free'. News24. https://www.news24.com/news24/southafrica/news/babita-deokaran-killers-weave-tale-of-stalking-and-murder-while-mastermind-remains-free-20230823

435 Wicks, J. 30 May 2023. '"Fraud", "forgery" and Tembisa tender kingpin's 300% markup: This is how he did it'. News24. https://www.news24.com/news24/investigations/silenced-fraud-forgery-and-tembisa-tender-kingpins-300-markup-this-is-how-he-did-it-20230530

436 Ibid.

437 Ibid.

438 Ibid.

439 Ibid.

440 Wicks, J. 31 May 2023. '"I know nothing": How a pool cleaner, unemployed guard were used to "cook" Tembisa tenders'. News24. https://www.news24.com/news24/investigations/silenced-i-know-nothing-how-a-pool-cleaner-unemployed-guard-were-used-to-cook-tembisa-tenders-20230531-2

441 Wicks, J. 29 May 2023. 'The big score: Tembisa tender kings "inflated" prices for embattled hospital by up to 2 000%'. News24. https://www.news24.com/news24/investigations/silenced-the-big-score-tembisa-tender-kings-inflated-prices-for-embattled-hospital-by-up-to-2-000-20230529-2

442 Wicks, J. 30 May 2023. '"Fraud", "forgery" and Tembisa tender kingpin's 300% markup: This is how he did it'. News24. https://www.news24.com/news24/investigations/silenced-fraud-forgery-and-tembisa-tender-kingpins-300-markup-this-is-how-he-did-it-20230530

443 Government Gazette. 1 September 2023. '136 of 2023 – Gauteng Department of Health and Tembisa Hospital'. Special Investigating Unit. https://www.siu.org.za/proclamation/136-of-2023-gauteng-department-of-health-and-its-provincial-hospital-in-tembisa/

Chapter 28

444 'Report on possible fraudulent transactions identified', authored by Babita Deokaran. 4 August 2021.

445 News24 Investigations. 6 March 2023. 'Tembisa tender mafia: Syndicates expand and look to other hospital feeding troughs'. News24. https://www.news24.com/news24/investigations/silenced-tembisa-tender-mafia-syndicates-expand-and-look-to-other-hospital-feeding-troughs-20230306

446 Ibid.

447 Ibid.

448 News24 Investigations. 28 November 2022. 'Mother of Tembisa tender "don" scores R30m Sea Point property as tenderpreneur network expands'. News24. https://www.news24.com/news24/investigations/silenced-mother-of-tembisa-tender-don-scores-r30m-sea-point-property-as-tenderpreneur-network-expands-20221128

449 Ibid.

450 Ibid.

Chapter 29

451 About the SIU. https://www.siu.org.za/about-us/

452 Press statement. 2 November 2023. 'Exploring the link between public procurement and innovation in Africa'. National Research Foundation. https://www.nrf.ac.za/exploring-the-link-between-public-procurement-and-innovation-in-africa/

453 Felix, J. 13 November 2024. 'Ramaphosa issued 50% of SIU proclamations since 2001, R1.4bn recovered so far in 2024'. News24. https://www.news24.com/news24/politics/ramaphosa-issued-50-of-siu-proclamations-since-2001-r14bn-recovered-so-far-in-2024-20241113

454 Wicks, J. 11 July 2024. 'SIU boss on death threats, rampant graft, and bent officials milking billions from "broken system"'. News24. https://www.news24.com/news24/investigations/siu-boss-on-death-threats-rampant-graft-and-bent-officials-milking-billions-from-broken-system-20240711

455 Ibid.

456 Ibid.

457 Ibid.

458 Ibid.

459 Ibid.

460 Ibid.

461 Ibid.

462 Ibid.

463 Ibid.

Chapter 30

464 Wicks, J. Pijoos, I. & Maketha, T. 23 December 2024. 'A tender tycoon, his R200 000 Rolex and dark "ties" to a double kidnapping exposed'. News24. https://www.news24.com/news24/southafrica/news/silenced-a-tender-tycoon-his-r200-000-rolex-and-dark-ties-to-a-double-kidnapping-exposed-20241223

465 Lancaster, L. 3 December 2024. 'South Africa's armed robbery problem drives kidnapping'. Institute for Security Studies. https://issafrica.org/iss-today/south-africa-s-armed-robbery-problem-drives-kidnapping

466 Wicks, J. Pijoos, I. & Maketha, T. 23 December 2024. 'A tender tycoon, his R200 000 Rolex and dark "ties" to a double kidnapping exposed'. News24. https://www.news24.com/news24/southafrica/news/silenced-a-tender-tycoon-his-r200-000-rolex-and-dark-ties-to-a-double-kidnapping-exposed-20241223

467 Ibid.

468 CAT VIP Protection – About the company. http://catvipprotection.com/Pages/The-Company.asp?mini-product=2

469 Ibid.

470 News24 Reporter. 14 November 2016. 'Murder convict escapee back in court for impersonating cops'. News24. https://www.news24.com/news24/murder-convict-escapee-back-in-court-for-impersonating-cops-20161114

471 'Report on possible fraudulent transactions identified', authored by Babita Deokaran. 4 August 2021.

472 News24 Investigations. 13 February 2023. 'Tembisa tender tycoon, his "mama cat", and their brazen blue-light brigade'. News24.https://www.news24.com/news24/investigations/silenced-tembisa-tender-tycoon-his-mama-cat-and-their-brazen-blue-light-brigade-20230213

473 Ibid.

474 Ibid.

475   Wicks, J. Pijoos, I. & Maketha, T. 23 December 2024. 'A tender tycoon, his R200 000 Rolex and dark "ties" to a double kidnapping exposed'. News24. https://www.news24.com/news24/southafrica/news/silenced-a-tender-tycoon-his-r200-000-rolex-and-dark-ties-to-a-double-kidnapping-exposed-20241223

476   Ibid.

477   Ibid.

Chapter 31

478   Damons, M. & Geffen, N. 2 June 2023. 'How bad is South Africa's murder rate?'. GroundUp. https://groundup.org.za/article/how-bad-murder-in-south-africa/

479   Staff Writer. 29 January 2023. 'South Africa ranks as one of the most violent and dangerous places in the world'. BusinessTech. https://businesstech.co.za/news/lifestyle/699927/south-africa-ranks-as-one-of-the-most-violent-and-dangerous-places-in-the-world/

480   Africa Check. 15 April 2023. 'Is it true that less than 10% of murder cases in South Africa are solved?'. https://africacheck.org/infofinder/explore-facts/it-true-less-10-murder-cases-south-africa-are-solved

481   Cowan, K. 18 March 2023. 'The Murray Murders'. News24. https://specialprojects.news24.com/the-murray-murders/index.html

482   Ibid.

483   Open Secrets. 19 September 2023. 'A Russian Doll Part 2: Who assassinated Frans Mathipa and how is the SANDF involved?' https://www.opensecrets.org.za/a-russian-doll-part-two-who-assassinated-frans-mathipa-and-how-is-the-sandf-involved/

484   Karrim, A. & Wicks, J. 13 July 2024. 'CCTV footage shows slaying of COJ corruption investigator, probing multimillion-rand graft'. News24. https://www.news24.com/news24/investigations/watch-cctv-footage-shows-slaying-of-coj-corruption-investigator-probing-multimillion-rand-graft-20240713

485   Wicks, J. 9 September 2024. 'Whistleblower murder: Vereeniging engineer slain after report of 4 500% Transnet contract price inflation'. News24. https://www.news24.com/news24/investigations/whistleblower-murder-vereeniging-engineer-slain-after-report-of-4-500-transnet-contract-price-inflation-20240909

486   Ibid.

487   Wicks, B. 25 February 2025. 'Family business: Alleged mastermind in Transnet whistleblower case unmasked'. News24. https://www.news24.com/news24/southafrica/news/family-business-alleged-mastermind-in-transnet-whistleblowing-unmasked-20250225

488   Wicks, J. 9 September 2024. 'Whistleblower murder: Vereeniging engineer slain after report of 4 500% Transnet contract price inflation'. News24. https://www.news24.com/news24/investigations/whistleblower-murder-vereeniging-engineer-slain-after-report-of-4-500-transnet-contract-price-inflation-20240909

Chapter 32

489   Wicks, J. 6 May 2024. 'Justice denied | Multimillion pension for hospital boss despite Babita Deokaran's R1bn graft find'. News24. https://www.news24.com/news24/investigations/justice-denied-multimillion-pension-for-hospital-boss-despite-babita-deokarans-r1bn-graft-find-20240506

490   Ibid.

491   Ibid.

492   Ibid.

493   Ibid.

494   Wicks, J. 3 July 2024. 'Disgraced Tembisa Hospital CEO's dubious appointment exposed'. News24. https://www.news24.com/news24/investigations/silenced-disgraced-tembisa-hospital-ceos-dubious-appointment-exposed-20240702

495   Ibid.

496   Ibid.

497 Ibid.

498 Ibid.

499 Tshwane, T. 24 April 2023. 'Gauteng Health bosses accused of bid-rigging in tender for kickbacks scheme'. AmaBhungane Centre for Investigative Journalism. https://www.news24.com/citypress/news/siu-probe-sparks-das-call-for-lesufi-to-remove-lesiba-malotana-as-gauteng-health-head-20241113

500 Ibid.

501 Press statement. Democratic Alliance. 'Cancer court action evokes memories of Esidimeni negligence'. https://www.da.org.za/2024/07/cancer-court-action-evokes-memories-of-esidimeni-negligence

502 Solomons, L. 8 September 2024. 'Watch | Desperate patient's viral videos prompt probe into Helen Joseph Hospital conditions'. News24. https://www.news24.com/news24/southafrica/news/desperate-patients-viral-videos-prompt-probe-into-helen-joseph-hospital-conditions-20240908

Conclusion

503 Cronje, J. 13 February 2025. 'New Eskom kickback scandal: R180m and counting in bribes for "low-value" contracts'. News24. https://www.news24.com/fin24/companies/new-eskom-kickback-scandal-r180m-and-counting-in-bribes-for-low-value-contracts-20250212

504 Wicks, J. 17 April 2023. 'Fort Hare murder accused ran tender empire, with help from his "Mumsy"'. News24. https://www.news24.com/news24/investigations/exclusive-fort-hare-murder-accused-ran-tender-empire-with-help-from-his-mumsy-20230417

505 Wicks, J. 9 September 2024. 'Whistleblower murder: Vereeniging engineer slain after report of 4 500% Transnet contract price inflation'. News24. https://www.news24.com/news24/investigations/whistleblower-murder-vereeniging-engineer-slain-after-report-of-4-500-transnet-contract-price-inflation-20240909

Index

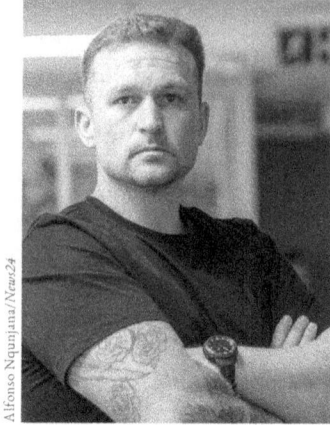

Jeff Wicks is a journalist with *News24*'s investigations team. With a career spanning nearly two decades, he has carved a niche for himself covering dark elements of the criminal underworld, organised crime and targeted killings.

Wicks has spearheaded several high-profile investigations, including those into the assassination of Anti-Gang Unit detective Charl Kinnear, a police-killing crew targeting figures in the gang world and tobacco trade, and corrupt cops who have infiltrated the rank and file of the police. For his investigation into the assassination of Babita Deokaran, he worked through over 60 000 emails and messages on her phone and visited numerous fake business addresses in person. He shared the information he had uncovered in an online documentary series, 'Silenced', which sparked public protests and investigations and led to the suspension and charging of key officials and politicians.

Wicks is a two-time winner of the Taco Kuiper Award for Investigative Journalism and, in 2024, was the recipient of the Nat Nakasa Award for courageous journalism. His work on Deokaran was short-listed for the Global Shining Light Award, which recognises watchdog journalism in developing or transitioning countries done under duress or in the direst of conditions.

He is the co-author of the bestseller *Eight Days in July: Inside the Zuma Unrest That Set South Africa Alight*, also published by Tafelberg.